C-881   **CAREER EXAMINATION SERIES**

This is your
PASSBOOK for...

Campus Public Safety Officer I

Test Preparation Study Guide
Questions & Answers

COPYRIGHT NOTICE

This book is SOLELY intended for, is sold ONLY to, and its use is RESTRICTED to individual, bona fide applicants or candidates who qualify by virtue of having seriously filed applications for appropriate license, certificate, professional and/or promotional advancement, higher school matriculation, scholarship, or other legitimate requirements of education and/or governmental authorities.

This book is NOT intended for use, class instruction, tutoring, training, duplication, copying, reprinting, excerption, or adaptation, etc., by:

1) Other publishers
2) Proprietors and/or Instructors of "Coaching" and/or Preparatory Courses
3) Personnel and/or Training Divisions of commercial, industrial, and governmental organizations
4) Schools, colleges, or universities and/or their departments and staffs, including teachers and other personnel
5) Testing Agencies or Bureaus
6) Study groups which seek by the purchase of a single volume to copy and/or duplicate and/or adapt this material for use by the group as a whole without having purchased individual volumes for each of the members of the group
7) Et al.

Such persons would be in violation of appropriate Federal and State statutes.

PROVISION OF LICENSING AGREEMENTS – Recognized educational, commercial, industrial, and governmental institutions and organizations, and others legitimately engaged in educational pursuits, including training, testing, and measurement activities, may address request for a licensing agreement to the copyright owners, who will determine whether, and under what conditions, including fees and charges, the materials in this book may be used them. In other words, a licensing facility exists for the legitimate use of the material in this book on other than an individual basis. However, it is asseverated and affirmed here that the material in this book CANNOT be used without the receipt of the express permission of such a licensing agreement from the Publishers. Inquiries re licensing should be addressed to the company, attention rights and permissions department.

All rights reserved, including the right of reproduction in whole or in part, in any form or by any means, electronic or mechanical, including photocopying, recording, or by any information storage and retrieval system, without permission in writing from the Publisher.

Copyright © 2024 by
National Learning Corporation

212 Michael Drive, Syosset, NY 11791
(516) 921-8888 • www.passbooks.com
E-mail: info@passbooks.com

PUBLISHED IN THE UNITED STATES OF AMERICA

PASSBOOK® SERIES

THE *PASSBOOK® SERIES* has been created to prepare applicants and candidates for the ultimate academic battlefield – the examination room.

At some time in our lives, each and every one of us may be required to take an examination – for validation, matriculation, admission, qualification, registration, certification, or licensure.

Based on the assumption that every applicant or candidate has met the basic formal educational standards, has taken the required number of courses, and read the necessary texts, the *PASSBOOK® SERIES* furnishes the one special preparation which may assure passing with confidence, instead of failing with insecurity. Examination questions – together with answers – are furnished as the basic vehicle for study so that the mysteries of the examination and its compounding difficulties may be eliminated or diminished by a sure method.

This book is meant to help you pass your examination provided that you qualify and are serious in your objective.

The entire field is reviewed through the huge store of content information which is succinctly presented through a provocative and challenging approach – the question-and-answer method.

A climate of success is established by furnishing the correct answers at the end of each test.

You soon learn to recognize types of questions, forms of questions, and patterns of questioning. You may even begin to anticipate expected outcomes.

You perceive that many questions are repeated or adapted so that you can gain acute insights, which may enable you to score many sure points.

You learn how to confront new questions, or types of questions, and to attack them confidently and work out the correct answers.

You note objectives and emphases, and recognize pitfalls and dangers, so that you may make positive educational adjustments.

Moreover, you are kept fully informed in relation to new concepts, methods, practices, and directions in the field.

You discover that you are actually taking the examination all the time: you are preparing for the examination by "taking" an examination, not by reading extraneous and/or supererogatory textbooks.

In short, this PASSBOOK®, used directedly, should be an important factor in helping you to pass your test.

CAMPUS PUBLIC SAFETY OFFICER I

DUTIES:
Campus Public Safety Officer positions may be located at any one of the State operated campuses of the State University where they perform public safety activities in a university environment. A primary assignment performed by incumbents of this position is that of desk officer, including communications related activities such as dispatching and operating a data terminal. When necessary, they also patrol buildings and facilities, enforce building regulations, issue parking permits, and give directions to and answer questions for clients and visitors to assist them in finding their way. They assist University Police as appropriate.

Campus Public Safety Officers are responsible for the detection and prevention of crime and for the enforcement of local laws, rules and regulations for the protection of persons, property, and the general maintenance of peace, order and security. Officers must develop and maintain a positive relationship with all segments of the campus community in order to obtain cooperation and support in conducting a successful campus law enforcement program. Typical activities include crowd control, foot and mobile patrols, traffic control and radio dispatching.

EXAMPLES OF DUTIES:
- Maintains order on campus at all times;
- Responds to campus emergencies and provides First Aid/CPR as needed;
- Patrols buildings, grounds and parking areas on foot or in a patrol vehicle to maintain order, protect persons and property, control traffic, and to prevent trespassing, theft or damage;
- Secures and checks all doors, windows and entrances to building to be sure that they are secure;
- Assures that all doors and entrances are unlocked for daily activities and classes;
- Makes operational checks of heating and cooling equipment, reporting any malfunctions;
- Controls and directs traffic on campus or campus related roads, grounds and parking areas;
- Investigates motor vehicle accidents that occur on campus or campus related property;
- Issues parking violation tickets;
- Enforces the Student Code of Conduct;
- Enforces fire codes, performs inspections of fire code compliance and issues reports;
- Provides assistance and training to students, faculty and staff (provides directions and information, assists motorists with lock-outs and other vehicular problems, etc.) on topics including, but not limited to, emergency response training, active shooter and other drills;
- Contacts Director of Buildings & Grounds regarding snow removal;
- Consults with the Vice President of College Safety and Security or other Community College Official regarding the status of the campus public safety/security program and make suggestions for improvement as required;
- Prepares records and reports related to the work performed and maintains an appropriate system of records and reports, including, but not limited to, reportable incidents and all required regulatory reporting under state and federal statutes and regulations.

SCOPE OF THE EXAMINATION:
The written test will cover knowledge, skills and/or abilities in such areas as:
1. Applying written information in a safety and security setting;
2. Following directions (maps);
3. Retaining and comprehending spoken information from calls for emergency services;
4. Preparing written material; and
5. Understanding and interpreting written material.

INTRODUCTION

This test guide provides a general description of the most common subject areas which will be tested and an explanation of the different types of questions you may see on the test.

Not all subject areas tested in the Safety and Security Series are covered in this test guide. The Examination Announcement will list the subject areas that will be included on the particular test you will be taking. Some of these subject areas may not be covered in this test guide.

The most common subject areas included in the Safety and Security Series are:

1. **APPLYING WRITTEN INFORMATION IN A SAFETY AND SECURITY SETTING:** These questions evaluate your ability to read, interpret and apply rules, regulations, directions, written narratives and other related material. You will be required to read a set of information and to appropriately apply the information to situations similar to those typically experienced in a public safety and security service setting. All information needed to answer the questions is contained in the rules, regulations, etc. which are cited.

2. **FOLLOWING DIRECTIONS (MAPS):** These questions test your ability to follow physical/geographic directions using street maps or building maps. You will have to read and understand a set of directions and then use them on a simple map.

3. **PREPARING WRITTEN MATERIAL:** These questions test for the ability to present information clearly and accurately, and to organize paragraphs logically and comprehensibly. For some questions, you will be given information in two or three sentences, followed by four restatements of the information. You must then choose the best version. For other questions, you will be given paragraphs with their sentences out of order. You must then choose, from among four choices, the best order for the sentences.

4. **PRINCIPLES AND PRACTICES OF SAFETY AND SECURITY:** These questions test for a knowledge of the proper principles and practices in the field of safety and security. The questions will cover such areas as selecting the best course of action to take in a safety or security related situation.

5. **SAFETY AND SECURITY METHODS AND PROCEDURES:** These questions test for knowledge of the methods and procedures utilized in safety and security related positions. The questions cover such areas as principles and practices of safety and security precautions in a building or grounds setting, accident prevention, proper response to safety or security related incidents, the investigation of incidents, and the inspection of buildings or grounds for potential safety and/or security problems.

INTRODUCTION – CONTINUED

6. **UNDERSTANDING AND INTERPRETING WRITTEN MATERIAL:** These questions test how well you comprehend written material. You will be provided with brief reading selections and will be asked questions about the selections. All the information required to answer the questions will be presented in the selections; you will not be required to have any special knowledge relating to the subject areas of the selections.

7. **SUPERVISION:** These questions test for knowledge of the principles and practices employed in planning, organizing, and controlling the activities of a work unit toward predetermined objectives. The concepts covered, usually in a situational question format, include such topics as assigning and reviewing work; evaluating performance; maintaining work standards; motivating and developing subordinates; implementing procedural change; increasing efficiency; and dealing with problems of absenteeism, morale, and discipline.

8. **ADMINISTRATIVE SUPERVISION:** These questions test for knowledge of the principles and practices involved in directing the activities of a large subordinate staff, including subordinate supervisors. Questions relate to the personal interactions between an upper level supervisor and his/her subordinate supervisors in the accomplishment of objectives. These questions cover such areas as assigning work to and coordinating the activities of several units, establishing and guiding staff development programs, evaluating the performance of subordinate supervisors, and maintaining relationships with other organizational sections.

The remainder of this test guide explains how you will be tested in each subject area listed above. A **TEST TASK** is provided for each subject area. This is an explanation of how a question is presented and how to correctly answer it. Read each explanation carefully. This test guide also provides at least one **SAMPLE QUESTION** for each subject area. The sample question is similar to the type of questions that will be presented on the actual test. This test guide provides the **SOLUTION** and correct answer to each sample question. You should study each sample question and solution in order to understand how the correct answer was determined.

At the end of this test guide we have included a **PRACTICE TEST** which includes additional examples of the types of questions you may see on your written test. Answers are provided in the Practice Test Key so that you can see how well you have done.

SUBJECT AREA 1

APPLYING WRITTEN INFORMATION IN A SAFETY AND SECURITY SETTING: These questions evaluate your ability to read, interpret and apply rules, regulations, directions, written narratives and other related material. You will be required to read a set of information and to appropriately apply the information to situations similar to those typically experienced in a public safety and security service setting. All information needed to answer the questions is contained in the rules, regulations, etc. which are cited.

TEST TASK: You will be given a set of rules, regulations, or other written information to read. You will then be asked a question which requires you to apply the rule to a given situation.

SAMPLE QUESTION:

RULE: While patrolling your grounds or building, keep a notebook and pencil with you. Keep the following emergency phone numbers in the notebook: police, fire department, nearby hospitals, alarm company, your supervisor, and the head of your building.

When you observe something out of the ordinary, take notes. Describe what is unusual, people who are unfamiliar, and any suspicious activity. If a crime or offense takes place, record what happened, who was involved, physical appearance of the suspect, clothing worn by the suspect, time and date, names and phone numbers of witnesses, where suspect was last seen, and any physical evidence found.

SITUATION: While you are doing your rounds at 11:20 p.m. you notice a door that has been left ajar. The door opens to the office of the Assistant Director of your facility. The door is typically closed and locked for the day when the Assistant Director leaves, usually between 5:00 and 6:00 p.m. The office is dark and no one is there.

QUESTION: Based solely on the above Rule and Situation, what, if anything, should be recorded in your notebook?

A. The office was dark when you entered it.
B. No one was in the office.
C. The door was open at 11:20 p.m.
D. No entry needs to be made.

The correct answer to this sample question is choice C.

SOLUTION: *The Situation states that while doing your rounds at 11:20 p.m., you notice a door left ajar. This door is typically closed and locked for the day between 5:00 and 6:00 p.m. by the Assistant Director. The question asks what, if anything, you should record about this incident in your notebook. To answer the question, evaluate all of the choices.*

Solution continued on next page.

SUBJECT AREA 1 – CONTINUED

Choice A states that you should record in your notebook the fact that the office was dark when you entered it. The Rule states that you should take notes when you observe something out of the ordinary. It is not out of the ordinary for the Assistant Director's office to be dark at 11:20 p.m. since the Assistant Director usually leaves for the day between 5:00 and 6:00 p.m. Choice A is incorrect.

Choice B states that you should record in your notebook the fact that no one was in the office. The Rule states that you should take notes when you observe something out of the ordinary. It is not out of the ordinary for the Assistant Director's office to be unoccupied at 11:20 p.m. since the Assistant Director is not usually at work after 6:00 p.m. Choice B is incorrect.

Choice C states that you should record in your notebook the fact that the door was open at 11:20 p.m. The Rule states that you should take notes when you observe something out of the ordinary. It is out of the ordinary for the Assistant Director's office door to be open at 11:20 p.m. because the door is typically closed and locked when the Assistant Director leaves for the day, usually between 5:00 and 6:00 p.m. Choice C is the correct answer.

Choice D states that you should make no entry in your notebook. The Rule states that you should take notes when you observe something out of the ordinary. It is out of the ordinary for the Assistant Director's office door to be open at 11:20 p.m. because the door is typically closed and locked when the Assistant Director leaves for the day, usually between 5:00 and 6:00 p.m. Choice D is incorrect.

SUBJECT AREA 2

FOLLOWING DIRECTIONS (MAPS): These questions test your ability to follow physical/geographic directions using street maps or building maps. You will have to read and understand a set of directions and then use them on a simple map.

TEST TASK: You will be provided with street maps or building maps. You will then be asked questions which require you to refer to the given maps and related information.

SAMPLE QUESTION:

DIRECTIONS: Base your answer to the following question on the sample information and sample map below. The map below shows a section of a city. The circled numbers are starting points and stopping points. Buildings are shown with letters. A roadblock is shown as a dark circle. One-way blocks are shown with an arrow pointing in the direction that you may travel on that block. For example:

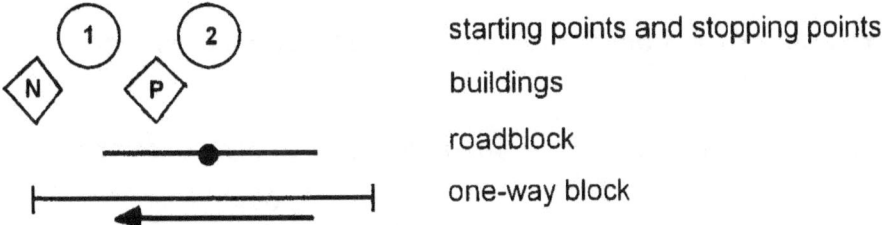

starting points and stopping points

buildings

roadblock

one-way block

You may not go through a roadblock or travel in the wrong direction on a one-way block. You are to answer the question by finding and following the SHORTEST CORRECT route between the two locations given. All blocks are equal in length.

NOTE 1: Blocks may be traveled in either direction UNLESS only one direction is shown by an arrow for that block.

NOTE 2: You "pass" a building when you travel the block NEAREST the building.

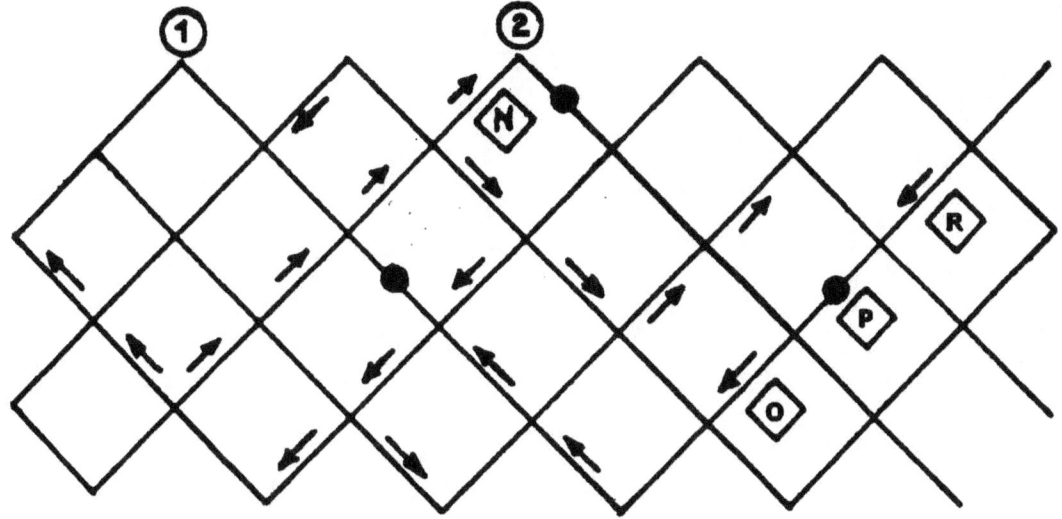

SUBJECT AREA 2 – CONTINUED

QUESTION: Which one of the following is a building you pass on the shortest correct route from point 1 to point 2?

A. N
B. O
C. P
D. R

The correct answer to this sample question is choice A.

SOLUTION:

Choice A is the correct answer to this question. The shortest correct route from point 1 to point 2 is four blocks and passes only building N.

Choice B is not correct. You do not pass building O on the shortest correct route from point 1 to point 2.

Choice C is not correct. You do not pass building P on the shortest correct route from point 1 to point 2.

Choice D is not correct. You do not pass building R on the shortest correct route from point 1 to point 2.

SUBJECT AREA 3

PREPARING WRITTEN MATERIAL: These questions test for the ability to present information clearly and accurately and for the ability to organize paragraphs logically and comprehensibly.

TEST TASK: There are two separate test tasks in this subject area.

- For the first, **Information Presentation**, you will be given information in two or three sentences, followed by four restatements of the information. You must then choose the best version.

- For the second, **Paragraph Organization**, you will be given paragraphs with their sentences out of order, and then be asked to choose, from among four choices, the best order for the sentences.

INFORMATION PRESENTATION SAMPLE QUESTION:

Martin Wilson failed to take proper precautions. His failure to take proper precautions caused a personal injury accident.

Which one of the following best presents the information above?

A. Martin Wilson failed to take proper precautions that caused a personal injury accident.
B. Proper precautions, which Martin Wilson failed to take, caused a personal injury accident.
C. Martin Wilson's failure to take proper precautions caused a personal injury accident.
D. Martin Wilson, who failed to take proper precautions, was in a personal injury accident.

The correct answer to this sample question is choice C.

SOLUTION:

Choice A conveys the incorrect impression that proper precautions caused a personal injury accident.

Choice B conveys the incorrect impression that proper precautions caused a personal injury accident.

Choice C best presents the original information: Martin Wilson failed to take proper precautions and this failure caused a personal injury accident.

Choice D states that Martin Wilson was in a personal injury accident. The original information states that Martin Wilson caused a personal injury accident, but it does not state that Martin Wilson was in a personal injury accident.

SUBJECT AREA 3 – CONTINUED

PARAGRAPH ORGANIZATION SAMPLE QUESTION:

The following question is based upon a group of sentences. The sentences are shown out of sequence, but when correctly arranged, they form a connected, well-organized paragraph. Read the sentences, and then answer the question about the best arrangement of these sentences.

1. Eventually, they piece all of this information together and make a choice.

2. Before actually deciding upon a human services job, people usually think about several possibilities.

3. They imagine themselves in different situations, and in so doing, they probably think about their interests, goals, and abilities.

4. Choosing among occupations in the field of human services is an important decision to make.

Which one of the following is the best arrangement of these sentences?

A. 2-4-1-3
B. 2-3-4-1
C. 4-2-1-3
D. 4-2-3-1

The correct answer to this sample question is choice D.

SOLUTION:

Choices A and C present the information in the paragraph out of logical sequence. In both A and C, sentence 1 comes before sentence 3. The key element in the organization of this paragraph is that sentence 3 contains the information to which sentence 1 refers; therefore, in logical sequence, sentence 3 should come before sentence 1.

Choice B also presents the information in the paragraph out of logical sequence. Choice B places the main idea of the paragraph (Sentence 4) in between two detail sentences (Sentences 1 and 3). The logical sequence of the information presented in the paragraph is therefore interrupted.

Choice D presents the information in the paragraph in the best logical sequence. Sentence 4 introduces the main idea of the paragraph: "choosing an occupation in the field of human services." Sentences 2-3-1 then follow up on this idea by describing, in order, the steps involved in making such a choice. Choice D is the best answer to this sample question.

SUBJECT AREA 4

PRINCIPLES AND PRACTICES OF SAFETY AND SECURITY: These questions test for a knowledge of the proper principles and practices in the field of safety and security. The questions will cover such areas as selecting the best course of action to take in a safety or security related situation.

TEST TASK: You will be presented with situations in which you must apply knowledge of the principles and practices of safety and security to answer the questions correctly.

SAMPLE QUESTION:

You are in charge of maintaining order in a room where a large number of people gather to transact business. A woman in the back of one of the lines starts to shout that she has been waiting for an hour and her line "has not moved at all." She continues to protest, and the rest of the crowd is getting restless.

Which one of the following actions would be best to take first in this situation?

A. Escort the woman to the head of the line and make sure her business is transacted promptly.
B. Tell the woman that unless she acts in a more orderly fashion, you will escort her out of the room.
C. Immediately remove the woman from the room.
D. Call the local police and detain the woman until the police arrive.

The correct answer to this sample question is choice B.

SOLUTION:

Choice A is not correct because escorting the woman to the head of the line and making sure her business is transacted promptly is not the best action to take first in this situation. This action could increase the restlessness of the other people who have also been waiting in the same line and will only serve to reinforce the woman's disruptive behavior.

Choice B is the correct answer because telling the woman that unless she acts in a more orderly fashion, you will escort her out of the room is the best action to take first in this situation. This action provides the woman with a clear warning to stop her disruptive behavior and advises her of the consequence should she continue to loudly protest the long wait.

Choice C is not correct because immediately removing the woman from the room is not the best action to take first in this situation. This action is too harsh based on the situation and could escalate the woman's disruptive behavior.

Choice D is not correct because calling the local police and detaining the woman until they arrive is not the best action to take first in this situation. This action is too harsh based on the situation and could escalate the woman's disruptive behavior.

SUBJECT AREA 5

SAFETY AND SECURITY METHODS AND PROCEDURES: These questions test for knowledge of the methods and procedures utilized in safety and security related positions. The questions cover such areas as principles and practices of safety and security precautions in a building or grounds setting, accident prevention, proper response to safety or security related incidents, the investigation of incidents, and the inspection of buildings or grounds for potential safety and/or security problems.

TEST TASK: You will be presented with questions in which you must apply knowledge of the methods and procedures utilized in safety and security related positions to answer the questions correctly.

SAMPLE QUESTION:

The most important purpose of patrolling the halls and grounds of a facility is to

A. discourage potential violations of rules or laws
B. give people on site the opportunity to obtain information or advice
C. maintain a routine observation of facility employees and their actions for your records
D. be able to provide assistance to local police authorities by accurately reporting whether unauthorized activity occurs in or near the facility

The correct answer to this sample question is choice A.

SOLUTION:

Choice A *is the correct answer because discouraging potential violations of rules or laws is the most important purpose of patrolling the halls and grounds of a facility. Your presence while patrolling the halls and grounds of a facility may be enough to deter potential rule or law violators.*

Choice B *is not correct because giving people on site the opportunity to obtain information or advice is not the most important purpose of patrolling the halls and grounds of a facility. Although giving people on site the opportunity to obtain information or advice may be an important purpose of patrolling the halls and grounds of a facility, it is not the most important purpose.*

Choice C *is not correct because maintaining a routine observation of facility employees and their actions for your records is not the most important purpose of patrolling the halls and grounds of a facility. Although maintaining a routine observation of facility employees and their actions for your records may be an important purpose of patrolling the halls and grounds of a facility, it is not the most important purpose.*

Choice D *is not correct because being able to provide assistance to local police authorities by accurately reporting whether unauthorized activity occurs in or near the facility is not the most important purpose of patrolling the halls and grounds of a facility. Although being able to provide assistance to local police authorities by accurately reporting whether unauthorized activity occurs in or near the facility may be an important purpose of patrolling the halls and grounds of a facility, it is not the most important purpose.*

SUBJECT AREA 6

UNDERSTANDING AND INTERPRETING WRITTEN MATERIAL: These questions test how well you comprehend written material. You will be provided with brief reading selections and will be asked questions about the selections. All the information required to answer the questions will be presented in the selections; you will not be required to have any special knowledge relating to the subject areas of the selections.

TEST TASK: You will be provided with brief reading passages and then will be asked questions relating to the passages. All the information required to answer the questions will be provided in the passages.

SAMPLE QUESTION: "Increasingly, behavior termed 'road rage' is being viewed as a public health issue, because of the number of deaths and injuries related to it. Such behavior is often a reaction to the feeling that one has been treated unfairly by another driver, and it is much less likely to occur if a driver is treated fairly. 'Fair play' on the road includes the observance not only of traffic regulations but also of the rules of courtesy. Courteous driving is based on common sense consideration for other drivers and a strong desire to make the roads safe for everyone. Good highway manners should become just as much a matter of habit as other kinds of manners."

Which one of the following statements is best supported by the above selection?

A. Courteous driving contributes to road safety.
B. Those who are generally polite are also courteous drivers.
C. Unlike driving courtesy, the observance of traffic regulations is a matter of habit.
D. Being courteous when driving is more important than observing traffic regulations.

The correct answer to this sample question is choice A.

SOLUTION: To answer this question correctly, you must evaluate each choice against the written selection and determine the one that is best supported by the written selection.

Choice A *states, "Courteous driving contributes to road safety." Choice A is supported by the statement in the written selection that, "Courteous driving is based on...a strong desire to make the roads safe for everyone." This is the correct answer.*

Choice B *states, "Those who are generally polite are also courteous drivers." Choice B is not supported by the written selection. The written selection does not mention "those who are generally polite" at all. Choice B is not the correct answer to this question.*

Choice C *states, "Unlike driving courtesy, the observance of traffic regulations is a matter of habit." Choice C is not supported by the written selection. The written selection makes no such bold statement. Instead, the written material mildly suggests that "Good highway manners should become just as much a matter of habit as other kinds of manners." Choice C is not the correct answer to this question.*

Choice D *states, "Being courteous when driving is more important than observing traffic regulations." Choice D is not supported by the written selection. The written selection states, "'Fair play' on the road includes the observance not only of traffic regulations but also of the rules of courtesy." The written selection does not state that being courteous is more important than observing traffic regulations. Choice D is not the correct answer to this question.*

SUBJECT AREA 7

SUPERVISION: These questions test for knowledge of the principles and practices employed in planning, organizing, and controlling the activities of a work unit toward predetermined objectives. The concepts covered, usually in a situational question format, include such topics as assigning and reviewing work; evaluating performance; maintaining work standards; motivating and developing subordinates; implementing procedural change; increasing efficiency; and dealing with problems of absenteeism, morale, and discipline.

TEST TASK: You will be presented with situations in which you must apply knowledge of the principles and practices of supervision in order to answer the questions correctly.

SAMPLE QUESTION:
Assume that the unit you supervise is given a new work assignment and that you are unsure about the proper procedure to use in performing this assignment. Which one of the following actions should you take FIRST in this situation?

A. Obtain input from your staff.
B. Consult other unit supervisors who have had similar assignments.
C. Use an appropriate procedure from a similar assignment that you are familiar with.
D. Discuss the matter with your supervisor.

The correct answer to this sample question is choice D.

SOLUTION:

Choice A is not correct. Since this assignment is new for your unit, your staff would not be expected to be more knowledgeable than you about the proper procedure.

Choice B is not correct. Although discussing this matter with other supervisors may increase your knowledge of the new assignment, similar assignments performed in other units may differ in some important way from your new assignment. Other units may also function differently from your unit, so the procedures used to perform similar assignments may differ accordingly.

Choice C is not correct. Since this assignment is new for your unit, you would have no way of knowing whether the procedure from a similar assignment is appropriate to use. You would need someone with the appropriate knowledge, usually your supervisor, to determine if the procedure from a similar assignment could be used before you actually employed this procedure in the performance of your new assignment.

Choice D is the correct answer to this question. Your supervisor is more likely to be informed about what procedure may be appropriate for work that he or she assigns to you than would other unit supervisors or your staff. Even if your supervisor does not know what procedure is appropriate, a decision regarding which procedure to use should be made with his or her participation, since he or she has the ultimate responsibility for your unit's work.

SUBJECT AREA 8

ADMINISTRATIVE SUPERVISION: These questions test for knowledge of the principles and practices involved in directing the activities of a large subordinate staff, including subordinate supervisors. Questions relate to the personal interactions between an upper level supervisor and his/her subordinate supervisors in the accomplishment of objectives. These questions cover such areas as assigning work to and coordinating the activities of several units, establishing and guiding staff development programs, evaluating the performance of subordinate supervisors, and maintaining relationships with other organizational sections.

TEST TASK: You will be presented with situations in which you must apply knowledge of the principles and practices of administrative supervision to answer the questions correctly. You will be placed in the role of a supervisor of a section, which is made up of several units. Each unit has a supervisor and several employees. All unit supervisors report directly to you.

SAMPLE QUESTION:

You have delegated a work project to two unit supervisors and have asked them to collaborate on it. Later, you observe two employees strongly arguing about which one of them is responsible for a certain activity within the work project. The arguing employees work for different units. Which one of the following actions is most appropriate for you to take in this situation?

A. Intercede in the employees' argument and settle it.
B. Meet with the unit supervisors of the two employees and inform them of the situation you observed.
C. Inform one unit supervisor of the situation and ask this supervisor to take care of it.
D. Set up a meeting that includes both unit supervisors and both employees to resolve the situation.

The correct answer to this sample question is choice B.

SOLUTION:

Choice A *is not correct.* In your position, you supervise properly by giving direction through your unit supervisors. By taking this choice, you are not allowing your unit supervisors to handle a problem involving their staff members. Also, it is not reasonable that you would be able to settle the employees' dispute. Earlier, you delegated the work project to the two unit supervisors, who would be responsible for assigning activities related to the project. The two unit supervisors must deal with the problem.

Choice B *is the correct answer to this question.* The two unit supervisors are collaborating on the work project and therefore giving the assignments. You should meet with them and tell them about the employees' argument. The unit supervisors should be informed about the point of contention and the fact that the two employees had a heated argument. The unit supervisors must then work out a way to handle the situation.

Choice C *is not correct.* Speaking to only one supervisor about the situation means that the second supervisor may be uninformed, or only partly informed, about the situation. You cannot be assured that the first supervisor will include the second supervisor in finding a way to settle the issue. If the first unit supervisor chooses to handle the situation on his own and speak to both employees, this supervisor would be giving direction to one employee from another unit. This is not good supervisory practice. Also, in taking Choice C, you are favoring one supervisor and slighting the other.

Choice D *is not correct.* The unit supervisors need to come up with a way of handling the situation that you observed. To do this, they must be informed without the employees present. Also, by including the employees in the meeting, you may get a replay of their earlier argument, which is not helpful.

PRACTICE TEST

Below and on the following pages are additional examples of the types of questions that will be on the written test for the Safety and Security Series. The answers are given on page 25. Good luck!

APPLYING WRITTEN INFORMATION IN A SAFETY AND SECURITY SETTING

DIRECTIONS: The following two questions evaluate your ability to read and interpret a specific rule and apply it to a given situation or situations. Each question or set of questions is given with a **RULE** along with a **SITUATION** or situations. You should base your answers to these questions upon the information provided and **NOT** upon any other information you may have on the subject.

1. **RULE:** A security officer is to obey all lawful regulations of the employer and all orders of a police officer in police matters. The security officer is to assist and cooperate with police officers in preserving the peace. Where police are on the scene, on duty and off duty security personnel should identify themselves as security officers and offer assistance. The police officer's directives and judgment shall prevail.

SITUATION: When leaving work for the day, you see that a motor vehicle accident has taken place on the highway near your workplace. You approach the accident in your car and see that a police officer is on the scene. You inform the police officer that you are a security officer. Traffic is stopped.

According to the above Rule, under which one of the following conditions, if any, should you take control of directing traffic in this Situation?

A. The police officer instructs you to direct traffic.
B. You regularly direct traffic as part of your job.
C. You should not direct traffic because you are off duty.
D. You should not direct traffic because the highway is not on facility property.

2. **RULE:** If a law enforcement officer is required to be at a mental health facility, the officer will be required to lock his weapon in a designated gun cabinet and retain the only key. In areas where gun cabinets are not available, the law enforcement officer shall be asked to remove the bullets from his weapon and retain the weapon. The only other allowable option is for the officer to lock the weapon in his patrol car.

SITUATION: During rounds as a security officer in a mental health facility with no gun control cabinets available, you come upon a law enforcement officer whom you know to be a firearms instructor. You allow the officer to enter the building with his weapon.

Based solely on the above Rule and Situation, in which one of the following cases is your action correct?

A. The officer has stated that his police agency prohibits an officer from locking a weapon in his patrol car.
B. The officer has stated that he would be willing to put his weapon in a gun cabinet.
C. The officer has shown you a letter stating he must attend a meeting at the facility today on the topic of firearm instruction.
D. The officer has removed the bullets from his weapon.

FOLLOWING DIRECTIONS (MAPS)

DIRECTIONS: The following map presents a diagram of a floor of an office building. You should become familiar with the map and interpret it with the legend provided. Use the map to answer the questions on the next page.

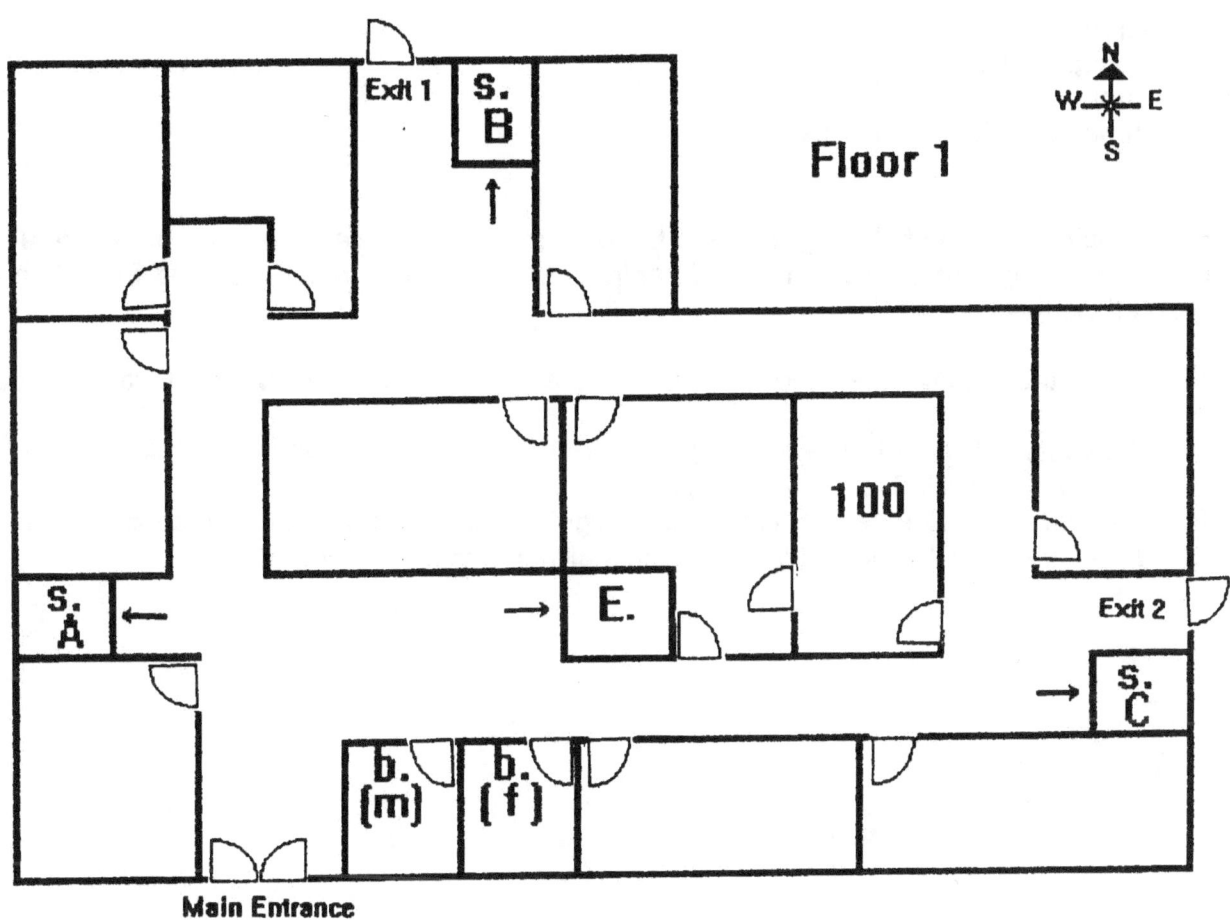

Legend:

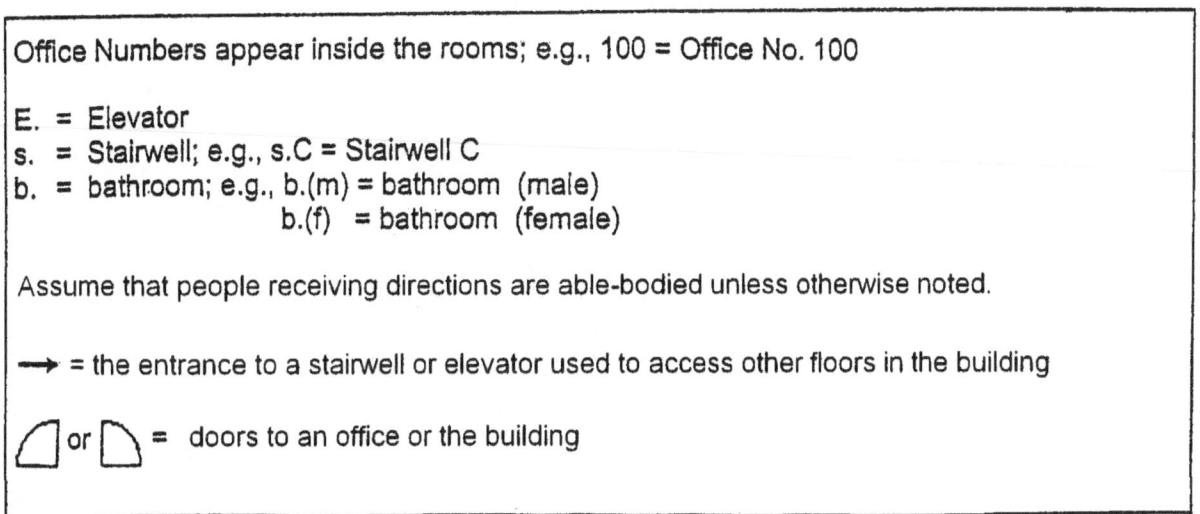

Office Numbers appear inside the rooms; e.g., 100 = Office No. 100

E. = Elevator
s. = Stairwell; e.g., s.C = Stairwell C
b. = bathroom; e.g., b.(m) = bathroom (male)
　　　　　　　　b.(f) = bathroom (female)

Assume that people receiving directions are able-bodied unless otherwise noted.

→ = the entrance to a stairwell or elevator used to access other floors in the building

◁ or ▷ = doors to an office or the building

FOLLOWING DIRECTIONS (MAPS) (Continued)

3. For a person in Office No. 100, which one of the following is the most direct route to leave the building in an emergency?

A. through exit 1
B. through exit 2
C. through stairwell C
D. through the Main Entrance

4. Which one of the following routes is the best to take if the elevator is out of service and a person standing directly inside the main entrance wants to get from Floor 1 to Floor 2 in the most efficient way?

A. Walk straight, take the second right, take the first left and take stairwell B to the second floor.
B. Walk straight, take the second right, walk straight, take the next right, take the first left and take stairwell C to the second floor.
C. Walk straight, take the first right, walk straight and take stairwell C to the second floor.
D. Walk straight, take the first left and take stairwell A to the second floor.

PREPARING WRITTEN MATERIAL

DIRECTIONS: Read the information given in the following two questions carefully. Then select the choice which presents the information most clearly, accurately, and completely.

5. Senator Martinez met with the county legislature. Then Senator Martinez announced that the meal subsidy program would start in June.

Which one of the following best presents the information given above?

A. After meeting with the county legislature, Senator Martinez announced that the meal subsidy program would start in June.
B. Senator Martinez met with the county legislature and announced that the meal subsidy program would start in June.
C. Senator Martinez announced that the meal subsidy program would start in June after a meeting with the county legislature.
D. Senator Martinez, who met with the county legislature, announced that the meal subsidy program would start in June.

6. Frank Colombe wrote the press release. He sent three copies to the Director. The Director then gave one of the copies to the Commissioner.

Which one of the following best presents the information given above?

A. Frank Colombe sent to the Director three copies of the press release he had written, who then gave a copy to the Commissioner.
B. Frank Colombe sent three copies of the press release he had written to the Director, who then gave one of the copies to the Commissioner.
C. The Director gave the Commissioner one of the three copies of the press release Frank Colombe had written and had been sent to him.
D. Of the three copies of the press release Frank Colombe had written and sent to the Director, one was then given to the Commissioner by him.

PREPARING WRITTEN MATERIAL (Continued)

DIRECTIONS: The following two (2) questions are based upon a group of sentences. The sentences are shown out of sequence, but when they are correctly arranged they form a connected, well-organized paragraph. Read the sentences and then answer the question about what order to arrange them in.

7.
1. The phosphates in detergents are carried into sewage systems, and from there into local rivers and streams, and eventually into large bodies of water.

2. The algae absorb much of the available oxygen that is necessary to sustain marine life.

3. There is no doubt that phosphates damage the environment through a complex chain of events.

4. Phosphates are nutrients, and, as such, they aid the growth of the algae living in the water.

5. This results not only in the death of fish and other aquatic life, but also in the too-thick growth of vegetation in the water.

Which one of the following is the best arrangement of these sentences?

A. 1-3-4-2-5
B. 1-4-2-5-3
C. 3-1-4-2-5
D. 3-4-2-1-5

8.
1. Never before has time been measured at a speed beyond the realm of experience.

2. Just how profound an effect it is having on society is as yet to be determined.

3. The computer has accelerated our sense of time beyond anything we have experienced before.

4. Though it is possible to conceive of an interval that brief and even to manipulate time at that speed, it is not possible to experience it.

5. It works in a time frame in which the nanosecond—a billionth of a second—is the primary measurement.

Which one of the following is the best arrangement of these sentences?

A. 1-2-3-5-4
B. 1-4-3-5-2
C. 3-2-5-4-1
D. 3-5-4-1-2

PRINCIPLES AND PRACTICES OF SAFETY AND SECURITY

9. You are on patrol in a radio-equipped car at night. You discover that a large drum of gasoline near a garage on the property is punctured and is rapidly spilling gasoline on the ground around the building.

Which one of the following actions should you take first in this situation?

A. Submit a written report of the incident to your supervisor.
B. Report the matter to headquarters.
C. Examine the puncture to see if it was accidental or deliberate.
D. Check other drums or containers around the building for punctures.

10. You hear shouting on the second floor of a building where you are on duty. Upon arriving at the scene, you see two building employees engaged in a fist fight in the hall.

Which one of the following actions should you take first in this situation?

A. Report the matter to the supervisors of the two employees.
B. Ask observers how the fight started.
C. Call for assistance.
D. Break up the fight.

SAFETY AND SECURITY METHODS AND PROCEDURES

11. Complaints relating to suspicious activity, especially at night, are often groundless. Which one of the following is the best way of handling such a complaint?

A. Analyze the nature of the complaint to make sure that it is justifiable before dispatching anyone to the scene.
B. Consider the complaint justified only if it corresponds to similar complaints in the same area.
C. Take no action on the complaint, but make a record of it.
D. Attend to the complaint immediately on the assumption that it is justified.

12. In the course of an investigation, you are interviewing a person who is over-talkative. Which one of the following is the best method for you to use in order to obtain the facts which you seek?

A. Tell the witness to talk only about the facts you are interested in.
B. Place a time limit on the witness's answers to your questions.
C. Make it clear that you want only "yes" or "no" answers to your questions.
D. Guide the conversation toward the subject of interest when the witness talks about subjects clearly not relevant to the interview.

UNDERSTANDING AND INTERPRETING WRITTEN MATERIAL

DIRECTIONS: The following two questions are related to the reading selection preceding each question. Base your answer to the question SOLELY on what is said in the selection – NOT on what you may happen to know about the subject discussed.

13. "The increasing demands upon our highways from a growing population and the development of forms of transportation not anticipated when the highways were first built have brought about congestion, confusion, and conflict, until the yearly toll of traffic accidents is now at an appalling level. If the death and disaster that traffic accidents bring throughout the year were concentrated into one calamity, we would shudder at the tremendous catastrophe. The loss is no less catastrophic because it is spread out over time and space."

Which one of the following statements concerning the yearly toll of traffic accidents is best supported by the passage above?

A. It is increasing the demands for safer means of transportation.
B. It has resulted in increased congestion, confusion, and conflict on our highways.
C. It has resulted mainly from the new forms of transportation.
D. It does not shock us as much as it should because the accidents do not all occur at the same time.

14. "Depression is one of the top public health problems in the United States, and its occurrence is on the rise. One in 20 Americans develops a case of depression serious enough to require professional treatment. The incidence of depression has been escalating among Baby Boomers (Americans born in the years 1946 through 1964). The reason for this increase is that the lifestyles of this generation have become increasingly demanding while offering little support. Also, stress and poor eating habits are now more the rule than the exception, and both can disrupt brain chemistry enough to bring on depression."

Which one of the following statements is best supported by the above selection?

A. We can expect a small proportion of the population to require treatment for depression at some time in their lives.
B. Baby Boomers have the highest rate of depression in the United States.
C. Lifestyle demands are the major cause of depression in the current generation.
D. Depression can cause a disruption in the chemistry of the brain.

SUPERVISION

DIRECTIONS: For the following two questions, assume that you are the newly appointed supervisor of a unit consisting of several employees. You report to a section head.

15. You have a suspicion that some of your employees are not working to the best of their abilities. Which one of the following actions should you take first in this situation?

A. Arrange for these employees to take a course in organizing priorities.
B. Determine which employee is the worst offender.
C. Assess the assignments and work methods of these employees.
D. Set up a meeting with these employees to learn about any work problems they are having.

16. As you are giving an employee a certain assignment, she expresses concern that it is too difficult. The employee is reluctant to accept the assignment. Which one of the following actions should you take first in this situation?

A. Insist that the employee take on the assignment.
B. Tell the employee that it is likely she has completed assignments of similar difficulty before.
C. Offer to share the tasks of the assignment with the employee.
D. Ask the employee why she sees the assignment as difficult.

ADMINISTRATIVE SUPERVISION

DIRECTIONS: For the following two questions, assume that you supervise a section composed of several units. Each unit has a supervisor and several employees. All unit supervisors report directly to you.

17. Assume that you are the head of a section made up of four units, each of which is responsible for similar work. The work volume of one of the units of the section has permanently decreased to the point that the supervisor of that unit now is responsible for much less work than any of the other three unit supervisors. Of the following, which determination should you as the section head make first in this situation?

A. Can other or additional tasks be assigned to this unit?
B. Can the unit supervisor function as assistant section head?
C. Can the unit supervisor's position be reclassified or reallocated?
D. Can the section be reorganized into three units?

18. In which one of the following circumstances should you try to reduce turnover in the section you supervise?

A. The turnover is higher than that of other sections.
B. The turnover reduces the number of highly experienced employees.
C. The turnover lowers the efficiency of the section.
D. The turnover requires unit supervisors to spend a moderate amount of time in training new employees.

PRACTICE TEST KEY

(1) A
(2) D
(3) B
(4) D
(5) A
(6) B
(7) C
(8) D
(9) B
(10) C
(11) D
(12) D
(13) D
(14) A
(15) C
(16) D
(17) A
(18) C

HOW TO TAKE A TEST

I. YOU MUST PASS AN EXAMINATION

A. *WHAT EVERY CANDIDATE SHOULD KNOW*

Examination applicants often ask us for help in preparing for the written test. What can I study in advance? What kinds of questions will be asked? How will the test be given? How will the papers be graded?

As an applicant for a civil service examination, you may be wondering about some of these things. Our purpose here is to suggest effective methods of advance study and to describe civil service examinations.

Your chances for success on this examination can be increased if you know how to prepare. Those "pre-examination jitters" can be reduced if you know what to expect. You can even experience an adventure in good citizenship if you know why civil service exams are given.

B. *WHY ARE CIVIL SERVICE EXAMINATIONS GIVEN?*

Civil service examinations are important to you in two ways. As a citizen, you want public jobs filled by employees who know how to do their work. As a job seeker, you want a fair chance to compete for that job on an equal footing with other candidates. The best-known means of accomplishing this two-fold goal is the competitive examination.

Exams are widely publicized throughout the nation. They may be administered for jobs in federal, state, city, municipal, town or village governments or agencies.

Any citizen may apply, with some limitations, such as the age or residence of applicants. Your experience and education may be reviewed to see whether you meet the requirements for the particular examination. When these requirements exist, they are reasonable and applied consistently to all applicants. Thus, a competitive examination may cause you some uneasiness now, but it is your privilege and safeguard.

C. *HOW ARE CIVIL SERVICE EXAMS DEVELOPED?*

Examinations are carefully written by trained technicians who are specialists in the field known as "psychological measurement," in consultation with recognized authorities in the field of work that the test will cover. These experts recommend the subject matter areas or skills to be tested; only those knowledges or skills important to your success on the job are included. The most reliable books and source materials available are used as references. Together, the experts and technicians judge the difficulty level of the questions.

Test technicians know how to phrase questions so that the problem is clearly stated. Their ethics do not permit "trick" or "catch" questions. Questions may have been tried out on sample groups, or subjected to statistical analysis, to determine their usefulness.

Written tests are often used in combination with performance tests, ratings of training and experience, and oral interviews. All of these measures combine to form the best-known means of finding the right person for the right job.

II. HOW TO PASS THE WRITTEN TEST

A. NATURE OF THE EXAMINATION

To prepare intelligently for civil service examinations, you should know how they differ from school examinations you have taken. In school you were assigned certain definite pages to read or subjects to cover. The examination questions were quite detailed and usually emphasized memory. Civil service exams, on the other hand, try to discover your present ability to perform the duties of a position, plus your potentiality to learn these duties. In other words, a civil service exam attempts to predict how successful you will be. Questions cover such a broad area that they cannot be as minute and detailed as school exam questions.

In the public service similar kinds of work, or positions, are grouped together in one "class." This process is known as *position-classification*. All the positions in a class are paid according to the salary range for that class. One class title covers all of these positions, and they are all tested by the same examination.

B. FOUR BASIC STEPS

1) Study the announcement

How, then, can you know what subjects to study? Our best answer is: "Learn as much as possible about the class of positions for which you've applied." The exam will test the knowledge, skills and abilities needed to do the work.

Your most valuable source of information about the position you want is the official exam announcement. This announcement lists the training and experience qualifications. Check these standards and apply only if you come reasonably close to meeting them.

The brief description of the position in the examination announcement offers some clues to the subjects which will be tested. Think about the job itself. Review the duties in your mind. Can you perform them, or are there some in which you are rusty? Fill in the blank spots in your preparation.

Many jurisdictions preview the written test in the exam announcement by including a section called "Knowledge and Abilities Required," "Scope of the Examination," or some similar heading. Here you will find out specifically what fields will be tested.

2) Review your own background

Once you learn in general what the position is all about, and what you need to know to do the work, ask yourself which subjects you already know fairly well and which need improvement. You may wonder whether to concentrate on improving your strong areas or on building some background in your fields of weakness. When the announcement has specified "some knowledge" or "considerable knowledge," or has used adjectives like "beginning principles of…" or "advanced … methods," you can get a clue as to the number and difficulty of questions to be asked in any given field. More questions, and hence broader coverage, would be included for those subjects which are more important in the work. Now weigh your strengths and weaknesses against the job requirements and prepare accordingly.

3) Determine the level of the position

Another way to tell how intensively you should prepare is to understand the level of the job for which you are applying. Is it the entering level? In other words, is this the position in which beginners in a field of work are hired? Or is it an intermediate or advanced level? Sometimes this is indicated by such words as "Junior" or "Senior" in the class title. Other jurisdictions use Roman numerals to designate the level – Clerk I, Clerk II, for example. The word "Supervisor" sometimes appears in the title. If the level is not indicated by the title, check the description of duties. Will you be working under very close supervision, or will you have responsibility for independent decisions in this work?

4) Choose appropriate study materials

Now that you know the subjects to be examined and the relative amount of each subject to be covered, you can choose suitable study materials. For beginning level jobs, or even advanced ones, if you have a pronounced weakness in some aspect of your training, read a modern, standard textbook in that field. Be sure it is up to date and has general coverage. Such books are normally available at your library, and the librarian will be glad to help you locate one. For entry-level positions, questions of appropriate difficulty are chosen – neither highly advanced questions, nor those too simple. Such questions require careful thought but not advanced training.

If the position for which you are applying is technical or advanced, you will read more advanced, specialized material. If you are already familiar with the basic principles of your field, elementary textbooks would waste your time. Concentrate on advanced textbooks and technical periodicals. Think through the concepts and review difficult problems in your field.

These are all general sources. You can get more ideas on your own initiative, following these leads. For example, training manuals and publications of the government agency which employs workers in your field can be useful, particularly for technical and professional positions. A letter or visit to the government department involved may result in more specific study suggestions, and certainly will provide you with a more definite idea of the exact nature of the position you are seeking.

III. KINDS OF TESTS

Tests are used for purposes other than measuring knowledge and ability to perform specified duties. For some positions, it is equally important to test ability to make adjustments to new situations or to profit from training. In others, basic mental abilities not dependent on information are essential. Questions which test these things may not appear as pertinent to the duties of the position as those which test for knowledge and information. Yet they are often highly important parts of a fair examination. For very general questions, it is almost impossible to help you direct your study efforts. What we can do is point out some of the more common of these general abilities needed in public service positions and describe some typical questions.

1) General information

Broad, general information has been found useful for predicting job success in some kinds of work. This is tested in a variety of ways, from vocabulary lists to questions about current events. Basic background in some field of work, such as sociology or economics, may be sampled in a group of questions. Often these are principles which have become familiar to most persons through exposure rather than through formal training. It is difficult to advise you how to study for these questions; being alert to the world around you is our best suggestion.

2) Verbal ability

An example of an ability needed in many positions is verbal or language ability. Verbal ability is, in brief, the ability to use and understand words. Vocabulary and grammar tests are typical measures of this ability. Reading comprehension or paragraph interpretation questions are common in many kinds of civil service tests. You are given a paragraph of written material and asked to find its central meaning.

3) Numerical ability

Number skills can be tested by the familiar arithmetic problem, by checking paired lists of numbers to see which are alike and which are different, or by interpreting charts and graphs. In the latter test, a graph may be printed in the test booklet which you are asked to use as the basis for answering questions.

4) Observation

A popular test for law-enforcement positions is the observation test. A picture is shown to you for several minutes, then taken away. Questions about the picture test your ability to observe both details and larger elements.

5) Following directions

In many positions in the public service, the employee must be able to carry out written instructions dependably and accurately. You may be given a chart with several columns, each column listing a variety of information. The questions require you to carry out directions involving the information given in the chart.

6) Skills and aptitudes

Performance tests effectively measure some manual skills and aptitudes. When the skill is one in which you are trained, such as typing or shorthand, you can practice. These tests are often very much like those given in business school or high school courses. For many of the other skills and aptitudes, however, no short-time preparation can be made. Skills and abilities natural to you or that you have developed throughout your lifetime are being tested.

Many of the general questions just described provide all the data needed to answer the questions and ask you to use your reasoning ability to find the answers. Your best preparation for these tests, as well as for tests of facts and ideas, is to be at your physical and mental best. You, no doubt, have your own methods of getting into an exam-taking mood and keeping "in shape." The next section lists some ideas on this subject.

IV. KINDS OF QUESTIONS

Only rarely is the "essay" question, which you answer in narrative form, used in civil service tests. Civil service tests are usually of the short-answer type. Full instructions for answering these questions will be given to you at the examination. But in case this is your first experience with short-answer questions and separate answer sheets, here is what you need to know:

1) Multiple-choice Questions

Most popular of the short-answer questions is the "multiple choice" or "best answer" question. It can be used, for example, to test for factual knowledge, ability to solve problems or judgment in meeting situations found at work.

A multiple-choice question is normally one of three types—
- It can begin with an incomplete statement followed by several possible endings. You are to find the one ending which *best* completes the statement, although some of the others may not be entirely wrong.
- It can also be a complete statement in the form of a question which is answered by choosing one of the statements listed.

- It can be in the form of a problem – again you select the best answer.

Here is an example of a multiple-choice question with a discussion which should give you some clues as to the method for choosing the right answer:

When an employee has a complaint about his assignment, the action which will *best* help him overcome his difficulty is to
    A. discuss his difficulty with his coworkers
    B. take the problem to the head of the organization
    C. take the problem to the person who gave him the assignment
    D. say nothing to anyone about his complaint

In answering this question, you should study each of the choices to find which is best. Consider choice "A" – Certainly an employee may discuss his complaint with fellow employees, but no change or improvement can result, and the complaint remains unresolved. Choice "B" is a poor choice since the head of the organization probably does not know what assignment you have been given, and taking your problem to him is known as "going over the head" of the supervisor. The supervisor, or person who made the assignment, is the person who can clarify it or correct any injustice. Choice "C" is, therefore, correct. To say nothing, as in choice "D," is unwise. Supervisors have and interest in knowing the problems employees are facing, and the employee is seeking a solution to his problem.

2) True/False Questions

The "true/false" or "right/wrong" form of question is sometimes used. Here a complete statement is given. Your job is to decide whether the statement is right or wrong.

SAMPLE: A roaming cell-phone call to a nearby city costs less than a non-roaming call to a distant city.

This statement is wrong, or false, since roaming calls are more expensive.
This is not a complete list of all possible question forms, although most of the others are variations of these common types. You will always get complete directions for answering questions. Be sure you understand *how* to mark your answers – ask questions until you do.

V. RECORDING YOUR ANSWERS

Computer terminals are used more and more today for many different kinds of exams.
For an examination with very few applicants, you may be told to record your answers in the test booklet itself. Separate answer sheets are much more common. If this separate answer sheet is to be scored by machine – and this is often the case – it is highly important that you mark your answers correctly in order to get credit.
An electronic scoring machine is often used in civil service offices because of the speed with which papers can be scored. Machine-scored answer sheets must be marked with a pencil, which will be given to you. This pencil has a high graphite content which responds to the electronic scoring machine. As a matter of fact, stray dots may register as answers, so do not let your pencil rest on the answer sheet while you are pondering the correct answer. Also, if your pencil lead breaks or is otherwise defective, ask for another.

Since the answer sheet will be dropped in a slot in the scoring machine, be careful not to bend the corners or get the paper crumpled.

The answer sheet normally has five vertical columns of numbers, with 30 numbers to a column. These numbers correspond to the question numbers in your test booklet. After each number, going across the page are four or five pairs of dotted lines. These short dotted lines have small letters or numbers above them. The first two pairs may also have a "T" or "F" above the letters. This indicates that the first two pairs only are to be used if the questions are of the true-false type. If the questions are multiple choice, disregard the "T" and "F" and pay attention only to the small letters or numbers.

Answer your questions in the manner of the sample that follows:

32. The largest city in the United States is
    A. Washington, D.C.
    B. New York City
    C. Chicago
    D. Detroit
    E. San Francisco

1) Choose the answer you think is best. (New York City is the largest, so "B" is correct.)
2) Find the row of dotted lines numbered the same as the question you are answering. (Find row number 32)
3) Find the pair of dotted lines corresponding to the answer. (Find the pair of lines under the mark "B.")
4) Make a solid black mark between the dotted lines.

VI. BEFORE THE TEST

Common sense will help you find procedures to follow to get ready for an examination. Too many of us, however, overlook these sensible measures. Indeed, nervousness and fatigue have been found to be the most serious reasons why applicants fail to do their best on civil service tests. Here is a list of reminders:

- Begin your preparation early – Don't wait until the last minute to go scurrying around for books and materials or to find out what the position is all about.
- Prepare continuously – An hour a night for a week is better than an all-night cram session. This has been definitely established. What is more, a night a week for a month will return better dividends than crowding your study into a shorter period of time.
- Locate the place of the exam – You have been sent a notice telling you when and where to report for the examination. If the location is in a different town or otherwise unfamiliar to you, it would be well to inquire the best route and learn something about the building.
- Relax the night before the test – Allow your mind to rest. Do not study at all that night. Plan some mild recreation or diversion; then go to bed early and get a good night's sleep.
- Get up early enough to make a leisurely trip to the place for the test – This way unforeseen events, traffic snarls, unfamiliar buildings, etc. will not upset you.
- Dress comfortably – A written test is not a fashion show. You will be known by number and not by name, so wear something comfortable.

- Leave excess paraphernalia at home – Shopping bags and odd bundles will get in your way. You need bring only the items mentioned in the official notice you received; usually everything you need is provided. Do not bring reference books to the exam. They will only confuse those last minutes and be taken away from you when in the test room.
- Arrive somewhat ahead of time – If because of transportation schedules you must get there very early, bring a newspaper or magazine to take your mind off yourself while waiting.
- Locate the examination room – When you have found the proper room, you will be directed to the seat or part of the room where you will sit. Sometimes you are given a sheet of instructions to read while you are waiting. Do not fill out any forms until you are told to do so; just read them and be prepared.
- Relax and prepare to listen to the instructions
- If you have any physical problem that may keep you from doing your best, be sure to tell the test administrator. If you are sick or in poor health, you really cannot do your best on the exam. You can come back and take the test some other time.

VII. AT THE TEST

The day of the test is here and you have the test booklet in your hand. The temptation to get going is very strong. Caution! There is more to success than knowing the right answers. You must know how to identify your papers and understand variations in the type of short-answer question used in this particular examination. Follow these suggestions for maximum results from your efforts:

1) Cooperate with the monitor

The test administrator has a duty to create a situation in which you can be as much at ease as possible. He will give instructions, tell you when to begin, check to see that you are marking your answer sheet correctly, and so on. He is not there to guard you, although he will see that your competitors do not take unfair advantage. He wants to help you do your best.

2) Listen to all instructions

Don't jump the gun! Wait until you understand all directions. In most civil service tests you get more time than you need to answer the questions. So don't be in a hurry. Read each word of instructions until you clearly understand the meaning. Study the examples, listen to all announcements and follow directions. Ask questions if you do not understand what to do.

3) Identify your papers

Civil service exams are usually identified by number only. You will be assigned a number; you must not put your name on your test papers. Be sure to copy your number correctly. Since more than one exam may be given, copy your exact examination title.

4) Plan your time

Unless you are told that a test is a "speed" or "rate of work" test, speed itself is usually not important. Time enough to answer all the questions will be provided, but this does not mean that you have all day. An overall time limit has been set. Divide the total time (in minutes) by the number of questions to determine the approximate time you have for each question.

5) Do not linger over difficult questions

If you come across a difficult question, mark it with a paper clip (useful to have along) and come back to it when you have been through the booklet. One caution if you do this – be sure to skip a number on your answer sheet as well. Check often to be sure that you have not lost your place and that you are marking in the row numbered the same as the question you are answering.

6) Read the questions

Be sure you know what the question asks! Many capable people are unsuccessful because they failed to *read* the questions correctly.

7) Answer all questions

Unless you have been instructed that a penalty will be deducted for incorrect answers, it is better to guess than to omit a question.

8) Speed tests

It is often better NOT to guess on speed tests. It has been found that on timed tests people are tempted to spend the last few seconds before time is called in marking answers at random – without even reading them – in the hope of picking up a few extra points. To discourage this practice, the instructions may warn you that your score will be "corrected" for guessing. That is, a penalty will be applied. The incorrect answers will be deducted from the correct ones, or some other penalty formula will be used.

9) Review your answers

If you finish before time is called, go back to the questions you guessed or omitted to give them further thought. Review other answers if you have time.

10) Return your test materials

If you are ready to leave before others have finished or time is called, take ALL your materials to the monitor and leave quietly. Never take any test material with you. The monitor can discover whose papers are not complete, and taking a test booklet may be grounds for disqualification.

VIII. EXAMINATION TECHNIQUES

1) Read the general instructions carefully. These are usually printed on the first page of the exam booklet. As a rule, these instructions refer to the timing of the examination; the fact that you should not start work until the signal and must stop work at a signal, etc. If there are any *special* instructions, such as a choice of questions to be answered, make sure that you note this instruction carefully.

2) When you are ready to start work on the examination, that is as soon as the signal has been given, read the instructions to each question booklet, underline any key words or phrases, such as *least, best, outline, describe* and the like. In this way you will tend to answer as requested rather than discover on reviewing your paper that you *listed without describing*, that you selected the *worst* choice rather than the *best* choice, etc.

3) If the examination is of the objective or multiple-choice type – that is, each question will also give a series of possible answers: A, B, C or D, and you are called upon to select the best answer and write the letter next to that answer on your answer paper – it is advisable to start answering each question in turn. There may be anywhere from 50 to 100 such questions in the three or four hours allotted and you can see how much time would be taken if you read through all the questions before beginning to answer any. Furthermore, if you come across a question or group of questions which you know would be difficult to answer, it would undoubtedly affect your handling of all the other questions.

4) If the examination is of the essay type and contains but a few questions, it is a moot point as to whether you should read all the questions before starting to answer any one. Of course, if you are given a choice – say five out of seven and the like – then it is essential to read all the questions so you can eliminate the two that are most difficult. If, however, you are asked to answer all the questions, there may be danger in trying to answer the easiest one first because you may find that you will spend too much time on it. The best technique is to answer the first question, then proceed to the second, etc.

5) Time your answers. Before the exam begins, write down the time it started, then add the time allowed for the examination and write down the time it must be completed, then divide the time available somewhat as follows:
    - If 3-1/2 hours are allowed, that would be 210 minutes. If you have 80 objective-type questions, that would be an average of 2-1/2 minutes per question. Allow yourself no more than 2 minutes per question, or a total of 160 minutes, which will permit about 50 minutes to review.
    - If for the time allotment of 210 minutes there are 7 essay questions to answer, that would average about 30 minutes a question. Give yourself only 25 minutes per question so that you have about 35 minutes to review.

6) The most important instruction is to *read each question* and make sure you know what is wanted. The second most important instruction is to *time yourself properly* so that you answer every question. The third most important instruction is to *answer every question*. Guess if you have to but include something for each question. Remember that you will receive no credit for a blank and will probably receive some credit if you write something in answer to an essay question. If you guess a letter – say "B" for a multiple-choice question – you may have guessed right. If you leave a blank as an answer to a multiple-choice question, the examiners may respect your feelings but it will not add a point to your score. Some exams may penalize you for wrong answers, so in such cases *only*, you may not want to guess unless you have some basis for your answer.

7) Suggestions
    a. Objective-type questions
        1. Examine the question booklet for proper sequence of pages and questions
        2. Read all instructions carefully
        3. Skip any question which seems too difficult; return to it after all other questions have been answered
        4. Apportion your time properly; do not spend too much time on any single question or group of questions

5. Note and underline key words – *all, most, fewest, least, best, worst, same, opposite,* etc.
6. Pay particular attention to negatives
7. Note unusual option, e.g., unduly long, short, complex, different or similar in content to the body of the question
8. Observe the use of "hedging" words – *probably, may, most likely,* etc.
9. Make sure that your answer is put next to the same number as the question
10. Do not second-guess unless you have good reason to believe the second answer is definitely more correct
11. Cross out original answer if you decide another answer is more accurate; do not erase until you are ready to hand your paper in
12. Answer all questions; guess unless instructed otherwise
13. Leave time for review

  b. Essay questions
   1. Read each question carefully
   2. Determine exactly what is wanted. Underline key words or phrases.
   3. Decide on outline or paragraph answer
   4. Include many different points and elements unless asked to develop any one or two points or elements
   5. Show impartiality by giving pros and cons unless directed to select one side only
   6. Make and write down any assumptions you find necessary to answer the questions
   7. Watch your English, grammar, punctuation and choice of words
   8. Time your answers; don't crowd material

8) Answering the essay question

Most essay questions can be answered by framing the specific response around several key words or ideas. Here are a few such key words or ideas:

M's: manpower, materials, methods, money, management
P's: purpose, program, policy, plan, procedure, practice, problems, pitfalls, personnel, public relations

  a. Six basic steps in handling problems:
   1. Preliminary plan and background development
   2. Collect information, data and facts
   3. Analyze and interpret information, data and facts
   4. Analyze and develop solutions as well as make recommendations
   5. Prepare report and sell recommendations
   6. Install recommendations and follow up effectiveness

  b. Pitfalls to avoid
   1. *Taking things for granted* – A statement of the situation does not necessarily imply that each of the elements is necessarily true; for example, a complaint may be invalid and biased so that all that can be taken for granted is that a complaint has been registered

2. *Considering only one side of a situation* – Wherever possible, indicate several alternatives and then point out the reasons you selected the best one
3. *Failing to indicate follow up* – Whenever your answer indicates action on your part, make certain that you will take proper follow-up action to see how successful your recommendations, procedures or actions turn out to be
4. *Taking too long in answering any single question* – Remember to time your answers properly

IX. AFTER THE TEST

Scoring procedures differ in detail among civil service jurisdictions although the general principles are the same. Whether the papers are hand-scored or graded by machine we have described, they are nearly always graded by number. That is, the person who marks the paper knows only the number – never the name – of the applicant. Not until all the papers have been graded will they be matched with names. If other tests, such as training and experience or oral interview ratings have been given, scores will be combined. Different parts of the examination usually have different weights. For example, the written test might count 60 percent of the final grade, and a rating of training and experience 40 percent. In many jurisdictions, veterans will have a certain number of points added to their grades.

After the final grade has been determined, the names are placed in grade order and an eligible list is established. There are various methods for resolving ties between those who get the same final grade – probably the most common is to place first the name of the person whose application was received first. Job offers are made from the eligible list in the order the names appear on it. You will be notified of your grade and your rank as soon as all these computations have been made. This will be done as rapidly as possible.

People who are found to meet the requirements in the announcement are called "eligibles." Their names are put on a list of eligible candidates. An eligible's chances of getting a job depend on how high he stands on this list and how fast agencies are filling jobs from the list.

When a job is to be filled from a list of eligibles, the agency asks for the names of people on the list of eligibles for that job. When the civil service commission receives this request, it sends to the agency the names of the three people highest on this list. Or, if the job to be filled has specialized requirements, the office sends the agency the names of the top three persons who meet these requirements from the general list.

The appointing officer makes a choice from among the three people whose names were sent to him. If the selected person accepts the appointment, the names of the others are put back on the list to be considered for future openings.

That is the rule in hiring from all kinds of eligible lists, whether they are for typist, carpenter, chemist, or something else. For every vacancy, the appointing officer has his choice of any one of the top three eligibles on the list. This explains why the person whose name is on top of the list sometimes does not get an appointment when some of the persons lower on the list do. If the appointing officer chooses the second or third eligible, the No. 1 eligible does not get a job at once, but stays on the list until he is appointed or the list is terminated.

X. HOW TO PASS THE INTERVIEW TEST

The examination for which you applied requires an oral interview test. You have already taken the written test and you are now being called for the interview test – the final part of the formal examination.

You may think that it is not possible to prepare for an interview test and that there are no procedures to follow during an interview. Our purpose is to point out some things you can do in advance that will help you and some good rules to follow and pitfalls to avoid while you are being interviewed.

What is an interview supposed to test?

The written examination is designed to test the technical knowledge and competence of the candidate; the oral is designed to evaluate intangible qualities, not readily measured otherwise, and to establish a list showing the relative fitness of each candidate – as measured against his competitors – for the position sought. Scoring is not on the basis of "right" and "wrong," but on a sliding scale of values ranging from "not passable" to "outstanding." As a matter of fact, it is possible to achieve a relatively low score without a single "incorrect" answer because of evident weakness in the qualities being measured.

Occasionally, an examination may consist entirely of an oral test – either an individual or a group oral. In such cases, information is sought concerning the technical knowledges and abilities of the candidate, since there has been no written examination for this purpose. More commonly, however, an oral test is used to supplement a written examination.

Who conducts interviews?

The composition of oral boards varies among different jurisdictions. In nearly all, a representative of the personnel department serves as chairman. One of the members of the board may be a representative of the department in which the candidate would work. In some cases, "outside experts" are used, and, frequently, a businessman or some other representative of the general public is asked to serve. Labor and management or other special groups may be represented. The aim is to secure the services of experts in the appropriate field.

However the board is composed, it is a good idea (and not at all improper or unethical) to ascertain in advance of the interview who the members are and what groups they represent. When you are introduced to them, you will have some idea of their backgrounds and interests, and at least you will not stutter and stammer over their names.

What should be done before the interview?

While knowledge about the board members is useful and takes some of the surprise element out of the interview, there is other preparation which is more substantive. It *is* possible to prepare for an oral interview – in several ways:

1) Keep a copy of your application and review it carefully before the interview

This may be the only document before the oral board, and the starting point of the interview. Know what education and experience you have listed there, and the sequence and dates of all of it. Sometimes the board will ask you to review the highlights of your experience for them; you should not have to hem and haw doing it.

2) Study the class specification and the examination announcement

Usually, the oral board has one or both of these to guide them. The qualities, characteristics or knowledges required by the position sought are stated in these documents. They offer valuable clues as to the nature of the oral interview. For example, if the job involves supervisory responsibilities, the announcement will usually indicate that knowledge of modern supervisory methods and the qualifications of the candidate as a supervisor will be tested. If so, you can expect such questions, frequently in the form of a hypothetical situation which you are expected to solve. NEVER go into an oral without knowledge of the duties and responsibilities of the job you seek.

3) Think through each qualification required

Try to visualize the kind of questions you would ask if you were a board member. How well could you answer them? Try especially to appraise your own knowledge and background in each area, *measured against the job sought*, and identify any areas in which you are weak. Be critical and realistic – do not flatter yourself.

4) Do some general reading in areas in which you feel you may be weak

For example, if the job involves supervision and your past experience has NOT, some general reading in supervisory methods and practices, particularly in the field of human relations, might be useful. Do NOT study agency procedures or detailed manuals. The oral board will be testing your understanding and capacity, not your memory.

5) Get a good night's sleep and watch your general health and mental attitude

You will want a clear head at the interview. Take care of a cold or any other minor ailment, and of course, no hangovers.

What should be done on the day of the interview?

Now comes the day of the interview itself. Give yourself plenty of time to get there. Plan to arrive somewhat ahead of the scheduled time, particularly if your appointment is in the fore part of the day. If a previous candidate fails to appear, the board might be ready for you a bit early. By early afternoon an oral board is almost invariably behind schedule if there are many candidates, and you may have to wait. Take along a book or magazine to read, or your application to review, but leave any extraneous material in the waiting room when you go in for your interview. In any event, relax and compose yourself.

The matter of dress is important. The board is forming impressions about you – from your experience, your manners, your attitude, and your appearance. Give your personal appearance careful attention. Dress your best, but not your flashiest. Choose conservative, appropriate clothing, and be sure it is immaculate. This is a business interview, and your appearance should indicate that you regard it as such. Besides, being well groomed and properly dressed will help boost your confidence.

Sooner or later, someone will call your name and escort you into the interview room. *This is it.* From here on you are on your own. It is too late for any more preparation. But remember, you asked for this opportunity to prove your fitness, and you are here because your request was granted.

What happens when you go in?

The usual sequence of events will be as follows: The clerk (who is often the board stenographer) will introduce you to the chairman of the oral board, who will introduce you to the other members of the board. Acknowledge the introductions before you sit down. Do not be surprised if you find a microphone facing you or a stenotypist sitting by. Oral interviews are usually recorded in the event of an appeal or other review.

Usually the chairman of the board will open the interview by reviewing the highlights of your education and work experience from your application – primarily for the benefit of the other members of the board, as well as to get the material into the record. Do not interrupt or comment unless there is an error or significant misinterpretation; if that is the case, do not hesitate. But do not quibble about insignificant matters. Also, he will usually ask you some question about your education, experience or your present job – partly to get you to start talking and to establish the interviewing "rapport." He may start the actual questioning, or turn it over to one of the other members. Frequently, each member undertakes the questioning on a particular area, one in which he is perhaps most competent, so you can expect each member to participate in the examination. Because time is limited, you may also expect some rather abrupt switches in the direction the questioning takes, so do not be upset by it. Normally, a board member will not pursue a single line of questioning unless he discovers a particular strength or weakness.

After each member has participated, the chairman will usually ask whether any member has any further questions, then will ask you if you have anything you wish to add. Unless you are expecting this question, it may floor you. Worse, it may start you off on an extended, extemporaneous speech. The board is not usually seeking more information. The question is principally to offer you a last opportunity to present further qualifications or to indicate that you have nothing to add. So, if you feel that a significant qualification or characteristic has been overlooked, it is proper to point it out in a sentence or so. Do not compliment the board on the thoroughness of their examination – they have been sketchy, and you know it. If you wish, merely say, "No thank you, I have nothing further to add." This is a point where you can "talk yourself out" of a good impression or fail to present an important bit of information. Remember, *you close the interview yourself*.

The chairman will then say, "That is all, Mr. _____, thank you." Do not be startled; the interview is over, and quicker than you think. Thank him, gather your belongings and take your leave. Save your sigh of relief for the other side of the door.

How to put your best foot forward

Throughout this entire process, you may feel that the board individually and collectively is trying to pierce your defenses, seek out your hidden weaknesses and embarrass and confuse you. Actually, this is not true. They are obliged to make an appraisal of your qualifications for the job you are seeking, and they want to see you in your best light. Remember, they must interview all candidates and a non-cooperative candidate may become a failure in spite of their best efforts to bring out his qualifications. Here are 15 suggestions that will help you:

1) Be natural – Keep your attitude confident, not cocky

If you are not confident that you can do the job, do not expect the board to be. Do not apologize for your weaknesses, try to bring out your strong points. The board is interested in a positive, not negative, presentation. Cockiness will antagonize any board member and make him wonder if you are covering up a weakness by a false show of strength.

2) Get comfortable, but don't lounge or sprawl

Sit erectly but not stiffly. A careless posture may lead the board to conclude that you are careless in other things, or at least that you are not impressed by the importance of the occasion. Either conclusion is natural, even if incorrect. Do not fuss with your clothing, a pencil or an ashtray. Your hands may occasionally be useful to emphasize a point; do not let them become a point of distraction.

3) Do not wisecrack or make small talk

This is a serious situation, and your attitude should show that you consider it as such. Further, the time of the board is limited – they do not want to waste it, and neither should you.

4) Do not exaggerate your experience or abilities

In the first place, from information in the application or other interviews and sources, the board may know more about you than you think. Secondly, you probably will not get away with it. An experienced board is rather adept at spotting such a situation, so do not take the chance.

5) If you know a board member, do not make a point of it, yet do not hide it

Certainly you are not fooling him, and probably not the other members of the board. Do not try to take advantage of your acquaintanceship – it will probably do you little good.

6) Do not dominate the interview

Let the board do that. They will give you the clues – do not assume that you have to do all the talking. Realize that the board has a number of questions to ask you, and do not try to take up all the interview time by showing off your extensive knowledge of the answer to the first one.

7) Be attentive

You only have 20 minutes or so, and you should keep your attention at its sharpest throughout. When a member is addressing a problem or question to you, give him your undivided attention. Address your reply principally to him, but do not exclude the other board members.

8) Do not interrupt

A board member may be stating a problem for you to analyze. He will ask you a question when the time comes. Let him state the problem, and wait for the question.

9) Make sure you understand the question

Do not try to answer until you are sure what the question is. If it is not clear, restate it in your own words or ask the board member to clarify it for you. However, do not haggle about minor elements.

10) Reply promptly but not hastily

A common entry on oral board rating sheets is "candidate responded readily," or "candidate hesitated in replies." Respond as promptly and quickly as you can, but do not jump to a hasty, ill-considered answer.

11) Do not be peremptory in your answers

A brief answer is proper – but do not fire your answer back. That is a losing game from your point of view. The board member can probably ask questions much faster than you can answer them.

12) Do not try to create the answer you think the board member wants

He is interested in what kind of mind you have and how it works – not in playing games. Furthermore, he can usually spot this practice and will actually grade you down on it.

13) Do not switch sides in your reply merely to agree with a board member

Frequently, a member will take a contrary position merely to draw you out and to see if you are willing and able to defend your point of view. Do not start a debate, yet do not surrender a good position. If a position is worth taking, it is worth defending.

14) Do not be afraid to admit an error in judgment if you are shown to be wrong

The board knows that you are forced to reply without any opportunity for careful consideration. Your answer may be demonstrably wrong. If so, admit it and get on with the interview.

15) Do not dwell at length on your present job

The opening question may relate to your present assignment. Answer the question but do not go into an extended discussion. You are being examined for a *new* job, not your present one. As a matter of fact, try to phrase ALL your answers in terms of the job for which you are being examined.

Basis of Rating

Probably you will forget most of these "do's" and "don'ts" when you walk into the oral interview room. Even remembering them all will not ensure you a passing grade. Perhaps you did not have the qualifications in the first place. But remembering them will help you to put your best foot forward, without treading on the toes of the board members.

Rumor and popular opinion to the contrary notwithstanding, an oral board wants you to make the best appearance possible. They know you are under pressure – but they also want to see how you respond to it as a guide to what your reaction would be under the pressures of the job you seek. They will be influenced by the degree of poise you display, the personal traits you show and the manner in which you respond.

ABOUT THIS BOOK

This book contains tests divided into Examination Sections. Go through each test, answering every question in the margin. We have also attached a sample answer sheet at the back of the book that can be removed and used. At the end of each test look at the answer key and check your answers. On the ones you got wrong, look at the right answer choice and learn. Do not fill in the answers first. Do not memorize the questions and answers, but understand the answer and principles involved. On your test, the questions will likely be different from the samples. Questions are changed and new ones added. If you understand these past questions you should have success with any changes that arise. Tests may consist of several types of questions. We have additional books on each subject should more study be advisable or necessary for you. Finally, the more you study, the better prepared you will be. This book is intended to be the last thing you study before you walk into the examination room. Prior study of relevant texts is also recommended. NLC publishes some of these in our Fundamental Series. Knowledge and good sense are important factors in passing your exam. Good luck also helps. So now study this Passbook, absorb the material contained within and take that knowledge into the examination. Then do your best to pass that exam.

EXAMINATION SECTION

EXAMINATION SECTION
TEST 1

DIRECTIONS: Each question or incomplete statement is followed by several suggested answers or completions. Select the one that BEST answers the question or completes the statement. *PRINT THE LETTER OF THE CORRECT ANSWER IN THE SPACE AT THE RIGHT.*

1. As a general rule, which of the following areas on a campus would be most in need of protection by a physical barrier?
   Areas

   A. set aside for group activities
   B. smaller than 40 feet in diameter
   C. with roof access
   D. less than 18 feet above ground

   1._____

2. For a campus officer to be armed, it is customary for him to complete a signed statement pledging himself to certain guidelines. Which of the following would typically be included in such a statement?
   I. The firearm will never be used as a club or similar weapon.
   II. Before shooting directly at a person, the officer will fire at least one warning shot.
   III. The firearm is only to be drawn when the officer's life, or the life of another, is threatened.
   IV. Shots directed at a perpetrator should be intended to disable, rather than kill.
   The CORRECT answer is:

   A. I, III   B. I, III, IV
   C. III *only*   D. II, III, IV

   2._____

3. An arrest that is made after the security officer sees the offense committed is known as an arrest on

   A. reasonable suspicion of probable cause
   B. view
   C. detention
   D. complaint

   3._____

4. The gate valve alarm of a sprinkler system has sounded. This means that the

   A. sprinkler system has been activated
   B. main water riser to the valve has been shut off
   C. storage water level has dropped below minimum requirements
   D. secondary water valve has been closed

   4._____

5. A *dry* fire — from burning wood, paper, or textiles — is classified as Class

   A. A   B. B   C. C   D. D

   5._____

6. The main DISADVANTAGE associated with the use of local alarms in security systems is that

   A. sometimes nobody is around to hear them
   B. they are dependent on electrical power
   C. they must be placed in multiple locations
   D. they don't deter criminals from breaking and entering

   6.____

7. Each of the following is a symptom exhibited by *huffers* of vapors produced by glue, gasoline, paint, or other substances EXCEPT

   A. slurred speech   B. violent behavior
   C. coughing   D. increased appetite

   7.____

8. Legally, a theft from the inside of a vehicle that has been locked and entered unlawfully is called

   A. robbery   B. grand larceny
   C. burglary   D. petty larceny

   8.____

9. Security problems that may be caused by severe heat include

   A. increased likelihood of loss of power
   B. electrical overheating
   C. greater ability for people to hide stolen property
   D. increased likelihood of fires

   9.____

10. Which of the following campus features does the most to necessitate a 24-hour radio dispatcher?
    A

    A. residential community
    B. contractual installation such as food service
    C. valuable collection
    D. high-rise building or buildings

    10.____

11. If rounds clocks are used by an officer on patrol,

    A. the clock areas should be evenly spaced
    B. each clock must be punched on every round, regardless of the order
    C. the clock locations should never be changed
    D. they should be punched in exactly the same order each time

    11.____

12. Because of the operating costs involved, a _____ alarm system is used primarily for government-owned facilities.

    A. remote   B. central station
    C. local   D. proprietary station

    12.____

13. When assisting victims at the scene of an accident, an officer may
    I. give nonprescription medication
    II. restrain a person who is having a seizure
    III. treat a victim for shock
    IV. give the person fluids if the person is conscious
    The CORRECT answer is:

    A. I only   B. II only   C. III, IV   D. IV only

    13.____

14. When a(n) _____ is NOT generally an occasion on which a person, automobile, or premises may be legally searched.

    A. subject is being held for questioning
    B. warrant has been obtained
    C. emergency situation exists
    D. lawful arrest has been made

15. After a crime has been committed, a(n) _____ makes the most useful interview subject.

    A. witness   B. victim   C. suspect   D. informant

16. A _____ lock generally offers the LEAST amount of security.

    A. combination   B. pin tumbler
    C. disc tumbler   D. cipher

17. Evacuation guidelines for most campus buildings provide for an area warden, stair guard, and a group leader who is appointed from among the building's management personnel. Typically, a group leader will be responsible for controlling and directing about _____ people, depending on the floor size and layout.

    A. 5   B. 15   C. 25   D. 35

18. The campus has just received a bomb threat, and a search is underway. When searching individual rooms, an officer should begin

    A. at the door and move in a circular path
    B. at the corners and move inward
    C. with the furniture and then check the fixtures
    D. at the ceiling and move to the floor

19. The highest percentage of crime on school campuses typically occurs in

    A. classrooms and private offices
    B. residence hall or dorms
    C. parking lots
    D. commercial installations such as bookstores and food service

20. For most security applications, a report listing the holder of keys must be filed

    A. twice daily   B. daily
    C. twice weekly   D. weekly

21. The best driving speed for vehicle patrol services is generally between _____ miles per hour.

    A. 5-10   B. 15-20   C. 25-30   D. 35-40

22. Which of the following statements is generally FALSE?

    A. An officer should never approach a group of people without requesting backup, even if it is not needed.
    B. The officer should never draw a weapon as a tactic for discouraging violence.
    C. An officer should never confront hostile persons alone.
    D. When using a flashlight, the officer should hold it sheltered close to his body.

23. In general, security personnel may make an arrest if they
    I. observe a suspect taking property
    II. know a felony has been committed but did not see it happen
    III. know a misdemeanor has been committed but did not see it happen
    The CORRECT answer is:

    A. I only   B. I, II   C. I, III   D. II, III

24. Which of the following may be a visible symptom of the abuse of opiates such as morphine, codeine, or heroin?

    A. Antisocial behavior
    B. Constricted eye functions
    C. Pale, sweaty skin
    D. Rapid speech

25. A security officer is the first to arrive at the scene of an accident that has caused injury. The victim has an open wound that is bleeding dark red, in a steady stream. After taking precautions against blood-borne disease, the officer should

    A. flush the wound with water
    B. apply a tourniquet
    C. apply antiseptic
    D. apply direct pressure to the wound

26. When approaching a subject for a weapons search, the officer should inform the subject that the search is to be conducted

    A. after the subject has been apprehended
    B. from behind, with one hand placed on the subject's shoulder
    C. from the patrol car, through a bullhorn or intercom
    D. from a safe distance of at least five feet

27. Which of the following elements should be included in a shift report?
    I. Detailed accounts of reported incidents
    II. Time and number of patrol rounds completed
    III. Information on condition of lighting
    IV. Weather conditions
    The CORRECT answer is:

    A. I only
    B. II, III, IV
    C. III, IV
    D. I, II

28. A(n) _____ internal alarm would probably be most effective in protecting a safe or vault.

    A. audio
    B. ultrasonic
    C. photoelectric
    D. capacitance

29. A call has come in from a passenger on a stranded elevator to the switchboard operator. After the operator receives the relevant information, security and maintenance personnel are contacted. Security personnel should report to the

    A. floor where the elevator is stranded
    B. maintenance personnel for direction
    C. bottom floor
    D. top floor

30. The post indicator alarm of a sprinkler system has sounded. This means the

    A. sprinkler system has been activated
    B. main water riser to the valve has been shut off
    C. storage water level has dropped below minimum requirements
    D. secondary water valve has been closed

31. The primary goal of a private security officer at the scene of a recent crime is

    A. containment
    B. witness interviews
    C. suspect apprehension
    D. evidence gathering

32. If a security officer encounters an accident victim who has gone into shock, the officer should do each of the following EXCEPT

    A. keep the victim warm
    B. raise the victim's head
    C. treat injuries
    D. loosen the victim's clothing

33. For a security officer, the foundation of good report writing is considered to be

    A. through patrolling
    B. good interviewing
    C. field note taking
    D. outlining skills

34. The fundamental difference between a crime called *malicious destruction of property* and one called *vandalism* is one of

    A. jurisdiction
    B. apparent motive
    C. the monetary amount of damage
    D. the type of property that was damaged

35. The most commonly used form of access control in setting such as college campuses is

    A. cipher locks
    B. compartmentalization
    C. flood lighting
    D. entry gate posts

36. The _____ should be allowed input into the decision to arm security personnel for specific situations or events.
    I. employers of security personnel
    II. public
    III. security agency
    IV. local law enforcement agency

    The CORRECT answer is:

    A. I, III
    B. I, IV
    C. II, III, IV
    D. II, IV

37. Which of the following activities generally offers the greatest degree of flexibility in the delivery of security services?

    A. Report writing
    B. Vehicle patrol
    C. Access control
    D. Foot patrol

38. Which of the following is NOT a security concern that is generally associated with flooding?   38.____
    A. Usefulness of parking areas
    B. Evacuation plans
    C. Bursting water pipes
    D. Looting

39. Which of the following is a use-of-force guideline for private security personnel?   39.____
    A. If equipment (such as a flashlight) is not designed for use as a weapon, it should never be used for that purpose.
    B. If necessary, use a weapon as a form of intimidation to forestall the necessity of having to use it.
    C. Saps or billyclubs should be displayed prominently on the officer's belt to discourage resistance.
    D. The officer should use whatever force is necessary to overcome perceived resistance.

40. An informant has come forward to offer information about a crime that has been committed on campus. The security officer believes it is important to understand the informant's motivation for coming forward.   40.____
    Generally, the officer should approach this subject
    A. at the beginning of the interview
    B. when the informant least expects it
    C. after the informant has given an account, but before the officer has asked any questions
    D. at the conclusion of the interview

KEY (CORRECT ANSWERS)

1.	D	11.	A	21.	B	31.	A
2.	A	12.	A	22.	D	32.	B
3.	B	13.	C	23.	B	33.	C
4.	D	14.	A	24.	B	34.	B
5.	A	15.	A	25.	D	35.	D
6.	A	16.	C	26.	D	36.	A
7.	D	17.	B	27.	B	37.	B
8.	C	18.	A	28.	D	38.	C
9.	D	19.	B	29.	A	39.	A
10.	A	20.	B	30.	B	40.	D

TEST 2

DIRECTIONS: Each question or incomplete statement is followed by several suggested answers or completions. Select the one that BEST answers the question or completes the statement. *PRINT THE LETTER OF THE CORRECT ANSWER IN THE SPACE AT THE RIGHT.*

1. The campus has just received a bomb threat, and a search is underway. When searching individual rooms, team members should be instructed to

    A. start the search in the center of the room and move outward from there
    B. search slowly, first searching the area from the floor to waist height
    C. place a marker on any suspicious looking item
    D. enter a room completely before beginning the search

1._____

2. When on a foot patrol assignment, an officer should

    A. turn the lights off whenever leaving a building
    B. stick to the shadows and avoid being seen
    C. observe the area to be patrolled before entering
    D. stick to the same pattern of patrolling

2._____

3. Chemical fires are classified as Class

    A. A   B. B   C. C   D. D

3._____

4. If campus security officers are to be armed, a _____ is typically most appropriate for their use.

    A. shotgun
    B. short-nosed .38-caliber revolver
    C. carbine
    D. long-nosed .357 magnum

4._____

5. Which of the following is NOT a guideline that should be followed by security personnel who are on foot patrol at night?

    A. Avoid being lit from the back
    B. View the area to be patrolled in advance, if possible
    C. When entering buildings and are moving from room to room, open doors as quietly as possible
    D. Keep the flashlight on thumb pressure only

5._____

6. Which of the following types of locks is most likely to be used with cabinets and desks?

    A. Combination lock   B. Disc tumbler lock
    C. Padlock   D. Cipher lock

6._____

7. When on patrol, security personnel have an obligation to report
    I. traffic patterns
    II. improper employee conduct
    III. observed hazards
    IV. poor housekeeping or maintenance practices

    The CORRECT answer is:

    A. I *only*   B. II, IV
    C. II, III, IV   D. III, IV

7._____

8. Towing policies for the enforcement of campus parking should include each of the following EXCEPT

   A. a contractual arrangement with a tow truck operator
   B. fines returnable to the local municipality, if possible
   C. the presence of a security officer at each towing incident
   D. a random pattern of towing that includes first-time offenders

9. Which of the following statements is generally TRUE?

   A. An officer should always display his badge prominently, especially when on night patrol.
   B. An officer should communicate with a dispatcher or other officers constantly while on duty.
   C. When approaching a vehicle, an officer should walk directly in front of the vehicle headlights.
   D. If a door has a window, an officer should look through it and examine the room before entering.

10. Which of the following is a sign that might be exhibited by a person who is on amphetamines or *uppers*?

    A. Loss of appetite
    B. Constricted pupils
    C. Rapid speech
    D. Uncontrolled laughing

11. Whenever possible, security policy guidelines for campus residence halls should include each of the following EXCEPT

    A. a periphery of high-intensity light around the exterior
    B. the use of interchangeable-core locking cylinders
    C. the use of only one main ground-floor entrance per building
    D. planting shrubs/trees outside first-floor rooms

12. An alarm system whose monitors are located in the main guard office is known as a _____ alarm system.

    A. remote
    B. central station
    C. local
    D. proprietary station

13. A security officer comes across a victim who has been badly burned. The officer should

    A. treat the victim for shock
    B. bandage the burn
    C. apply cold water to the burn
    D. apply an ointment or salve

14. Which of the following interview subjects typically presents a security officer with the least amount of difficulty?
    A(n)

    A. witness   B. victim   C. suspect   D. informant

15. Access control to any campus will be ineffective in any case if _____ are not provided.

    A. physical barriers
    B. weapons
    C. floodlights
    D. secure locks

16. Generally, security personnel may detain a person if
    I. it is known that the subject has information regarding a crime
    II. there is probable cause to believe the person has unlawfully taken property that can be recovered by holding the person for a reasonable period of time
    III. it is suspected that the person will commit a crime in the near future

    The CORRECT answer is:

    A. I, II
    B. II only
    C. III only
    D. I, III

17. In general, departmental record control should place a _____ day limit on the time allotted for the removal of files from the office by security personnel.

    A. 1
    B. 2-3
    C. 5-7
    D. 10-15

18. Keys to gates, buildings, and other secured equipment must generally be issued and returned by officers

    A. every day
    B. every week
    C. every month
    D. annually

19. A crime has just been committed and a security officer is the first to arrive at the scene. Before the police arrive, a handful of campus officials arrive and request to enter the crime scene.
    The best way to handle this is to

    A. keep them out by any means necessary
    B. request their cooperation in remaining outside the scene until the police have arrived
    C. refer them to the security supervisor
    D. defer to their wishes

20. Which of the following phrases has a different meaning from the others?

    A. Incident report
    B. Post journal
    C. Shift report
    D. Post log

21. In order to be effective, combination locks used for access control should have AT LEAST _____ numbers.

    A. 3
    B. 4
    C. 5
    D. 6

22. The simplest, most effective, and trouble-free peripheral alarm system for low-risk applications would probably involve

    A. magnetic switches
    B. button switches
    C. metallic foil tape
    D. audio switches

23. During a bomb search, a suspicious-looking package is found. Security personnel should

    A. move the package to a secure location
    B. place the package in water
    C. prevent anyone from touching the package
    D. place a tag on the package

24. When assisting a victim at the scene of an accident, an officer may
    I. describe an injury to the victim
    II. lift an injured person to a sitting position
    III. try to remove a foreign object from the victim's eye
    IV. attempt to keep the victim warm
    The CORRECT answer is:

    A. I only   B. II, III   C. IV only   D. III, IV

25. Each of the following is a symptom of shock EXCEPT

    A. slow pulse   B. intense thirst
    C. dilated pupils   D. irregular breathing

26. When on vehicle patrol, an officer should

    A. park directly in front of the building to be inspected
    B. observe from a distance or in a drive-by before driving into an area
    C. use spotlights to meet inspection requirements
    D. keep all windows closed while driving

27. Which of the following is a guideline to be followed by security personnel who are required to testify in court?

    A. Avoid asking attorneys to repeat their questions
    B. Never use the phrase *I think*
    C. Answer all questions as completely as possible
    D. Avoid looking directly at the judge or jury

28. Of the following types of arrest, the one that is most troublesome for security officers to justify is one that is made on

    A. reasonable suspicion of probable cause
    B. view
    C. detention
    D. complaint

29. The primary DISADVANTAGE associated with the use of central station alarm monitors is that

    A. time is lost from the time the signal is received until personnel arrive at the alarm area
    B. they do not provide a link to outside law enforcement agencies
    C. intruders are tipped off that the alarm has been activated
    D. they do not pin down the exact location of the alarm site

30. When writing any report, a security officer should

    A. write in the third person
    B. make sure there is at least one copy made
    C. use a formal outline
    D. use as few words as possible

31. Generally, campus property such as audio-visual equipment and office machinery should be inventoried at LEAST

   A. monthly
   B. quarterly
   C. annually
   D. every two years

32. Security personnel who carry firearms should generally be required to requalify themselves at a firing range every

   A. 4 months
   B. 6 months
   C. year
   D. two years

33. Which of the following campus building areas is generally LEAST likely to be used for the placement of a bomb?

   A. Elevator shafts
   B. Toilets
   C. Roofs
   D. Electrical panels

34. If padlocks are used in security systems, it is recommended that they be made of

   A. aluminum
   B. case-hardened steel
   C. cast iron
   D. hardened steel

35. An officer should make certain assumptions about foot patrol assignments. Which of the following is NOT one of these?

   A. Some form of communication is available for the officer to obtain assistance or request instructions.
   B. Most foot patrol assignments are single-officer duties.
   C. Only buildings that are open for public access will be included in the assignment.
   D. Back-up officers are available but are at some distance.

36. Which of the following statements about security personnel arrests is/are generally TRUE?
   I. The subject does not have to be under control in order for there to be an arrest.
   II. Detaining a person is a technical arrest.
   III. An arrest is made with the arresting persons identifying themselves and make a statement such as *you are under arrest*, and either touch the suspect or the suspect agrees.
   IV. The authority for the arrest must be known by the suspect.
   The CORRECT answer is:

   A. I, II, IV
   B. II, III, IV
   C. III, IV
   D. I, III

37. As a general rule, an area that is less than _____ from another structure should be protected by a physical barrier.

   A. 14 feet
   B. 25 feet
   C. 64 feet
   D. 100 yards

38. Security concerns associated with extreme cold include each of the following EXCEPT

   A. delayed communication
   B. physical danger from frozen surfaces
   C. increased opportunity for concealing objects under clothes
   D. integrity of plumbing systems

39. Fires from flammable liquids or grease are classified as Class 39.___

    A. A B. B C. C D. D

40. When interviewing the victim of a crime, which of the following is a guideline that should generally be followed by a security officer? 40.___

    A. Make sure at least one other officer is present.
    B. Maintain a calm, steady demeanor.
    C. Get the facts by any means necessary.
    D. Keep the victim away from others who are familiar to him/her.

KEY (CORRECT ANSWERS)

1. B	11. D	21. B	31. C
2. C	12. D	22. A	32. A
3. D	13. A	23. C	33. C
4. B	14. D	24. C	34. D
5. C	15. A	25. A	35. C
6. B	16. B	26. B	36. B
7. C	17. B	27. B	37. A
8. D	18. A	28. A	38. A
9. B	19. B	29. A	39. B
10. C	20. A	30. B	40. B

EXAMINATION SECTION
TEST 1

DIRECTIONS: Each question or incomplete statement is followed by several suggested answers or completions. Select the one that BEST answers the question or completes the statement. *PRINT THE LETTER OF THE CORRECT ANSWER IN THE SPACE AT THE RIGHT.*

Questions 1-3.

DIRECTIONS: Questions 1 through 3 are to be answered SOLELY on the basis of the following passage.

    On May 15 at 10:15 A.M., Mr. Price was returning to his home at 220 Kings Walk when he discovered two of his neighbor's apartment doors slightly opened. One neighbor, Mrs. Kagan, who lives alone in Apartment 1C, was away on vacation. The other apartment, IB, is occupied by Martin and Ruth Stone, an elderly couple, who usually take a walk everyday at 10:00 A.M. Fearing a robbery might be taking place, Mr. Price runs downstairs to Mr. White in Apartment BI to call the police. Police Communications Technician Johnson received the call at 10:20 A.M. Mr. Price gave his address and stated that two apartments were possibly being burglarized. Communications Technician Johnson verified the address in the computer and then asked Mr. Price for descriptions of the suspects. He explained that he had not seen anyone, but he believed that they were still inside the building. Communications Technician Johnson immediately notified the dispatcher who assigned two patrol cars at 10:25 A.M., while Mr. Price was still on the phone. Communications Technician Johnson told Mr. Price that the police were responding to the location.

1. Who called Communications Technician Johnson?

   A. Mrs. Kagan   B. Mr. White
   C. Mrs. Stone   D. Mr. Price

2. What time did Communications Technician Johnson receive the call?
_____ A.M.

   A. 10:00   B. 10:15   C. 10:20   D. 10:25

3. Which tenant was away on vacation?
The tenant in Apartment

   A. 1C   B. IB   C. BI   D. ID

4. Dispatcher Watkins receives the following information regarding a complaint.
   Place of occurrence: St. James Park
   Complaint: Large group of intoxicated males throwing beer bottles and playing loud music
   Complainant: Oscar Aker
   Complainant's Address: 13 St. James Square, Apt. 2B
Dispatcher Watkins is not certain if this incident should be reported to 911 or Mr. Aker's local precinct. Dispatcher Watkins is about to notify his supervisor of the call. Which one of the following expresses the above information MOST clearly and accurately?

A. Mr. Aker, who lives at 13 St. James Square, Apt. 2B, called to make a complaint of a large group of intoxicated males who are throwing beer bottles and playing loud music in St. James Park.
B. Mr. Aker, who lives at 13 St. James Square, called to complain about a large group of intoxicated males, in Apt. 2B. They are throwing beer bottles and playing loud music in St. James Park.
C. Mr. Aker of 13 St. James Square, Apt. 2B, called to complain about loud music. There were a large group of intoxicated males throwing beer bottles in St. James Park.
D. As a result of intoxicated males throwing beer bottles Mr. Aker of 13 St. James Square, Apt. 2B, called to complain. A large group was playing loud music in St. James Park.

5. Communications Operator Davis recorded the following information from a caller:

Crime:	Rape
Time of Rape:	11:30 A.M.
Place of Rape:	Ralph's Dress Shop, 200 Lexington Avenue
Victim:	Linda Castro - employee at Ralph's Dress Shop
Description of Suspect:	Male, white
Weapon:	Knife

Communications Operator Davis needs to be clear and accurate when relaying information to the patrol car. Which one of the following expresses the above information MOST clearly and accurately?

A. Linda Castro was at 200 Lexington Avenue when she was raped at knife point by a white male. At 11:30 A.M., she is an employee of Ralph's Dress Shop.
B. At 11:30 A.M., Linda Castro reported that she was working in Ralph's Dress Shop located at 200 Lexington Avenue. A white male raped her while she was working at knife point.
C. Linda Castro, an employee of Ralph's Dress Shop, located at 200 Lexington Avenue, reported that at 11:30 A.M. a white male raped her at knife point in the dress shop.
D. At 11:30 A.M., a white male pointed a knife at Linda Castro. He raped an employee of Ralph's Dress Shop, which is located at 200 Lexington Avenue.

Question 6.

DIRECTIONS: Question 6 is to be answered SOLELY on the basis of the following information.

Police Communications Technicians frequently receive low priority calls, which are calls that do not require an immediate police response. When a low priority call is received, the Police Communications Technician should transfer the caller to a tape-recorded message which states *there will be a delay in police response.*

6. Police Communications Technicians should transfer to the low priority taped message a call reporting a

A. hubcap missing from an auto
B. child has just swallowed poison

C. group of youths fighting with knives
D. woman being assaulted

Questions 7-9.

DIRECTIONS: Questions 7 through 9 are to be answered SOLELY on the basis of the following passage.

On Tuesday, March 20 at 11:55 P.M., Dispatcher Uzel receives a call from a female stating that she immediately needs the police. The dispatcher asks the caller for her address. The excited female answers, *I can not think of it right now.* The dispatcher tries to calm down the caller. At this point, the female caller tells the dispatcher that her address is 1934 Bedford Avenue. The caller then realizes that 1934 Bedford Avenue is her mother's address and gives her address as 3455 Bedford Avenue. Dispatcher Uzel enters the address into the computer and tells the caller that the cross streets are Myrtle and Willoughby Avenues. The caller answers, *I don't live near Willoughby Avenue.* The dispatcher repeats her address at 3455 Bedford Avenue. Then the female states that her name is Linda Harris and her correct address is 5534 Bedford Avenue. Dispatcher Uzel enters the new address into the computer and determines the cross streets to be Utica Avenue and Kings Highway. The caller agrees that these are the cross streets where she lives.

7. What is the caller's CORRECT address? 7.____

   A. Unknown
   B. 1934 Bedford Avenue
   C. 3455 Bedford Avenue
   D. 5534 Bedford Avenue

8. What are the cross streets of the correct address? 8.____

   A. Myrtle Avenue and Willoughby Avenue
   B. Utica Avenue and Kings Highway
   C. Bedford Avenue and Myrtle Avenue
   D. Utica Avenue and Willoughby Avenue

9. Why did the female caller telephone Dispatcher Uzel? 9.____

   A. She needed the cross streets for her address.
   B. Her mother needed assistance.
   C. The purpose of the call was not mentioned.
   D. She did not know where she lived.

Question 10.

DIRECTIONS: Question 10 is to be answered SOLELY on the basis of the following information.

When performing vehicle license plate checks, Operators should do the following in the order given:
   I. Request the license plate in question.
   II. Repeat the license plate back to the patrol car officers.
   III. Check the license plate locally in the computer.
   IV. Advise the patrol car officers of the results of the local check.
   V. Check the license plate nationally in the computer.
   VI. Advise the patrol car officers of the results of the nationwide check.

10. Operator Johnson gets a request from a patrol car officer for a license plate check on a suspicious car. The patrol car officer tells Operator Johnson that the license plate number is XYZ-843, which Operator Johnson repeats back to the patrol car officer. Operator Johnson checks the license plate locally and determines that the car was stolen in the New York City area.
What should Operator Johnson do NEXT?

   A. Repeat the license plate back to patrol car officers.
   B. Check the license plate nationally.
   C. Advise the patrol car officers of the results of the local check.
   D. Advise the patrol ear officers of the results of the nationwide check.

11. Police Communications Technician Hughes receives a call from the owner of The Diamond Dome Jewelry Store, reporting a robbery. He obtains the following information from the caller:
   Place of Occurrence: The Diamond Dome Jewelry Store, 10 Exchange Place
   Time of Occurrence: 10:00 A.M.
   Crime: Robbery of a $50,000 diamond ring
   Victim: Clayton Pelt, owner of The Diamond Dome Jewelry Store
   Description of Suspect: Male, white, black hair, blue suit and gray shirt
   Weapon: Gun
   Communications Technician Hughes is about to relay the information to the dispatcher. Which one of the following expresses the above information MOST clearly and accurately?

   A. Clayton Pelt reported that at 10:00 A.M. his store, The Diamond Dome Jewelry Store, was robbed at gunpoint. At 10 Exchange Place, a white male with black hair took a $50,000 diamond ring. He was wearing a blue suit and gray shirt.
   B. At 10:00 A.M., a black-haired male robbed a $50,000 diamond ring from The Diamond Dome Jewelry Store, which is owned by Clayton Pelt. A white male was wearing a blue suit and gray shirt and had a gun at 10 Exchange Place.
   C. At 10:00 A.M., Clayton Pelt, owner of The Diamond Dome Jewelry Store, which is located at 10 Exchange Place, was robbed of a $50,000 diamond ring at gunpoint. The suspect is a white male with black hair wearing a blue suit and gray shirt.
   D. In a robbery that occurred at gunpoint, a white male with black hair robbed The Diamond Dome Jewelry Store, which is located at 10 Exchange Place. Clayton Pelt, the owner who was robbed of a $50,000 diamond ring, said he was wearing a blue suit and a gray shirt at 10:00 A.M.

12. Dispatcher Sanders receives the following information from the computer: Place of Occurrence: Bushwick Housing Projects, rear of Building 12B
   Time of Occurrence: 6:00 P.M.
   Crime: Mugging
   Victim: Hispanic female
   Suspect: Unknown
   Dispatcher sanders is about to relay the information to the patrol car.
   Which one of the following expresses the above information MOST clearly and accurately?

A. In the rear of Building 12B, a Hispanic female was mugged. An unknown suspect was in the Bushwick Housing Projects at 6:00 P.M.
B. At 6:00 P.M., a Hispanic female was mugged by an unknown suspect in the rear of Building 12B, in the Bushwick Housing Projects.
C. At 6:00 P.M., a female is in the rear of Building 12B in the Bushwick Housing Projects. An unknown suspect mugged a Hispanic female.
D. A suspect's identity is unknown in the rear of Building 12B in the Bushwick Housing Project at 6:00 P.M. A Hispanic female was mugged.

Questions 13-15.

DIRECTIONS: Questions 13 through 15 are to be answered SOLELY on the basis of the following passage.

Dispatcher Clark, who is performing a 7:30 A.M. to 3:30 P.M. tour of duty, receives a call from Mrs. Gold. Mrs. Gold states there are four people selling drugs in front of Joe's Cleaners, located at the intersection of Main Street and Broadway. After checking the location in the computer, Dispatcher Clark asks the caller to give a description of each person. She gives the following descriptions: one white male wearing a yellow shirt, green pants, and red sneakers; one Hispanic male wearing a red and white shirt, black pants, and white sneakers; one black female wearing a green and red striped dress and red sandals; and one black male wearing a green shirt, yellow pants, and green sneakers. She also states that the Hispanic male, who is standing near a blue van, has the drugs inside a small black shoulder bag. She further states that she saw the black female hide a gun inside a brown paper bag and place it under a black car parked in front of Joe's Cleaners. The drug selling goes on everyday at various times. During the week, it occurs from 7 A.M. to 1 P.M. and from 5 P.M. to 12 A.M., but on weekends it occurs from 3 P.M. until 7 A.M.

13. Which person was wearing red sneakers?

    A. Black male   B. Hispanic male
    C. Black female   D. White male

14. Mrs. Gold stated the drugs were located

    A. under the blue van
    B. inside the black shoulder bag
    C. under the black car
    D. inside the brown paper bag

15. At what time does Mrs. Gold state the drugs are sold on weekends?

    A. 7:30 A.M. - 3:30 P.M.   B. 7:00 A.M. - 1:00 P.M.
    C. 5:00 P.M. - 12:00 A.M.   D. 3:00 P.M. - 7:00 A.M.

16. Police Communications Technician Bentley receives a call of an auto being stripped. He obtains the following information from the caller:
    Place of Occurrence: Corner of West End Avenue and W. 72nd Street
    Time of Occurrence: 10:30 P.M.
    Witness: Mr. Simpson
    Suspects: Two white males
    Crime: Auto stripping
    Action Taken: Suspects fled before police arrived

Communications Technician Bentley is about to enter the incident into the computer and send the information to the dispatcher.
Which one of the following expresses the above information MOST clearly and accurately?

- A. At 10:30 P.M., Mr. Simpson witnessed two white males stripping an auto parked at the corner of West End Avenue and W. 72nd Street. The suspects fled before the police arrived.
- B. An auto was parked at the corner of West End Avenue and W. 72nd Street. Two white males who were stripping at 10:30 P.M. were witnessed by Mr. Simpson. Before the police arrived, the suspects fled.
- C. Mr. Simpson saw two white males at the corner of West End Avenue and W. 72nd Street. Fleeing the scene before the police arrived, the witness saw the suspects strip an auto.
- D. Before the police arrived at 10:30 P.M. on the corner of West End Avenue and W. 72nd Street, Mr. Simpson witnessed two white males. The suspects, who stripped an auto, fled the scene.

17. 911 Operator Washington receives a call of a robbery and obtains the following information regarding the incident:

Place of Occurrence:	First National Bank, 45 West 96th Street
Time of Occurrence:	2:55 P.M.
Amount Taken:	$10,000
Description of Suspect:	Male, black, wearing a leather jacket, blue jeans, and white shirt
Weapon:	Gun

911 Operator Washington is about to enter the call into the computer.
Which one of the following expresses the above information MOST clearly and accurately?

- A. At 2:55 P.M., the First National Bank, located at 45 West 96th Street, was robbed at gunpoint of $10,000. The suspect is a black male and is wearing a leather jacket, blue jeans, and a white shirt.
- B. Ten thousand dollars was robbed from the First National Bank at 2:55 P.M. A black male was wearing a leather jacket, blue jeans, and a white shirt at 45 West 96th Street. He also had a gun.
- C. At 2:55 P.M., a male was wearing a leather jacket, blue jeans, and a white shirt. The First National Bank located at 45 West 96th Street was robbed by a black male. Ten thousand dollars was taken at gunpoint.
- D. Robbing the First National Bank, a male wore a leather jacket, blue jeans, and a white shirt at gunpoint. A black male was at 45 W. 96th Street. At 2:55 P.M., $10,000 was taken.

Questions 18-20.

DIRECTIONS: Questions 18 through 20 are to be answered SOLELY on the basis of the following passage.

Police Communications Technician Gordon receives a call from a male stating there is a bomb set to explode in the gym of Public School 85 in two hours. Realizing the urgency of the call, the Communications Technician calls the radio dispatcher, who assigns Patrol Car 43A to the scene. Communications Technician Gordon then notifies her supervisor, Miss Smith, who first reviews the tape of the call, then calls the Operations Unit which is notified of all serious incidents, and she reports the facts. The Operations Unit notifies the Mayor's Information Agency and Borough Headquarters of the emergency situation.

18. Who did Communications Technician Gordon notify FIRST? 18.____

    A. Supervisor Smith
    B. Operations Unit
    C. Patrol Car 43A
    D. Radio dispatcher

19. The Operations Unit was notified 19.____

    A. to inform school personnel of the bomb
    B. so they can arrive at the scene before the bomb is scheduled to go off
    C. to evacuate the school
    D. due to the seriousness of the incident

20. Who did Miss Smith notify? 20.____

    A. Patrol Car 43A
    B. Operations Unit
    C. Mayor's Information Agency
    D. Borough Headquarters

KEY (CORRECT ANSWERS)

1.	D	11.	C
2.	C	12.	B
3.	A	13.	D
4.	A	14.	B
5.	C	15.	D
6.	A	16.	A
7.	D	17.	A
8.	B	18.	D
9.	C	19.	D
10.	C	20.	B

TEST 2

DIRECTIONS: Each question or incomplete statement is followed by several suggested answers or completions. Select the one that BEST answers the question or completes the statement. *PRINT THE LETTER OF THE CORRECT ANSWER IN THE SPACE AT THE RIGHT.*

1. A Police Communications Technician receives a call reporting a large gathering. She obtained the following information:
   Place of Occurrence: Cooper Square Park
   Time of Occurrence: 1:15 A.M.
   Occurrence: Youths drinking and playing loud music
   Complainant: Mrs. Tucker, 20 Cooper Square
   Action Taken: Police scattered the crowd
   Communications Technician Carter is about to relay the information to the dispatcher. Which one of the following expresses the above information MOST clearly and accurately?

   A. The police responded to Cooper Square Park because Mrs. Tucker, who called 911, lives at 20 Cooper Square. The group of youths was scattered due to drinking and playing loud music at 1:15 A.M.
   B. Mrs. Tucker, who lives at 20 Cooper Square, called 911 to make a complaint of a group of youths who were drinking and playing loud music in Cooper Square Park at 1:15 A.M. The police responded and scattered the crowd.
   C. Loud music and drinking in Cooper Square Park by a group of youths caused the police to respond and scatter the crowd. Mrs. Tucker called 911 and complained. At 1:15 A.M., she lives at 20 Cooper Square.
   D. Playing loud music and drinking, Mrs. Tucker called the police. The police scattered a group of youths in Cooper Square Park at 1:15 A.M. Mrs. Tucker lives at 20 Cooper Square.

2. Dispatcher Weston received a call from the owner of a gas station and obtained the following information:
   Place of Occurrence: Blin's Gas Station, 1800 White Plains Road
   Time of Occurrence: 10:30 A.M.
   Occurrence: Left station without paying
   Witness: David Perilli
   Description of Auto: A white Firebird, license plate GEB275
   Suspect: Male, white, wearing blue jeans and a black T-shirt
   Dispatcher Weston is about to enter the information into the computer.
   Which one of the following expresses the above information MOST clearly and accurately?

   A. At 10:30 A.M., David Perilli witnessed a white male wearing blue jeans and a black T-shirt leave Blin's Gas Station, located at 1800 White Plains Road, without paying. The suspect was driving a white Firebird with license plate GEB275.
   B. Wearing blue jeans and a black T-shirt, David Perilli witnessed a white male leave Blin's Gas Station without paying. He was driving a white Firebird with license plate GEB275. This occurred at 1800 White Plains Road at 10:30 A.M.
   C. David Perilli witnessed a male wearing blue jeans and a black T-shirt driving a white Firebird. At 10:30 A.M., a white male left Blin's Gas Station, located at 1800 White Plains Road, without paying. His license plate was GEB275.

D. At 10:30 A.M., David Perilli witnessed a white male leaving Blin's Gas Station without paying. The driver of a white Firebird, license plate GEB275, was wearing blue jeans and a black T-shirt at 1800 White Plains Road.

Questions 3-4.

DIRECTIONS: Questions 3 and 4 are to be answered SOLELY on the basis of the following information.

Police Communications Technicians are required to assist callers who need non-emergency assistance. The callers are referred to non-emergency agencies. Listed below are some non-emergency situations and the agencies to which they should be referred.

Agency
Local Precinct   Unoccupied suspicious car
Environmental Protection Agency   Open fire hydrant
Sanitation Department   Abandoned car
S.P.C.A.   Injured, stray or sick animal
Transit Authority   Transit Authority travel information

3. Communications Technician Carter received a call from Mr. Cane, who stated that a car without license plates had been parked in front of his house for five days. Mr. Crane should be referred to the

    A. A.S.P.C.A.
    B. Transit Authority
    C. Sanitation Department
    D. Environmental Protection Agency

4. Mrs. Dunbar calls to report that a dog has been hit by a car and is lying at the curb in front of her house. Mrs. Dunbar should be referred to the

    A. Sanitation Department
    B. Local Precinct
    C. Environmental Protection Agency
    D. A.S.P.C.A.

5. Operator Bryant received a call of a robbery and obtained the following information:
    Place of Occurrence: Deluxe Deli, 303 E. 30th Street
    Time of Occurrence: 5:00 P.M.
    Crime: Robbery of $300
    Victim: Bonnie Smith, cashier of Deluxe Deli
    Description of Suspect: White, female, blonde hair, wearing black slacks and a red shirt
    Weapon: Knife
Operator Bryant is about to enter this information into the computer.
Which one of the following expresses the above information MOST clearly and accurately?

- A. Bonnie Smith, the cashier of the Deluxe Deli reported at 5:00 P.M. that she was robbed of $300 at knifepoint at 303 East 30th Street. A white female with blonde hair was wearing black slacks and a red shirt.
- B. At 5:00 P.M., a blonde-haired female robbed the 303 East 30th Street store. At the Deluxe Deli, cashier Bonnie Smith was robbed of $300 by a white female at knifepoint. She was wearing black slacks and a red shirt.
- C. In a robbery that occurred at knifepoint, a blonde-haired white female robbed $300 from the Deluxe Deli. Bonnie Smith, cashier of the 303 East 30th Street store, said she was wearing black slacks and a red shirt at 5:00 P.M.
- D. At 5:00 P.M., Bonnie Smith, cashier of the Deluxe Deli, located at 303 East 30th Street, was robbed of $300 at knifepoint. The suspect is a white female with blonde hair wearing black slacks and a red shirt.

6. 911 Operator Landers receives a call reporting a burglary that happened in the past. He obtained the following information from the caller:

Place of Occurrence:	196 Simpson Street
Date of Occurrence:	June 12
Time of Occurrence:	Between 8:30 A.M. and 7:45 P.M.
Victim:	Mr. Arnold Frank
Items Stolen:	$300 cash, stereo, assorted jewelry, and a VCR

911 Operator Landers is about to enter the incident into the computer.
Which one of the following expresses the above information MOST clearly and accurately?

- A. Mr. Arnold Frank stated that on June 12, between 8:30 A.M. and 7:45 P.M., someone broke into his home at 196 Simpson Street and took $300 in cash, a stereo, assorted jewelry, and a VCR.
- B. Mr. Arnold Frank stated between 8:30 A.M. and 7:45 P.M., he lives at 196 Simpson Street. A stereo, VCR, $300 in cash, and assorted jewelry were taken on June 12.
- C. Between 8:30 A.M. and 7:45 P.M. on June 12, Mr. Arnold Frank reported someone broke into his home. At 196 Simpson Street, a VCR, $300 in cash, a stereo, and assorted jewelry were taken.
- D. A stereo, VCR, $300 in cash, and assorted jewelry were taken between 8:30 M. and 7:45 P.M. On June 12, Mr. Arnold Frank reported he lives at 196 Simpson Street.

Questions 7-9.

DIRECTIONS: Questions 7 through 9 are to be answered SOLELY on the basis of the following passage.

Communications Operator Harris receives a call from Mrs. Stein who reports that a car accident occurred in front of her home. She states that one of the cars belongs to her neighbor, Mrs. Brown, and the other car belongs to Mrs. Stein's son, Joseph Stein. Communications Operator Harris enters Mrs. Stein's address into the computer and receives information that no such address exists. She asks Mrs. Stein to repeat her address. Mrs. Stein repeats her address and states that gasoline is leaking from the cars and that smoke is coming from their engines. She further states that people are trapped in the cars and then hangs up.

Communications Operator Harris notifies her supervisor, Jones, that she received a call but was unable to verify the address and that the caller hung up. Mrs. Jones listens to the tape of the call and finds that the caller stated 450 Park Place not 415 Park Place. She advises Communications Operator Harris to enter the correct address, then notify Emergency Service Unit to respond to the individuals trapped in the cars, the Fire Department for the smoke condition, and Emergency Medical Service for any possible injuries.

7. Who did Communications Operator Harris notify concerning the problem with the caller's address?

   A. Mrs. Brown
   B. Joseph Stein
   C. Joseph Brown
   D. Mrs. Jones

8. Which agency was Communications Operator Harris advised to notify concerning individuals trapped in the cars?

   A. Emergency Medical Service
   B. Fire Department
   C. Emergency Service Unit
   D. NYC Police Department

9. Which agency did Supervisor Jones advise Communications Operator Harris to notify for the smoke condition?

   A. NYC Police Department
   B. Emergency Medical Service
   C. Fire Department
   D. Emergency Service Unit

Question 10.

DIRECTIONS: Question 10 is to be answered SOLELY on the basis of the following information.

When a Police Communications Technician receives a call concerning a bank robbery, a Communications Technician should do the following in the order given:

   I. Get address and name of the bank from the caller.
   II. Enter the address into the computer.
   III. Use the *Hotline* button to alert the dispatcher of the serious incident going into the computer.
   IV. Get back to the caller and get the description of the suspect and other pertinent information.
   V. Enter additional information into the computer and send it to the dispatcher.
   VI. Upgrade the seriousness of the incident so it appears first on dispatcher's screen.
   VII. Notify the Supervising Police Communications Technician of the bank robbery.

10. Police Communications Technician Brent receives a call from Mr. Ross stating that while he was on line at the Trust Bank, at West 34th Street and 9th Avenue, he witnessed a bank robbery. Communications Technician Brent enters the address into the computer, then presses the *Hotline* button and alerts the dispatcher that there was a bank robbery at the Trust Bank on West 34th Street and 9th Avenue. Mr. Ross continues to state that the robber is a white male in his 30's wearing a light blue shirt and blue jeans.
After obtaining other pertinent information, the NEXT step Communications Technician Brent should take is to

    A. enter additional information into the computer and send it to the dispatcher
    B. upgrade the seriousness of the incident so it appears first on the dispatcher's screen
    C. notify his supervisor of the bank robbery
    D. use the *Hotline* button to alert the dispatcher of a serious incident going into the computer

10.____

11. Dispatcher Wilson receives a call regarding drugs being sold in the lobby of an apartment building. He obtains the following information:
Place of Occurrence: 305 Willis Avenue
Time of Occurrence: 2:00 P.M.
Witnesses: Roy Rodriguez and Harry Armstrong
Suspect: Melvin Talbot, left the scene before the police arrived
Crime: Drug sale
Dispatcher Wilson is about to enter this incident into the computer.
Which one of the following expresses the above information MOST clearly and accurately?

    A. Roy Rodriguez and Harry Armstrong reported that they witnessed Melvin Talbot selling drugs in the lobby of 305 Willis Avenue at 2:00 P.M. The suspect left the scene before the police arrived.
    B. In the lobby, Roy Rodriguez reported at 2:00 P.M. he saw Melvin Talbot selling drugs with Harry Armstrong. He left the lobby of 305 Willis Avenue before the police arrived.
    C. Roy Rodriguez and Harry Armstrong witnessed drugs being sold at 305 Willis Avenue. Before the police arrived at 2:00 P.M., Melvin Talbot left the lobby.
    D. Before the police arrived, witnesses stated that Melvin Talbot was selling drugs. At 305 Willis Avenue, in the lobby, Roy Rodriguez and Harry Armstrong said he left the scene at 2:00 P.M.

11.____

12. Operator Rogers receives a call of a car being stolen. He obtains the following information:
Place of Occurrence: Parking lot at 1723 East 20th Street
Time of Occurrence: 2:30 A.M.
Vehicle Involved: 1988 Toyota Corolla
Suspects: Male, Hispanic, wearing a red T-shirt
Crime: Auto theft
Witness: Janet Alonzo
Operator Rogers is entering the information into the computer.
Which one of the following expresses the above information MOST clearly and accurately?

12.____

A. At 2:30 A.M., wearing a red T-shirt, Janet Alonzo witnessed a 1988 Toyota Corolla being stolen by a male Hispanic in the parking lot at 1723 East 20th Street.
B. A male Hispanic, wearing a red T-shirt, was in the parking lot at 1723 East 20th Street." At 2:30 A.M., Janet Alonzo witnessed a 1988 Toyota Corolla being stolen.
C. At 2:30 A.M., Janet Alonzo witnessed a 1988 Toyota Corolla in the parking lot at 1723 East 20th Street being stolen by a male Hispanic who is wearing a red T-shirt.
D. Janet Alonzo witnessed a 1988 Toyota Corolla in the parking lot being stolen. At 2:30 A.M., a male Hispanic was wearing a red T-shirt at 1723 East 20th Street.

Question 13.

DIRECTIONS: Question 13 is to be answered SOLELY on the basis of the following information.

There are times when Police Communications Technicians have to reassign officers in a patrol car from a less serious incident which does not require immediate police response to an incident of a more serious nature which does require immediate police response. Police Communications Technicians must choose among the assigned patrol cars and determine which one is assigned to the least serious incident, then reassign that one to the situation which requires immediate police response.

Communications Technician Reese is working the 13th Division which covers the 79th Precinct. There are only four patrol cars working in the 79th Precinct. They are assigned as follows:

79A is assigned to a car accident with injuries involving an intoxicated driver.

79B is assigned to a group of teenagers playing loud music in a park.

79C is assigned to a group of teenagers trying to steal liquor in a liquor store, who are possibly armed with guns.

79D is assigned to a suspicious man in a bank, with possible intentions to rob the bank.

13. If Communications Technician Reese receives a call of an incident that requires immediate police response, which patrol car should be reassigned?

    A. 79A   B. 79B   C. 79C   D. 79D

Questions 14-16.

DIRECTIONS: Questions 14 through 16 are to be answered SOLELY on the basis of the following information.

On May 12, at 3:35 P.M., Police Communications Technician Connor receives a call from a child caller requesting an ambulance for her mother, whom she cannot wake. The child did not know her address, but gave Communications Technician Connor her apartment number and telephone number. Communications Technician Connor's supervisor, Ms. Bendel, is advised of the situation and consult's Cole's Directory, a listing published by the Bell Telephone Company, to obtain an address when only the telephone number is known. The telephone number is unlisted. Ms. Bendel asks Communications Technician Taylor to call Telco Security to obtain an address from their telephone number listing. Communications Technician Taylor speaks to Ms. Morris of Telco Security and obtains the address. Communications Technician Connor, who is still talking with the child, is given the address by Communications Technician Taylor. She enters the information into the computer system and transfers the caller to the Emergency Medical Service.

14. What information did Communications Technician Connor obtain from the child caller? 14.____

   A. Telephone number and apartment number
   B. Name and address
   C. Address and telephone number
   D. Apartment number and address

15. Communications Technician Taylor obtained the address from 15.____

   A. Communications Technician Connor
   B. Ms. Morris
   C. Supervisor Bendel
   D. the child caller

16. The caller's address was obtained by calling 16.____

   A. Cole's Directory
   B. Telco Security
   C. Emergency Medical Service
   D. The Telephone Company

Question 17.

DIRECTIONS: Question 17 is to be answered SOLELY on the basis of the following information.

The following incidents appear on the Police Communications Technician's computer screen which were called in by three different callers at the same time:
   I. At 3040 Hill Avenue between Worth and Centre Streets, there are two people fighting in the third floor hallway. One of them has a shiny metal object.
   II. In a building located on Hill Avenue between Worth and Centre Streets, a man and a woman are having an argument on the third floor. The woman has a knife in her hand.
   III. In front of Apartment 3C on the third floor, a husband and wife are yelling at each other. The wife is pointing a metal letter opener at her husband. The building is located on the corner of Hill Avenue and Worth Street.

17. A Police Communications Technician may be required to combine into one incident many calls that appear on the computer screen if they seem to be reporting the same incident. Which of the above should a Police Communications Technician combine into one incident? 17.____

   A. I and II   B. I and III
   C. II and III   D. I, II, and III

Questions 18-19.

DIRECTIONS: Questions 18 and 19 are to be answered SOLELY on the basis of the following information.

Police Communications Technicians must be able to identify and assign codes to the crimes described in the calls they receive. All crimes are coded by number and by priority. The priority code number indicates the seriousness of the crime. The lower the priority number, the more serious the crime.

Listed below is a chart of several crimes and their definitions. The corresponding crime code and priority code number are given.

CRIME	DEFINITION	CRIME CODE	PRIORITY CODE
Criminal Mischief:	Occurs when a person intentionally damages another person's property	29	6
Harrassment:	Occurs when a person intentionally annoys another person by striking, shoving, or kicking them without causing injury	27	8
Aggravated Harrassment:	Occurs when a person intentionally annoys another person by using any form of communication	28	9
Theft of Service:	Occurs when a person intentionally avoids payment for services given	25	7

18. Communications Technician Rogers received a call from Mrs. Freeman, who stated that her next door neighbor, whom she had an argument with, has thrown a rock through her apartment window.
    Which one of the following is the CORRECT crime code?

    A. 29   B. 28   C. 27   D. 25

19. Communications Technician Tucker received a call from a man who stated that he is a waiter at the Frontier Diner. He states that one of his customers was refusing to pay for his meal.
    Which one of the following is the CORRECT priority code number for this crime?

    A. 6   B. 7   C. 8   D. 9

Dispatcher Matthews received a call of a bomb threat. He obtained the following information;
Address of Occurrence: 202 Church Avenue
Location: 2nd floor men's room
Time of Call: 12:00 P.M.
Time of Occurrence: 2:00 P.M.
Terrorist Organization: People *Against Government*

Caller: Anonymous male member of *People* Against Government
Action Taken: Supervisor Jones notified of the bomb threat

Dispatcher Matthews is about to enter the information into the computer.
Which one of the following expresses the above information MOST clearly and accurately?

- A. An anonymous male called Dispatcher Matthews and told him that a bomb is set to go off at 202 Church Avenue in the 2nd floor men's room at 2:00 P.M. Dispatcher Matthews notified Supervisor Jones that the caller is from *People Against Government* at 12:00 P.M.
- B. Dispatcher Matthews received a call in the 2nd floor men's room of a bomb threat from an anonymous male member of the *People Against Government* terrorist organization. He notified Supervisor Jones at 12:00 P.M. that a bomb is set to go off at 2:00 P.M. at 202 Church Avenue.
- C. Dispatcher Matthews received a call at 202 Church Avenue from the *People Against Government,* a terrorist organization. An anonymous male stated that a bomb is set to go off at 2:00 P.M. in the 2nd floor men's room. At 12:00 P.M., Dispatcher Matthews notified Supervisor Jones of the call.
- D. At 12:00 P.M., Dispatcher Matthews received a call from an anonymous male caller who states that he is from a terrorist organization known as *People Against Government.* He states that a bomb has been placed in the 2nd floor men's room of 202 Church Avenue and is set to go off at 2:00 P.M. Dispatcher Matthews notified Supervisor Jones of the bomb threat.

KEY (CORRECT ANSWERS)

1.	B	11.	A
2.	A	12.	C
3.	C	13.	B
4.	D	14.	A
5.	D	15.	B
6.	A	16.	B
7.	D	17.	D
8.	C	18.	A
9.	C	19.	B
10.	A	20.	D

EXAMINATION SECTION
TEST 1

DIRECTIONS: Questions 1 through 5 are to be answered on the basis of the information, instructions, and sample question given below. Each question contains a GENERAL RULE, EXCEPTIONS, a PROBLEM, and the ACTION actually taken.

The GENERAL RULE explains what the special officer (security officer) should or should not do.

The EXCEPTIONS describe circumstances under which a special officer (security officer) should take action contrary to the GENERAL RULE.

However, an unusual emergency may justify taking an action that is not covered either by the GENERAL RULE or by the stated EXCEPTIONS.

The PROBLEM describes a situation requiring some action by the special officer (security officer).

ACTION describes what a special officer (security officer) actually did in that particular case.

Read carefully the GENERAL RULE and EXCEPTIONS, the PROBLEM, and the ACTION, and the mark A, B, C, or D in the space at the right in accordance with the following instructions:

I. If an action is clearly justified under the general rule, mark your answer A.
II. If an action is not justified under the general rule, but is justified under a stated exception, mark your answer B.
III. If an action is not justified either by the general rule or by a stated exception, but does seem strongly justified by an unusual emergency situation, mark your answer C.
IV. If an action does not seem justified for any of these reasons, mark your answer D.

SAMPLE QUESTION:

GENERAL RULE: A special officer (security officer) is not empowered to stop a person and search him for hidden weapons.
EXCEPTION: He may stop a person and search him if he has good reason to believe that he may be carrying a hidden weapon. Good reasons to believe he may be carrying a hidden weapon include (a) notification through official channels that a person may be armed, (b) a statement directly to the special officer (security officer) by the person himself that he is armed, and (c) the special officer's (security officer's) own direct observation.

PROBLEM: A special officer (security officer) on duty at a hospital clinic is notified by a woman patient at the clinic that a man sitting near her is making muttered threats that he has a gun and is going to shoot his doctor if the doctor gives him any trouble. Although the woman is upset, she seems to be telling the truth, and two other waiting patients con-

firm this. However, the special officer (security officer) approaches the man and sees no sign of a hidden weapon. The man tells the officer that he has no weapon.
ACTION: The special officer (security officer) takes the man aside into an empty office and proceeds to frisk him for a concealed weapon.

ANSWER: The answer cannot be A, because the general rule is that a special officer (security officer) is not empowered to search a person for hidden weapons. The answer cannot be B, because the notification did not come through official channels, the man did not tell the special officer (security officer) that he had a weapon, and the special officer (security officer) did not observe any weapon. However, since three people have confirmed that the man has said he has a weapon and is threatening to use it, this is pretty clearly an emergency situation that calls for action. Therefore, the answer is C.

1. GENERAL RULE: A special officer (security officer) on duty at a certain entrance is not to leave his post unguarded at any time.
   EXCEPTION: He may leave the post for a brief period if he first summons a replacement. He may also leave if it is necessary for him to take prompt emergency action to prevent injury to persons or property.
   PROBLEM: The special officer (security officer) sees a man running down a hall with a piece of iron pipe in his hand, chasing another man who is shouting for help. By going in immediate pursuit, there is a good chance that the special officer (security officer) can stop the man with the pipe.
   ACTION: The special officer (security officer) leaves his post unguarded and pursues the man.

   The CORRECT answer is:

   A. IB. IIC. IIID. IV

2. GENERAL RULE: Special officers (security officers) assigned to a college campus are instructed not to arrest students for minor violations such as disorderly conduct; instead, the violation should be stopped and the incident should be reported to the college authorities, who will take disciplinary action.
   EXCEPTION: A special officer (security officer) may arrest a student or take other appropriate action if failure to do so is likely to result in personal injury or property damage, or disruption of school activities, or if the incident involves serious criminal behavior.
   PROBLEM: A special officer (security officer) is on duty in a college building where evening classes are being held. He is told that two students are causing a disturbance in a classroom. He arrives and finds that a fist fight is in progress and the classroom is in an uproar. The special officer (security officer) separates the two students who are fighting and takes them out of the room. Both of them seem to be intoxicated. They both have valid student ID cards.
   ACTION: The special officer (security officer) takes down their names and addresses for his report, then tells them to leave the building with a warning not to return this evening.

   The CORRECT answer is:

   A. IB. IIC. IIID. IV

3. **GENERAL RULE:** A special officer (security officer) is not permitted to carry a gun while on duty.
   EXCEPTION: A special officer (security officer) who disarms a person must keep the weapon in his possession for the brief period before he can turn it over to the proper authorities. A special officer (security officer) who is NOT on duty may, like any other citizen, own and carry a gun if he has a proper permit from the Police Department.
   PROBLEM: A special officer (security officer) is assigned to a post where there have been a series of violent incidents in the past few days. He feels that these incidents could have been controlled much more easily if the people involved had seen that the special officer (security officer) had a gun. He has a gun at home, for which he has a valid permit.
   ACTION: The special officer (security officer) brings his gun when he goes on duty. He does not plan to use it, but just show people that he has it so that they will not start any trouble.

   The CORRECT answer is:

   A. I B. II C. III D. IV

4. **GENERAL RULE:** No one except a licensed physician or someone acting directly under a physician's orders may legally administer medicine to another person.
   EXCEPTION: In a first aid situation, the special officer (security officer) is allowed to help a person sufferingから a heart condition or other disease to take medicine which the person has in his possession, provided that the person is conscious and requests this assistance.
   PROBLEM: A special officer (security officer) on duty at a public building is told that a man has collapsed in the elevator. When the special officer (security officer) arrives at the scene, the man is barely conscious. He cannot speak, but he points to his pocket. The special officer (security officer) finds a pill bottle that says *one capsule in ease of need*. The man nods.
   ACTION: The special officer (security officer) puts one capsule in the man's hand and guides the man's hand to his mouth.

   The CORRECT answer is:

   A. I B. II C. III D. IV

5. **GENERAL RULE:** In case of a fire drill or fire alarm, special officers (security officers) on patrol in a building are to remain in their assigned areas to assist in the evacuation of persons from the building and to make sure that no one takes advantage of the situation by stealing property that is left unguarded.
   EXCEPTION: Should there be an actual fire, special officers (security officers) will follow whatever instructions are given by the firefighters or police officers who arrive on the scene to take charge.
   PROBLEM: A special officer (security officer) is on duty patroling the fifth floor of a building when a fire alarm sounds. The fire is in a supply closet at one end of the fifth floor. All personnel have been evacuated from the floor. Neither police nor firemen have yet shown up.
   ACTION: The special officer (security officer) stays on the fifth floor at a safe distance from the supply closet.

   The CORRECT answer is:

   A. I B. II C. III D. IV

KEY (CORRECT ANSWERS)

1. B
2. A
3. D
4. B
5. A

EXAMINATION SECTION
TEST 1

DIRECTIONS: Each question or incomplete statement is followed by several suggested answers or completions. Select the one that BEST answers the question or completes the statement. *PRINT THE LETTER OF THE CORRECT ANSWER IN THE SPACE AT THE RIGHT.*

Questions 1-4.

DIRECTIONS: Questions 1 through 4 are based on the picture entitled *Contents of a Woman's Handbag.* Assume that all of the contents are shown in the picture.

CONTENTS OF A WOMAN'S HANDBAG

1. Where does Gladys Constantine live?

    A. Chalmers Street in Manhattan
    B. Summer Street in Manhattan
    C. Summer Street in Brooklyn
    D. Chalmers Street in Brooklyn

2. How many keys were in the handbag?

    A. 2   B. 3   C. 4   D. 5

3. How much money was in the handbag? _____ dollar(s).

    A. Exactly five   B. More than five
    C. Exactly ten   D. Less than one

4. The sales slip found in the handbag shows the purchase of which of the following?

    A. The handbag   B. Lipstick
    C. Tissues   D. Prescription medicine

Questions 5-8.

DIRECTIONS: Questions 5 through 8 are based on the floor plan below.

FLOOR PLAN

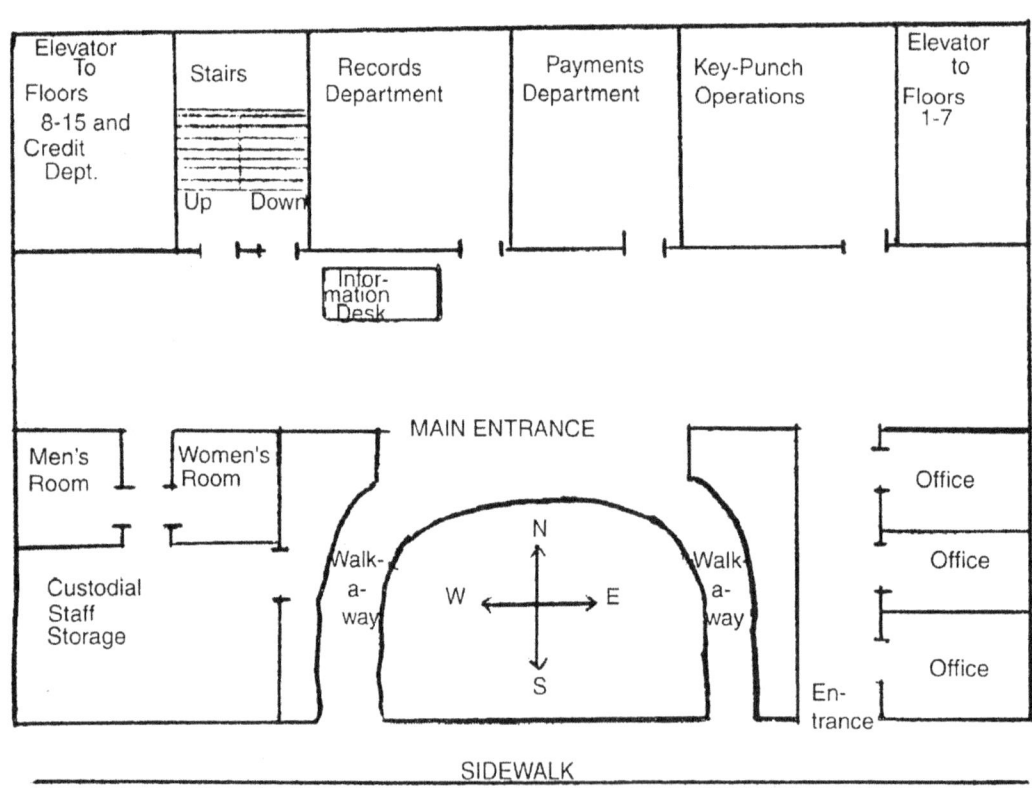

5. A special officer (security officer) on duty at the main entrance must be aware of other outside entrances to his area of the building. These unguarded entrances are usually kept locked, but they are important in case of fire or other emergency.
   Besides the main entrance, how many OTHER entrances shown on the floor plan directly face Forty-ninth Street?
   _____ other entrances.

   A. No B. One C. Two D. Three

6. A person who arrives at the main entrance and asks to be directed to the Credit Department SHOULD be told to

   A. take the elevator on the left
   B. take the elevator on the right
   C. go to a different entrance
   D. go up the stairs on the left

7. On the east side of the entrance can be found

   A. a storage room   B. offices
   C. toilets   D. stairs

8. The space DIRECTLY BEHIND the Information Desk in the floor plan is occupied by

   A. up and down stairs   B. key punch operations
   C. toilets   D. the records department

Questions 9-12.

DIRECTIONS: Answer Questions 9 to 12 on the basis of the information given in the passage below.

The public often believes that the main job of a uniformed officer is to enforce laws by simply arresting people. In reality, however, many of the situations that an officer deals with do not call for the use of his arrest power. In the first place, an officer spends much of his time <u>preventing</u> crimes from happening, by spotting potential violations or suspicious behavior and taking action to prevent illegal acts. In the second place, many of the situations in which officers are called on for assistance involve elements like personal arguments, husband-wife quarrels, noisy juveniles, or mentally disturbed persons. The majority of these problems do not result in arrests and convictions, and often they do not even involve illegal behavior. In the third place, even in situations where there seems to be good reason to make an arrest, an officer may have to exercise very good judgment. There are times when making an arrest too soon could touch off a riot, or could result in the detention of a minor offender while major offenders escaped, or could cut short the gathering of necessary on-the-scene evidence.

9. The above passage IMPLIES that most citizens

   A. will start to riot if they see an arrest being made
   B. appreciate the work that law enforcement officers do
   C. do not realize that making arrests is only a small part of law enforcement
   D. never call for assistance unless they are involved in a personal argument or a husband-wife quarrel

10. According to the passage, one way in which law enforcement officers can prevent crimes from happening is by

   A. arresting suspicious characters
   B. letting minor offenders go free
   C. taking action on potential violations
   D. refusing to get involved in husband-wife fights

11. According to the passage, which of the following statements is NOT true of situations involving mentally disturbed persons?

   A. It is a waste of time to call on law enforcement officers for assistance in such situations.
   B. Such situations may not involve illegal behavior
   C. Such situations often do not result in arrests.
   D. Citizens often turn to law enforcement officers for help in such situations.

12. The last sentence in the passage mentions *detention of minor offenders.*
    Of the following, which BEST explains the meaning of the word *detention* as used here?

   A. Sentencing someone
   B. Indicting someone
   C. Calling someone before a grand jury
   D. Arresting someone

Questions 13-28.

DIRECTIONS: In answering Questions 13 through 28, assume that *you* means a special officer (security officer) on duty. Your basic responsibilities are safeguarding people and property and maintaining order in the area to which you are assigned. You are in uniform, and you are not armed. You keep in touch with your supervisory station either by telephone or by a two-way radio (walkie-talkie).

13. It is a general rule that if the security alarm goes off showing that someone has made an unlawful entrance into a building, no officer responsible for security shall proceed to investigate alone. Each officer must be accompanied by at least one other officer.
    Of the following, which is the MOST probable reason for this rule?

   A. It is dangerous for an officer to investigate such a situation alone.
   B. The intruder might try to bribe an officer to let him go.
   C. One officer may be inexperienced and needs an experienced partner.
   D. Two officers are better than one officer in writing a report of the investigation.

14. You are on weekend duty on the main floor of a public building. The building is closed to the public on weekends, but some employees are sometimes asked to work weekends. You have been instructed to use cautious good judgment in opening the door for such persons.
    Of the following, which one MOST clearly shows the poorest judgment?

A. Admitting an employee who is personally known to you without asking to see any identification except the permit slip signed by the employee's supervisor
B. Refusing to admit someone whom you do not recognize but who claims left his identification at home
C. Admitting to the building only those who can give a detailed description of their weekend work duties
D. Leaving the entrance door locked for a while to make regulation security checks of other areas in the building with the result that no one can either enter or leave during these periods

15. You are on duty at a public building. An office employee tells you that she left her purse in her desk when she went out to lunch, and she has just discovered that it is gone. She has been back from lunch for half an hour and has not left her desk during this period. What should you do FIRST?

    A. Warn all security personnel to stop any suspicious-looking person who is seen with a purse
    B. Ask for a description of the purse
    C. Call the Lost and Found and ask if a purse has been turned in
    D. Obtain statements from any employees who were in the office during the lunch hour

16. You are patrolling your assigned area in a public building. You hear a sudden crash and the sound of running footsteps. You investigate and find that someone has forced open a locked entrance to the building. What is the FIRST thing you should do?

    A. Close the door and try to fix the lock so that no one else can get in
    B. Use your two-way radio to report the emergency and summon help
    C. Chase after the person whose running footsteps you heard
    D. Go immediately to your base office and make out a brief written report

17. You and another special officer (security officer) are on duty in the main waiting area at a welfare center. A caseworker calls both of you over and whispers that one of the clients, Richard Roe, may be carrying a gun. Of the following, what is the BEST action for both of you to take?

    A. You should approach the man, one on each side, and one of you should say loudly and clearly, *"Richard Roe, you are under arrest."*
    B. Both of you should ask the man to go with you to a private room, and then find out if he is carrying a gun
    C. Both of you should grab him, handcuff him, and take him to the nearest precinct station house
    D. Both of you should watch him carefully but not do anything unless he actually pulls a gun

18. You are on duty at a welfare center. You are told that a caseworker is being threatened by a man with a knife. You go immediately to the scene, and you find the caseworker lying on the floor with blood spurting from a wound in his arm. You do not know who the attacker is. What should you do FIRST?

    A. Ask the caseworker for a description of the attacker so that you can set out in pursuit and try to catch him
    B. Take down the names and addresses of any witnesses to the incident

C. Give first aid to the caseworker, if you can, and immediately call for an ambulance
D. Search the people standing around in the room for the knife

19. As a special officer (security officer), you have been patrolling a special section of a hospital building for a week. Smoking is not allowed in this section because the oxygen tanks in use here could easily explode. However, you have observed that some employees sneak into the linen-supply room in this section in order to smoke without anybody seeing them.
Of the following, which is the BEST way for you to deal with this situation?

    A. Whenever you catch anyone smoking, call his supervisor immediately
    B. Request the Building Superintendent to put a padlock on the door of the linen-supply room
    C. Ignore the smoking because you do not want to get a reputation for interfering in the private affairs of other employees
    D. Report the situation to your supervisor and follow his instructions

20. You are on duty at a hospital. You have been assigned to guard the main door, and you are responsible for remaining at your post until relieved. On one of the wards for which you are not responsible, there is a patient who was wounded in a street fight. This patient is under arrest for killing another man in this fight, and he is supposed to be under round-the-clock police guard. A nurse tells you that one of the police officers assigned to guard the patient has suddenly taken ill and has to periodically leave his post to go to the washroom. The nurse is worried because she thinks the patient might try to escape.
Of the following, which is the BEST action for you to take?

    A. Tell the nurse to call you whenever the police officer leaves his post so that you can keep an eye on the patient while the officer is gone
    B. Assume that the police officer probably knows his job, and that there is no reason for you to worry
    C. Alert your supervisor to the nurse's report
    D. Warn the police officer that the nurse has been talking about him

21. You are on night duty at a hospital where you are responsible for patrolling a large section of the main building. Your supervisor tells you that there have been several nighttime thefts from a supply room in your section and asks you to be especially alert for suspicious activity near this supply room.
Of the following, which is the MOST reasonable way to carry out your supervisor's direction?

    A. Check the supply room regularly at half-hour intervals
    B. Make frequent checks of the supply room at irregular intervals
    C. Station yourself by the door of the supply room and stay at this post all night
    D. Find a hidden spot from which you can watch the supply room and stay there all night

22. You are on duty at a vehicle entrance to a hospital. Parking space on the hospital grounds is strictly limited, and no one is ever allowed to park there unless they have an official parking permit. You have just stopped a driver who does not have a parking permit, but he explains that
he is a doctor and he has a patient in the hospital. What should you do?

A. Let him park since he has explained that he is a doctor
B. Ask in a friendly way, *"Can I check your identification?"*
C. Call the Information Desk to make sure there is such a patient in the hospital
D. Tell the driver politely but firmly that he will have to park somewhere else

23. You are on duty at a public building. A man was just mugged on a stairway. The mugger took the man's wallet and started to run down the stairs but tripped and fell. Now the mugger is lying unconscious at the bottom of the stairs and bleeding from the mouth.
The FIRST thing you should do is to

   A. search him to see if he is carrying any other stolen property
   B. pick him up and carry him away from the stairs
   C. try and revive him for questioning
   D. put in a call for an ambulance and police assistance

24. After someone breaks into an employee's locker at a public building, you interview the employee to determine what is missing from the locker. The employee becomes hysterical and asks why you are *wasting time with all these questions* instead of going after the thief.
The MOST reasonable thing for you to do is

   A. tell the employee that it is very important to have an accurate description of the missing articles
   B. quietly tell the employee to calm down and stop interfering with your work
   C. explain to the employee that you are only doing what you were told to do and that you don't make the rules
   D. assure the employee that there are a lot of people working on the case and that someone else is probably arresting the thief right now

25. You are on duty at a public building. An employee reports that a man has just held her up and taken her money. The employee says that the man was about 25 years old, with short blond hair and a pale complexion and was wearing blue jeans.
Of the following additional facts, which one would probably be MOST valuable to officers searching the building for the suspect?

   A. The man was wearing dark glasses.
   B. He had on a green jacket.
   C. He was about 5 feet 8 inches tall.
   D. His hands and fingernails were very dirty.

26. When the fire alarm goes off, it is your job as a special officer (security officer) to see that all employees leave the building quickly by the correct exits. A fire alarm has just sounded, and you are checking the offices on one of the floors. A supervisor in one office tells you, *"This is probably just another fire drill. I've sent my office staff out, but I don't want to stop my own work."*
What should you do?

   A. Insist politely but firmly that the supervisor must obey the fire rules.
   B. Tell the supervisor that it is all right this time but that the rules must be followed in the future.
   C. Tell the supervisor that he is under arrest.
   D. Allow the supervisor to do as he sees fit since he is in charge of his own office.

27. You are on duty on the main floor of a public building. You have been informed that a briefcase has just been stolen from an office on the tenth floor. You see a man getting off the elevator with a briefcase that matches the description of the one that was stolen. What is the FIRST action you should take? 27.____

   A. Arrest the man and take him to the nearest public station
   B. Stop the man and say politely that you want to take a look at the briefcase
   C. Take the briefcase from the man and tell him that he cannot have it back unless he can prove that it is his
   D. Do not stop the man but note down his description and the exact time he got off the elevator

28. You are on duty at a welfare center. You have been told that two clients are arguing with a caseworker and making loud threats. You go to the scene, but the caseworker tells you that everything is now under control. The two clients, who are both mean-looking characters, are still there but seem to be acting normally.
   What SHOULD you do? 28.____

   A. Apologize for having made a mistake and go away.
   B. Arrest the two men for having caused a disturbance.
   C. Insist on standing by until the interview is over, then escort the two men from the building.
   D. Leave the immediate scene but watch for any further developments.

29. You are on duty at a welfare center. A client comes up to you and says that two men just threatened him with a knife and made him give them his money. The client has alcohol on his breath and he is shabbily dressed. He points out the two men he says took the money.
   Of the following, which is the BEST action to take? 29.____

   A. Arrest the two men on the client's complaint.
   B. Ignore the client's complaint since he doesn't look as if he could have had any money.
   C. Suggest to the client that he may be imagining things.
   D. Investigate and find out what happened.

Questions 30-35.

DIRECTIONS: Answer Questions 30 through 35 on the basis of the information given in the passage below. Assume that all questions refer to the same state described in the passage.

The courts and the police consider an "offense" as any conduct that is punishable by a fine or imprisonment. Such offenses include many kinds of acts - from behavior that is merely annoying, like throwing a noisy party that keeps everyone awake, all the way up to violent acts like murder. The law classifies offenses according to the penalties that are provided for them. In one state, minor offenses are called "violations." A violation is punishable by a fine of not more than $250 or imprisonment of not more than. 15 days, or both. The annoying behavior mentioned above is an example of a violation. More serious offenses are classified as "crimes." Crimes are classified by the kind of penalty that is provided. A "misdemeanor" is a crime that is punishable by a fine of not more than $1,000 or by imprisonment of not more than one year, or both. Examples of misdemeanors include stealing something with a value *of $100 or less, turning in a false alarm, or illegally possessing less than 1/8 of an ounce of a dangerous drug. A "felony" is a criminal offense punishable by imprisonment of more than one year. Murder is clearly a felony.*

30. According to the above passage, any act that is punishable by imprisonment or by a fine is called a(n)   30.____

    A. offense   B. violation   C. crime   D. felony

31. According to the above passage, which of the following is classified as a crime?   31.____

    A. Offense punishable by 15 days imprisonment
    B. Minor offense
    C. Violation
    D. Misdemeanor

32. According to the above passage, if a person guilty of burglary can receive a prison sentence of 7 years or more, burglary would be classified as a   32.____

    A. violation   B. misdemeanor
    C. felony   D. violent act

33. According to the above passage, two offenses that would BOTH be classified as misdemeanors are   33.____

    A. making unreasonable noise and stealing a $90 bicycle
    B. stealing a $75 radio and possessing 1/16 of an ounce of heroin
    C. holding up a bank and possessing 1/4 of a pound of marijuana
    D. falsely reporting a fire and illegally double-parking

34. The above passage says that offenses are classified according to the penalties provided for them.   34.____
    On the basis of clues in the passage, who probably decides what the maximum penalties should be for the different kinds of offenses?

    A. The State lawmakers   B. The City police
    C. The Mayor   D. Officials in Washington, B.C.

35. Of the following, which BEST describes the subject matter of the passage?   35.____

    A. How society deals with criminals
    B. How offenses are classified
    C. Three types of criminal behavior
    D. The police approach to offenders

KEY (CORRECT ANSWERS)

1.	C	16.	B
2.	C	17.	B
3.	B	18.	C
4.	D	19.	D
5.	B	20.	C
6.	A	21.	B
7.	B	22.	D
8.	D	23.	D
9.	C	24.	A
10.	C	25.	C
11.	A	26.	A
12.	D	27.	B
13.	A	28.	D
14.	C	29.	D
15.	B	30.	A

31. D
32. C
33. B
34. A
35. B

TEST 2

DIRECTIONS: Each question or incomplete statement is followed by several suggested answers or completions. Select the one that BEST answers the question or completes the statement. *PRINT THE LETTER OF THE CORRECT ANSWER IN THE SPACE AT THE RIGHT.*

Questions 1-5.

DIRECTIONS: Questions 1 through 5 are based on the drawing below showing a view of a waiting area in a public building.

1. A desk is shown in the drawing. Which of the following is on the desk? A(n) 1.____

    A. plant   B. telephone
    C. In-Out file   D. *Information* sign

43

2. On which floor is the waiting area?

   A. Basement
   B. Main floor
   C. Second floor
   D. Third floor

3. The door IMMEDIATELY TO THE RIGHT of the desk is a(n)

   A. door to the Personnel Office
   B. elevator door
   C. door to another corridor
   D. door to the stairs

4. Among the magazines on the tables in the waiting area are

   A. TIME and NEWSWEEK
   B. READER'S DIGEST and T.V. GUIDE
   C. NEW YORK and READER'S DIGEST
   D. TIME and T.V. GUIDE

5. One door is partly open. This is the door to

   A. the Director's office
   B. the Personnel Manager's office
   C. the stairs
   D. an unmarked office

Questions 6-9.

DIRECTIONS: Questions 6 through 9 are based on the drawing below showing the contents of a male suspect's pockets.

CONTENTS OF A MALE SUSPECT'S POCKETS

6. The suspect had a slip in his pockets showing an appointment at an out-patient clinic on   6._____

    A. February 9, 2013   B. September 2, 2013
    C. February 19, 2013   D. September 12, 2013

7. The MP3 player that was found on the suspect was made by   7._____

    A. RCA   B. GE   C. Sony   D. Zenith

8. The coins found in the suspect's pockets have a TOTAL value of   8._____

    A. 56¢   B. 77¢   C. $1.05   D. $1.26

9. All except one of the following were found in the suspect's pockets.   9._____
   Which was NOT found? A

    A. ticket stub   B. comb
    C. subway fare   D. pen

Questions 10-18

DIRECTIONS: In answering Questions 10 through 18, assume that *you* means a special officer (security officer) on duty. Your basic responsibilities are safeguarding people and property and maintaining order in the area to which you are assigned. You are in uniform, and you are not armed. You keep in touch with your supervisory station either by telephone or by a two-way radio (a walkie-talkie).

10. You are on duty at a center run by the Department of Social Services. Two teenaged   10._____
    boys are on their way out of the center. As they go past you, they look at you and laugh, and one makes a remark to you in Spanish. You do not understand Spanish, but you suspect it was a nasty remark.
    What SHOULD you do?

    A. Give the boys a lecture about showing respect for a uniform.
    B. Tell the boys that they had better stay away from the center from now on.
    C. Call for an interpreter and insist that the boy repeat the remark to the interpreter.
    D. Let the boys go on their way since they have done nothing requiring your intervention.

11. You are on duty at a shelter run by the Department of Social Services. You know that   11._____
    many of the shelter clients have drinking problems, drug problems, or mental health problems. You get a call for assistance from a caseworker who says a fight has broken out. When you arrive on the scene, you see that about a dozen clients are engaged in a free-for-all and that two or three of them have pulled knives.
    The BEST course of action is to

    A. call for additional assistance and order all bystanders away from the area
    B. jump into the center of the fighting group and try to separate the fighters
    C. pick up a heavy object and start swinging at anybody who has a knife
    D. try to find out what clients started the fight and place them under arrest

12. You have been assigned to duty at a children's shelter run by the Department of Social Services. The children range in age from 6 to 15, and many of them are at the shelter because they have no homes to go to.
    Of the following, which is the BEST attitude for you to take in dealing with these youngsters?

    A. Assume that they admire and respect anyone in uniform and that they will not usually give you much trouble
    B. Assume that they fear and distrust anyone in uniform and that they are going to give you a hard time unless you act tough
    C. Expect that many of them are going to become juvenile delinquents because of their bad backgrounds and that you should be suspicious of everything they do
    D. Expect that many of them may be emotionally upset and that you should be alert for unusual behavior

13. You are on duty outside the emergency room of a hospital. You notice that an old man has been sitting on a bench outside the room for a long time. He arrived alone, and he has not spoken to anyone at all.
    What SHOULD you do?

    A. Pay no attention to him since he is not bothering anyone.
    B. Tell him to leave since he does not seem to have any business there.
    C. Ask him if you can help him in any way.
    D. Do not speak to him, but keep an eye on him.

14. You are patrolling a section of a public building. An elderly woman carrying a heavy shopping bag asks you if you would watch the shopping bag for her while she keeps an appointment in the building.
    What SHOULD you do?

    A. Watch the shopping bag for her since her appointment probably will not take long.
    B. Refuse her request, explaining that your duties keep you on the move.
    C. Agree to her request just to be polite, but then continue your patrol after the woman is out of sight.
    D. Find a bystander who will agree to watch the shopping bag for her.

15. You are on duty at a public building. It is nearly 6:00 P.M., and most employees have left for the day.
    You see two well-dressed men carrying an office calculating machine out of the building. You SHOULD

    A. stop them and ask for an explanation
    B. follow them to see where they are going
    C. order them to put down the machine and leave the building immediately
    D. take no action since they do not look like burglars

16. You are on duty patrolling a public building. You have just tripped on the stairs and turned your ankle. The ankle hurts and is starting to swell.
    What is the BEST thing to do?

A. Take a taxi to a hospital emergency room, and from there have a hospital employee call your supervisor to explain the situation.
B. First try soaking your foot in cold water for half an hour, then go off duty if you really cannot walk at all.
C. Report the situation to your supervisor, explaining that you need prompt medical attention for your ankle.
D. Find a place where you can sit until you are due to go off duty, then have a doctor look at your ankle.

17. One of your duties as a special officer (security officer) on night patrol in a public building is to check the washrooms to see that the taps are turned off and that there are no plumbing leaks.
Of the following possible reasons for this inspection, which is probably the MOST important reason?

    A. If the floor gets wet, someone might slip and fall the next morning.
    B. A running water tap might be a sign that there is an intruder in the building.
    C. A washroom flood could leak through the ceilings and walls below and cause a lot of damage.
    D. Leaks must be reported quickly so that repairs can be scheduled as soon as possible.

17.____

18. You are on duty at a public building. A department supervisor tells you that someone has left a suspicious-looking package in the hallway on his floor. You investigate, and you hear ticking in the parcel. You think it could be a bomb.
The FIRST thing you should do is to

    A. rapidly question employees on this floor to get a description of the person who left the package
    B. write down the description of the package and the name of the department supervisor
    C. notify your security headquarters that there may be a bomb in the building and that all personnel should be evacuated
    D. pick up the package carefully and remove it from the building as quickly as you can

18.____

Questions 19-22.

DIRECTIONS: Answer Questions 19 through 22 on the basis of the Fact Situation and the Report of Arrest form below. Questions 19 through 22 ask how the report form should be filled in based on the information given in the Fact Situation.

FACT SITUATION

Jesse Stein is a special officer (security officer) who is assigned to a welfare center at 435 East Smythe Street, Brooklyn. He was on duty there Thursday morning, February 1. At 10:30 A.M., a client named Jo Ann Jones, 40 years old, arrived with her ten-year-old son, Peter. Another client, Mary Alice Wiell, 45 years old, immediately began to insult Mrs. Jones. When Mrs. Jones told her to "go away," Mrs. Wiell pulled out a long knife. The special officer (security officer) intervened and requested Mrs. Wiell to drop the knife. She would not, and he had to use necessary force to disarm her. He arrested her on charges of disorderly conduct, harassment, and possession of a dangerous weapon. Mrs. Wiell lives at 118 Heally Street,

Brooklyn, Apartment 4F, and she is unemployed. The reason for her aggressive behavior is not known.

```
REPORT OF ARREST
01) _____     (08) _____
    (Prisoner's surname) (first) (initial)      (Precinct)
02) _____     (09) _____
    (Address)                                (Date of arrest)
                                             (Month, Day)
03) _____ (04) _____ (05) ____  (10) _____
    (Date of birth)   (Age)   (Sex)          (Time of arrest)
06) _____ (07) _____  (11) _____
    (Occupation)      (Where employed)       (Place of arrest)

(12) _____
     (Specific offenses)

(13) _____     (14) _____
     (Arresting Officer)                      (Officer's No.)
```

19. What entry should be made in Blank 01?

    A. Jo Ann Jones   B. Jones, Jo Ann
    C. Mary Wiell   D. Wiell, Mary A.

20. Which of the following should be entered in Blank 04?

    A. 40   B. 40's   C. 45   D. Middle-aged

21. Which of the following should be entered in Blank 09?

    A. Wednesday, February 1, 10:30 A.M.
    B. February 1
    C. Thursday morning, February 2
    D. Morning, February 4

22. Of the following, which would be the BEST entry to make in Blank 11?

    A. Really Street Welfare Center
    B. Brooklyn
    C. 435 E. Smythe St., Brooklyn
    D. 118 Heally St., Apt. 4F

Questions 23-27.

DIRECTIONS: Answer Questions 23 through 27 on the basis of the information given in the Report of Loss or Theft that appears below.

```
REPORT OF LOSS OR THEFT         Date: 12/4      Time: 9:15 a.m.
Complaint made by:  Richard Aldridge           ☐ Owner
                    306 S. Walter St.          ☒ Other - explain:
                                               Head of Accty. Dept.

Type of property:  Computer                    Value: $550.00
Description: Dell
Location: 768 N Margin Ave., Accounting Dept., 3rd Floor
Time: Overnight 12/3 - 12/4
Circumstances: Mr. Aldridge reports he arrived at work 8:45 A.M.,
found office door open and machine missing. Nothing else reported
missing. I investigated and found signs of forced entry: door lock
was broken.          Signature of Reporting Officer: B.L. Ramirez
Notify:
    ☐ Building & Grounds Office, 768 N. Margin Ave.
    ☐ Lost Property Office, 110 Brand Ave.
    ☒ Security Office, 703 N. Wide Street
```

23. The person who made this complaint is

    A. a secretary   B. a security officer
    C. Richard Aldridge   D. B.L. Ramirez

24. The report concerns a computer that has been

    A. lost   B. damaged   C. stolen   D. sold

25. The person who took the computer probably entered the office through

    A. a door   B. a window   C. the roof   D. the basement

26. When did the head of the Accounting Department first notice that the computer was missing?

    A. December 4 at 9:15 A.M.   B. December 4 at 8:45 A.M.
    C. The night of December 3   D. The night of December 4

27. The event described in the report took place at

    A. 306 South Walter Street   B. 768 North Margin Avenue
    C. 110 Brand Avenue   D. 703 North Wide Street

8 (#2)

Questions 28-33.

DIRECTIONS: Answer Questions 28 through 33 on the basis of the instructions, the code, and the sample question given below.

Assume that a special officer (security officer) at a certain location is equipped with a two-way radio to keep him in constant touch with his security headquarters. Radio messages and replies are given in code form, as follows:

Radio Code for Situation	J	P	M	F	B
Radio Code for Action to be Taken	o	r	a	z	q
Radio Response for Action Being Taken	1	2	3	4	5

Assume that each of the above capital letters is the radio code for a particular type of situation, that the small letter below each capital letter is the radio code for the action a special officer (security officer) is directed to take, and that the number directly below each small letter is the radio response a special officer (security officer) should make to indicate what action was actually taken.

In each of the following Questions 28 through 33, the code letter for the action directed (Column 2) and the code number for the action taken (Column 3) should correspond to the capital letters in Column 1.

If only Column 2 is different from Column 1, mark your answer A.

If only Column 3 is different from Column 1, mark your answer B.

If both Column 2 and Column 3 are different from Column 1, mark your answer C.

If both Columns 2 and 3 are the same as Column 1, mark your answer D.

SAMPLE QUESTION

Column I	Column 2	Column 3
JPFMB	orzaq	12453

The code letters in Column 2 are correct, but the numbers 53 in Column 3 should be 35. Therefore, the answer is B.

	Column 1	Column 2	Column 3	
28.	PBFJM	rqzoa	25413	28._____
29.	MPFBJ	zrqao	32541	29._____
30.	JBFPM	oqzra	15432	30._____
31.	BJPMF	qaroz	51234	31._____
32.	PJFMB	rozaq	21435	32._____
33.	FJBMP	zoqra	41532	33._____

50

Questions 34-40.

DIRECTIONS: Questions 34 through 40 are based on the instructions given below. Study the instructions and the sample question; then answer Questions 34 through 40 on the basis of this information

INSTRUCTIONS:

In each of the following Questions 34 through 40, the 3-line name and address in Column 1 is the master-list entry, and the 3-line entry in Column 2 is the information to be checked against the master list.

If there is one line that does not match, mark your answer A.

If there are two lines that do not match, mark your answer B.

If all three lines do not match, mark your answer C.

If the lines all match exactly, mark your answer D.

SAMPLE QUESTION:

Column 1	Column 2
Mark L. Field	Mark L. Field
11-09 Prince Park Blvd.	11-99 Prince Park
Bronx, N.Y. 11402	Bronx, N.Y. 11401

The first lines in each column match exactly. The second lines do not match, since 11-09 does not match 11-99 and Blvd. does not match Way. The third lines do not match either, since 11402 does not match 11401. Therefore, there are two lines that do not match and the correct answer is B.

	Column 1	Column 2	
34.	Jerome A. Jackson 1243 14th Avenue New York, N.Y. 10023	Jerome A. Johnson 1234 14th Avenue New York, N.Y. 10023	34.____
35.	Sophie Strachtheim 33-28 Connecticut Ave. Far Rockaway, N.Y. 11697	Sophie Strachtheim 33-28 Connecticut Ave. Far Rockaway, N.Y. 11697	35.____
36.	Elisabeth N.T. Gorrell 256 Exchange St. New York, N.Y. 10013	Elizabeth N.T. Gorrell 256 Exchange St. New York, N.Y. 10013	36.____
37.	Maria J. Gonzalez 7516 E. Sheepshead Rd. Brooklyn, N.Y. 11240	Maria J. Gonzalez 7516 N. Shepshead Rd. Brooklyn, N.Y. 11240	37.____
38.	Leslie B. Brautenweiler 21 57A Seller Terr. Flushing, N.Y. 11367	Leslie B. Brautenwieler 21-75A Seiler Terr. Flushing, N.J. 11367	38.____

39. Rigoberto J. Peredes	Rigoberto J. Peredes	39.____
    157 Twin Towers, #18F	157 Twin Towers, #18F
    Tottenville, S.I., N.Y.	Tottenville, S.I., N.Y.

40. Pietro F. Albino	Pietro F. Albina	40.____
    P.O. Box 7548	P.O. Box 7458
    Floral Park, N.Y. 11005	Floral Park, N.Y. 11005

KEY (CORRECT ANSWERS)

1. D	11. A	21. B	31. A
2. C	12. D	22. C	32. D
3. B	13. C	23. C	33. A
4. D	14. B	24. C	34. B
5. B	15. A	25. A	35. D
6. A	16. C	26. B	36. A
7. C	17. C	27. B	37. A
8. D	18. C	28. D	38. C
9. D	19. D	29. C	39. D
10. D	20. C	30. B	40. B

EVALUATING INFORMATION AND EVIDENCE
EXAMINATION SECTION
TEST 1

DIRECTIONS: Each question or incomplete statement is followed by several suggested answers or completions. Select the one that BEST answers the question or completes the statement. *PRINT THE LETTER OF THE CORRECT ANSWER IN THE SPACE AT THE RIGHT.*

Question 1-4.

DIRECTIONS: Questions 1 through 4 measure your ability (1) to determine whether statements from witnesses say essentially the same thing and (2) to determine the evidence needed to make it reasonably certain that a particular conclusion is true.
To do well in this part of the test, you do NOT have to have a working knowledge of police procedures and techniques or to have any more familiarity with crimes and criminal behavior than that acquired from reading newspapers, listening to radio, or watching TV. In order to do well in this part, you must read carefully and reason closely. Sloppy reading or sloppy reasoning will lead to a low score.

1. In which of the following do the two statements made say essentially the same thing in two different ways?
   I. All members of the pro-x group are free from persecution.
      No person that is persecuted is a member of the pro-x group.
   II. Some responsible employees of the police department are not supervisors.
       Some police department supervisors are not responsible employees.
   The CORRECT answer is:
   A. I only
   B. II only
   C. Both I and II
   D. Neither I nor II

1._____

2. In which the following do the two statements made say essentially the same thing in two different ways?
   I. All Nassau County police officers weigh less than 225 pounds.
      No police officer weighs more than 225 pounds.
   II. No police officer is an alcoholic.
       No alcoholic is a police officer.
   The CORRECT answer is:
   A. I only
   B. II only
   C. Both I and II
   D. Neither I nor II

2._____

3. <u>Summary of Evidence Collected to Date</u>: All pimps in the precinct own pink-colored cars and carry knives.
   <u>Prematurely Drawn Conclusion</u>: Any person in the precinct who carries a knife is a pimp.

3._____

Which one of the following additional pieces of evidence, if any, would make it *reasonably certain* that the conclusion drawn is TRUE?
A. Each person who carries a knife owns a pink-colored car.
B. All persons who own pink-colored cars pimp.
C. No one who carries a knife has a vocation other than pimping.
D. None of the above

4. Summary of Evidence Collected to Date: 4.____
   a. Some of the robbery suspects have served time as convicted felons.
   b. Some of the robbery suspects are female.
   Prematurely Drawn Conclusion: Some of the female suspects have never served time as convicted felons.
   Which one of the following additional pieces of evidence, if any, would make it *reasonably certain* that the conclusion drawn is TRUE?
   A. The number of female suspects is the same as the number of robber suspects who have served time as convicted felons.
   B. The number of female suspects is smaller than the number of convicted felons.
   C. The number of suspects that have served time is smaller than the number of suspects that have been convicted of a felony.
   D. None of the above

Questions 5-8.

DIRECTIONS: Questions 5 through 8 measure your ability to orient yourself within a given section of a town, neighborhood, or particular area. Each of the questions describes a starting point and a destination. Assume that you are driving a patrol car in the area shown on the map accompanying the questions. Use the map as a basis for choosing the shortest way to get from one point to another without breaking the law.

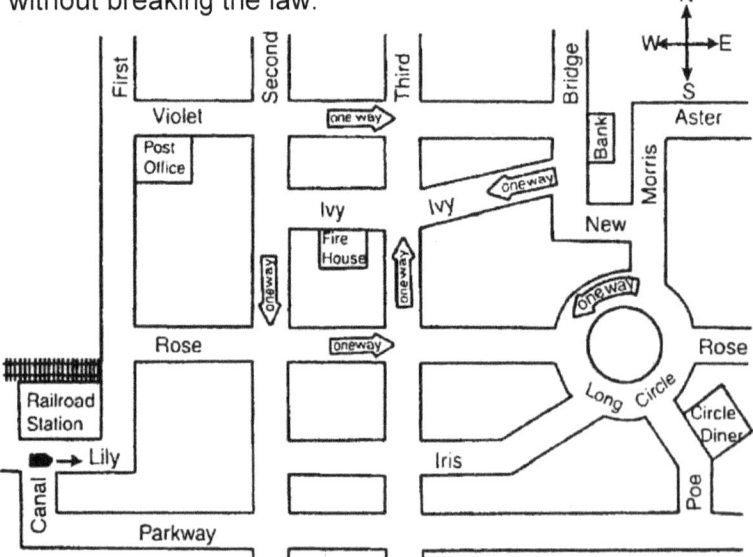

A street marked one way is one-way for the full length, even when there are breaks or jogs in the street. EXCEPTION: A street that does not have the same name over the full length.

5. A patrol car at the train station is sent to the bank to investigate a robbery. 5.____
   The SHORTEST way to get there without breaking any traffic laws is to go
   A. east on Lily, north on First, east on Rose, north on Third, and east on Ivy to bank
   B. east on Lily, north on First, east on Violet, and south on Bridge to bank
   C. south on Canal, east on Parkway, north on Poe, around Long Circle to Morris, west on New, and north on Bridge to bank
   D. south on Canal, east on Parkway, north on Third, and east on Ivy to bank

6. At the bank, the patrol car receives a call to hurry to the post office. 6.____
   The SHORTEST way to get there without breaking any traffic laws is to go
   A. west on Ivy, south on Second, west on Rose, and north on First to post office
   B. west on Ivy, south on Second, west on Rose, and south on First to post office
   C. south on Bridge, east on New, south on Morris, around Long Circle, south on Poe, west on Parkway, north on Canal, east on Lily, and north on First to post office
   D. north on Bridge, west on Violet, and south on First to post office

7. On leaving the post office, the police officers decide to go to the Circle Diner. 7.____
   The SHORTEST way to get there without breaking any traffic laws is to go
   A. south on First, left on Rose, right on Second, left on Parkway, and right on Poe to diner
   B. south on First, left on Rose, around Long Circle, and right on Poe to diner
   C. south on First, left on Rose, right on Second, right on Iris, around Long Circle, and left on Poe to diner
   D. west on Violet, right on Bridge, right on new, right on Morris, around Long Circle, and left on Poe to diner

8. During lunch break, a fire siren sounds and the police officers rush to their patrol 8.____
   car and head to the firehouse.
   The SHORTEST way to get there without breaking any traffic laws is to go
   A. north on Poe, around Long Circle, west on Iris, north on Third, and west on Ivy to firehouse
   B. north on Poe, around Long Circle,, north on Morris, west on New, north on Bridge, and west on Ivy to firehouse
   C. north on Poe, around Long Circle, west on Rose, north on Third, and west on Ivy to firehouse
   D. south on Poe, west on Parkway, north on Third, and east on Ivy to firehouse

Questions 9-13.

DIRECTIONS: Questions 9 through 13 measure your ability to understand written descriptions of events. Each question presents you with a description of an accident, a crime, or an event and asks you which of four drawings BEST represent it.

4 (#1)

In the drawings, the following symbols are used (these symbols and their meanings will be repeated in the test):

A moving vehicle is represented by this symbol: (front) ⬠ (rear)

A parked vehicle is represented by this symbol: (front) ◀ (rear)

A pedestrian or a bicyclist is represented by this symbol: •

The path and direction of travel of a vehicle or pedestrian is indicated by a solid line: ⟶

EXCEPTION: The path and direction of travel of each vehicle or person directly involved in a collision from the point of impact is indicated by a dotted line: --→

9. A driver pulling out from between two parked cars on Magic is struck by a vehicle heading east which turns left onto Maple and flees. 9.____
Which of the following depicts the accident?

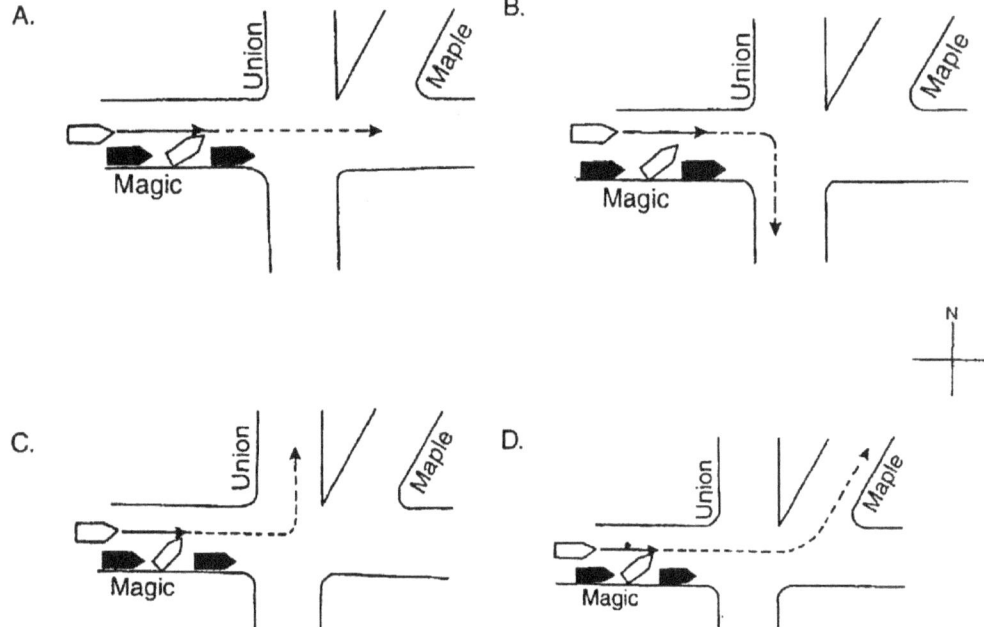

10. As Mr. Jones is driving south on Side St., he falls asleep at the wheel. His car goes out of control and sideswipes an oncoming car, goes through an intersection, and hits a pedestrian on the southeast corner of Main Street. Which of the following depicts the accident?

10.____

A.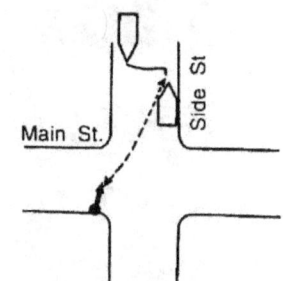

B.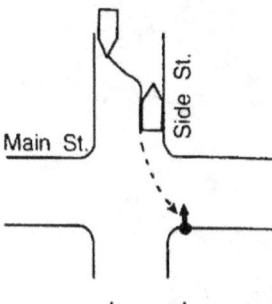

C.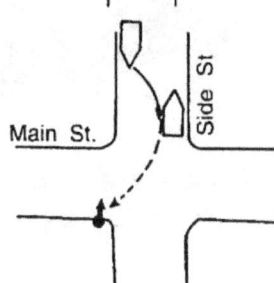

D.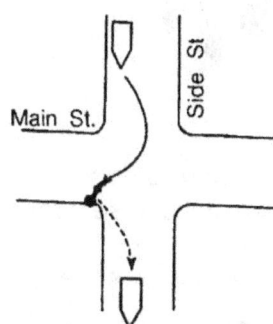

11. A car traveling south on Baltic skids through a red light at the intersection of Baltic and Atlantic, sideswipes a car stopped for a light in the northbound lane, skids 180 degrees, and stops on the west sidewalk of Baltic. Which of the following depicts the accident?

11.____

A.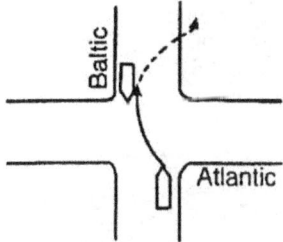

B.

C.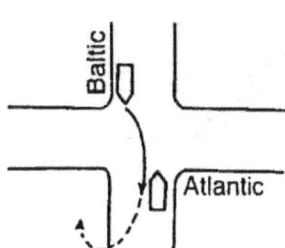

D.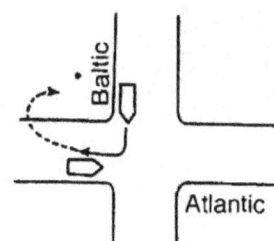

12. When found, the right front end of an automobile was smashed and bent around a post, and the hood was buckled.
Which of the following cars on a service lot is the car described?

12._____

A.
B.
C.
D.

13. An open floor safe with its door bet out of shape was found at the scene. It was empty. An electric drill and several envelopes and papers were found on the floor near the safe.
Which of the following shows the scene described?

13._____

A.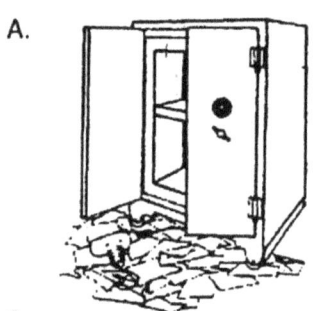
B.
C.
D.

Questions 14-16.

DIRECTIONS: In Questions 14 through 16, you are to pick the word or phrase CLOSEST in meaning to the word or phrase printed in capital letters.

14. HAZARDOUS
    A. uncertain   B. threatening   C. difficult   D. dangerous

14._____

15. NEGLIGENT   15.____
    A. careless   B. fearless   C. ruthless   D. useless

16. PROVOKE   16.____
    A. accuse   B. arouse   C. insist   D. suspend

Questions 17-20.

DIRECTIONS: Questions 17 through 20 measure your ability to do arithmetic related to police
              work. Each question presents a separate arithmetic problem to be solved.

17. To the nearest hour, how long can a specialized police vehicle with a 40-gallon   17.____
    fuel tank be on the road before heading for a service facility, assuming that the
    vehicle consumes 8 gallons per hour and must head for a service facility when
    there are only 8 gallons in the tank?
    A. 3   B. 4   C. 5   D. None of the above

18. A man with a history of vagrancy was found dead under a bridge with the   18.____
    following U.S. currency in a band around his belly:
    7 $5 bills, 3 $10 bills, 11 $20 bills, 9 $50 bills, 4 $100 bills
    What is the TOTAL amount of the money that was found in the band?
    A. $1,015   B. $1,135   C. $2,719   D. None of the above

19. X is 110 dimes; Y is 1,111 pennies.   19.____
    Which of the following statements about the values of X and Y above is TRUE?
    A. X is greater than Y.
    B. Y is greater than X.
    C. X equals Y.
    D. The relationship of X to Y cannot be determined from the information given.

20. Which of the following individuals drinking hard liquor in a bar was 21 years   20.____
    old at the time of the incident?
    A. One born August 26, 1989. Date of incident is March 17, 2010.
    B. One born January 6, 1989. Date of incident is New Year's Eve 2009.
    C. One born 3/17/89. Date of incident is 2/14/10
    D. None of the above

KEY (CORRECT ANSWERS)

1.	A	11.	C
2.	B	12.	D
3.	C	13.	B
4.	D	14.	D
5.	B	15.	A
6.	C	16.	B
7.	B	17.	B
8.	B	18.	B
9.	D	19.	B
10.	B	20.	D

EXAMINATION SECTION
TEST 1

DIRECTIONS: Each question or incomplete statement is followed by several suggested answers or completions. Select the one that BEST answers the question or completes the statement. *PRINT THE LETTER OF THE CORRECT ANSWER IN THE SPACE AT THE RIGHT.*

Questions 1-10.   MEMORY

DIRECTIONS: Questions 1 through 10 are to be answered SOLELY on the basis of the following passage, which contains a story about an incident involving police officers. You will have ten minutes to read and study the story. You may not write or make any notes while studying it. After ten minutes, close the memory booklet and do not look at it again. Then, answer the questions that follow.

You are one of a number of police officers who have been assigned to help control a demonstration inside Baldwin Square, a major square in the city. The demonstration is to protest the U.S. involvement in Iraq. As was expected, the demonstration has become nasty. You and nine other officers have been assigned to keep the demonstrators from going up Bell Street which enters the Square from the northwest. During the time you have been assigned to Bell Street, you have observed a number of things.

Before the demonstration began, three vans and a wagon entered the Square from the North on Howard Avenue. The first van was a 1989 blue Ford, plate number 897-JLK. The second van was a 1995 red Ford, plate number 899-LKK. The third van was a 1997 green Dodge step-van, plate number 997-KJL. The wagon was a blue 1998 Volvo with a luggage rack on the roof, plate number 989-LKK. The Dodge had a large dent in the left-hand rear door and was missing its radiator grill. The Ford that was painted red had markings under the paint which made you believe that it had once been a telephone company truck. Equipment for the speakers' platform was unloaded from the van, along with a number of demonstration signs. As soon as the vans and wagon were unloaded, a number of demonstrators picked up the signs and started marching around the square. A sign reading *U.S. Out Now* was carried by a woman wearing red jeans, a black tee shirt, and blue sneakers. A man with a beard, a blue shirt, and Army pants began carrying a poster reading *To Hell With Davis*. A tall, Black male and a Hispanic male had been carrying a large sign with *This Is How Vietnam Started* in big black letters with red dripping off the bottom of each letter.

A number of the demonstrators are wearing black armbands and green tee shirts with the peace symbol on the front. A woman with very short hair who was dressed in green and yellow fatigues is carrying a triangular-shaped blue sign with white letters. The sign says *Out Of Iraq*.

A group of 12 demonstrators have been carrying six fake coffins back and forth across the Square between Apple Street on the West and Webb Street on the East. They are shouting *Death to Hollis and his Henchmen*. Over where Victor Avenue enters the Square from the South, a small group of demonstrators (two men and three women) just started painting slogans on the walls surrounding the construction of the First National Union Bank and Trust.

1. Which street is on the opposite side of the Square from Victor Avenue? 1._____
   A. Bell B. Howard C. Apple D. Webb

2. How many officers are assigned with you? 2._____
   A. 8 B. 6 C. 9 D. 5

3. Howard Avenue enters the Square from which direction? 3._____
   A. Northwest B. North C. East D. Southwest

4. The van that had PROBABLY been a telephone truck had plate number 4._____
   A. 899-LKK B. 989-LKK C. 897-JKL D. 997-KJL

5. What is the color of the sign carried by the woman with very short hair? 5._____
   A. Blue B. White C. Black D. Red

6. The man wearing the army pants has a(n) 6._____
   A. Afro B. beard
   C. triangular-shaped sign D. black armband

7. Which vehicle had plate number 989-LKK? The 7._____
   A. red Ford B. blue Ford C. Volvo D. Dodge

8. The bank under construction is located _____ of the Square. 8._____
   A. north B. south C. east D. west

9. How many people are painting slogans on the walls surrounding the construction site? 9._____
   A. 4 B. 5 C. 6 D. 7

10. What is the name of the bank under construction? 10._____
    A. National Union Bank and Trust
    B. First National Bank and Trust
    C. First Union National Bank and Trust
    D. First National Union Bank and Trust

KEY (CORRECT ANSWERS)

1. B 6. B
2. C 7. C
3. B 8. B
4. A 9. B
5. A 10. D

TEST 2

DIRECTIONS: Each question or incomplete statement is followed by several suggested answers or completions. Select the one that BEST answers the question or completes the statement. *PRINT THE LETTER OF THE CORRECT ANSWER IN THE SPACE AT THE RIGHT.*

Questions 1-15.

DIRECTIONS: Questions 1 through 15 are to be answered SOLELY on the basis of the Memory Booklet given below.

MEMORY BOOKLET

The following passage contains a story about an incident involving police officers. You will have ten minutes to read and study the story. You may not write or make any notes while studying it. The first questions in the examination will be based on the passage. After ten minutes, close the memory booklet, and do not look at it again. Then, answer the questions that follow.

Police Officers Boggs and Thomas are patrolling in a radio squad car on a late Saturday afternoon in the spring. They are told by radio that a burglary is taking place on the top floor of a six-story building on the corner of 5th Street and Essex and that they should deal with the incident.

The police officers know the location and know that the Gold Jewelry Company occupies the entire sixth floor. They also know that, over the weekends, the owner has gold bricks in his office safe worth $500,000.

When the officers arrive at the location, they lock their radio car. They then find the superintendent of the building who opens the front door for them. He indicates he has neither seen nor heard anything suspicious in the building. However, he had just returned from a long lunch hour. The officers take the elevator to the sixth floor. As the door of the elevator with the officers opens on the sixth floor, the officers hear the door of the freight elevator in the rear of the building closing and the freight elevator beginning to move. They leave the elevator and proceed quickly through the open door of the office of the Gold Jewelry Company. They see that the office safe is open and empty. The officers quickly proceed to the rear staircase. They run down six flights of stairs, and they see four suspects leaving through the rear entrance of the building.

They run through the rear door and out of the building after the suspects. The four suspects are running quickly through the parking lot at the back of the building. The suspects then make a right-hand turn onto 5th Street and are clearly seen by the officers. The officers see one white male, one Hispanic male, one Black male, and one white female.

The white male has a beard and sunglasses. He is wearing blue jeans, a dark red and blue jacket, and white jogging shoes. He is carrying a large green duffel bag over his shoulder.

The Hispanic male limps slightly and has a dark moustache. He is wearing dark brown slacks, a dark green sweat shirt, and brown shoes. He is carrying a large blue duffel bag.

The Black male is clean-shaven, wearing black corduroy pants, a multi-colored shirt, a green beret, and black boots. He is carrying a tool box.

The white female has long dark hair and is wear-ing light-colored blue jeans, a white blouse, sneakers, and a red kerchief around her neck. She is carrying a shotgun.

The officers chase the suspects for three long blocks without getting any closer to them. At the intersection of 5th Street and Pennsylvania Avenue, the suspects separate. The white male and the Black male rapidly get into a 1992 brown Ford stationwagon. The stationwagon has a roof rack on top and a Connecticut license plate with the letters *JEAN* on it. The stationwagon departs even before the occupants close the door completely.

The Hispanic male and the white female get into an old blue Dodge van. The van has a CB antenna on top, a picture of a cougar on the back doors, a dented right rear fender, and a New Jersey license plate. The officers are not able to read the plate numbers on the van.

The officers then observe the stationwagon turn left and enter an expressway going to Connecticut. The van turns right onto Illinois Avenue and proceeds toward the tunnel to New Jersey.

The officers immediately run back to their radio car to radio in what happened.

1. Which one of the following suspects had sunglasses on? 1.____

   A. White male B. Hispanic male
   C. Black male D. White female

2. Which one of the following suspects was carrying a shotgun? 2.____

   A. White male B. Hispanic male
   C. Black male D. White female

3. Which one of the following suspects was wearing a green beret? 3.____

   A. White male B. Hispanic male
   C. Black male D. White femal

4. Which one of the following suspects limped slightly? 4.____

   A. White male B. Hispanic male
   C. Black male D. White female

5. Which one of the following BEST describes the stationwagon used? 5.____
   A

   A. 1992 brown Ford B. 1992 blue Dodge
   C. 1979 brown Ford D. 1979 blue Dodge

6. Which one of the following BEST describes the suspect or suspects who used the stationwagon?
   A

   A. Black male and a Hispanic male
   B. white male and a Hispanic male
   C. Black male and a white male
   D. Black male and a white female

7. The van had a license plate from which of the following states?

   A. Connecticut   B. New Jersey
   C. New York   D. Pennsylvania

8. The license plate on the stationwagon read as follows:

   A. JANE   B. JOAN   C. JEAN   D. JUNE

9. The van used had a dented _____ fender.

   A. left rear   B. right rear
   C. right front   D. left front

10. When last seen by the officers, the van was headed toward

    A. Connecticut   B. New Jersey
    C. Pennsylvania   D. Long Island

11. The female suspect's hair can BEST be described as

    A. long and dark-colored   B. short and dark-colored
    C. long and light-colored   D. short and light-colored

12. Which one of the following suspects was wearing a multicolored shirt?

    A. White male   B. Hispanic male
    C. Black male   D. White female

13. Blue jeans were worn by the _____ male suspect and the suspect.

    A. Hispanic; white female   B. Black; Hispanic male
    C. white; white female   D. Black; white male

14. The color of the duffel bag carried by the Hispanic male suspect was

    A. blue   B. green   C. brown   D. red

15. The Hispanic male suspect was wearing

    A. brown shoes   B. black shoes
    C. black boots   D. jogging shoes

KEY (CORRECT ANSWERS)

1. A
2. D
3. C
4. B
5. A

6. C
7. B
8. C
9. B
10. B

11. A
12. C
13. C
14. A
15. A

SCANNING MAPS

One section of the exam tests your ability to orient yourself within a given region on a map. Using the map accompanying questions 1 through 3; choose the best way of getting from one point to another.

The New Bridge is closed to traffic because it has a broken span.

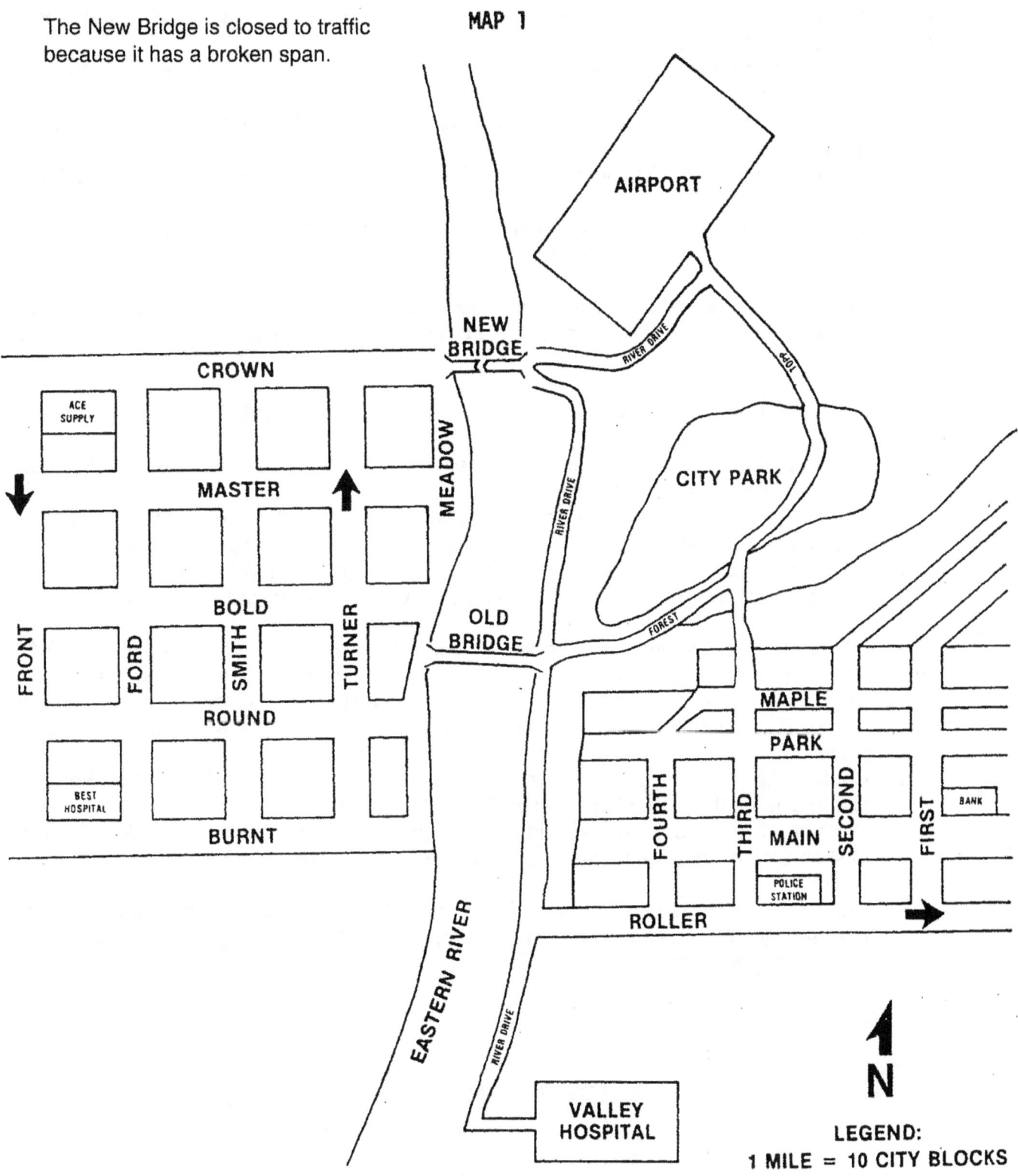

MAP 1

LEGEND:
1 MILE = 10 CITY BLOCKS

Arrows (→) indicate on-way traffic and direction of traffic. A street marked by an arrow is one way for the entire length of the street.

67

SAMPLE QUESTIONS

1. Officers in a patrol car which is at the Airport receive a call for assistance at Best Hospital. The shortest route without breaking the law is:
    A. Southwest on River Drive, right on Forest, cross Old Bridge, south on Meadow, and west on Burnt to hospital entrance.
    B. Southwest on River Drive, right on New Bridge, left on Meadow, west on Burnt to hospital entrance.
    C. Southwest on River Drive, right on Old Bridge, left on Turner, right on Burnt to hospital entrance.
    D. North on River Drive to Topp, through City Park to Forest, cross Old Bridge, left on Meadow, west on Burnt to hospital entrance.

2. After returning to the police station, the officers receive a call to pick up injured persons at an accident site (located on the east side of New Bridge) and return to Valley Hospital. The shortest route without breaking the law is:

    A. West on Roller, north on River Drive, left to accident scene at New Bridge, then north on River Drive to hospital entrance.
    B. North on Third, left on Forest, north on River Drive, left to accident scene at new Bridge, then south on River Drive to hospital entrance.
    C. East on Roller, left on First, west on Maple, north on Third, left on Forest, north on River Drive to accident scene at New Bridge, then south on River Drive to hospital entrance.
    D. North on Third, left on Forest, cross Old Bridge, north on Meadow to New Bridge, south on Meadow, east over Old Bridge, then south on River Drive to hospital entrance.

3. While at the Valley Hospital, the officers receive a call asking them to pick up materials at the Ace Supply and return them to the police station. The shortest route without breaking the law is:
    A. North on River Drive, cross New Bridge, west on Crown to Ace Supply, then south on Front, east on Burnt, north on Meadow, cross Old Bridge, east on Forest, south on Third to police station.
    B. North on River Drive, right on Roller to police station, then north on Third, left on Forest, cross Old Bridge, north on Meadow, west on Crown to Ace Supply.
    C. North on River Drive, cross Old Bridge, north on Meadow, west on Crown to Ace Supply, then east on Crown, south on Meadow, cross Old Bridge, east on Forest, south on Third to police station.
    D. North on River Drive, cross Old Bridge, south on Meadow, west on Burnt, north on Front to Ace Supply, then east on Crown, south on Meadow, cross Old Bridge, east on Forest, south on Third to police station.

KEY (CORRECT ANSWERS)

1. A
2. B
3. C

MAP READING
EXAMINATION SECTION
TEST 1

DIRECTIONS: Each question or incomplete statement is followed by several suggested answers or completions. Select the one that BEST answers the question or completes the Statement. *PRINT THE LETTER OF THE CORRECT ANSWER IN THE SPACE AT THE RIGHT.*

Questions 1-5.

DIRECTIONS: Questions 1 through 5 are to be answered SOLELY on the basis of the following information and map.

An employee may be required to assist civilians who seek travel directions or referral to city agencies and facilities.

The following is a map of part of a city, where several public offices and other institutions are located. Each of the squares represents one city block. Street names are as shown. If there is an arrow next to the street name, it means the street is one-way only in the direction of the arrow. If there is no arrow next to the street name, two-way traffic is allowed.

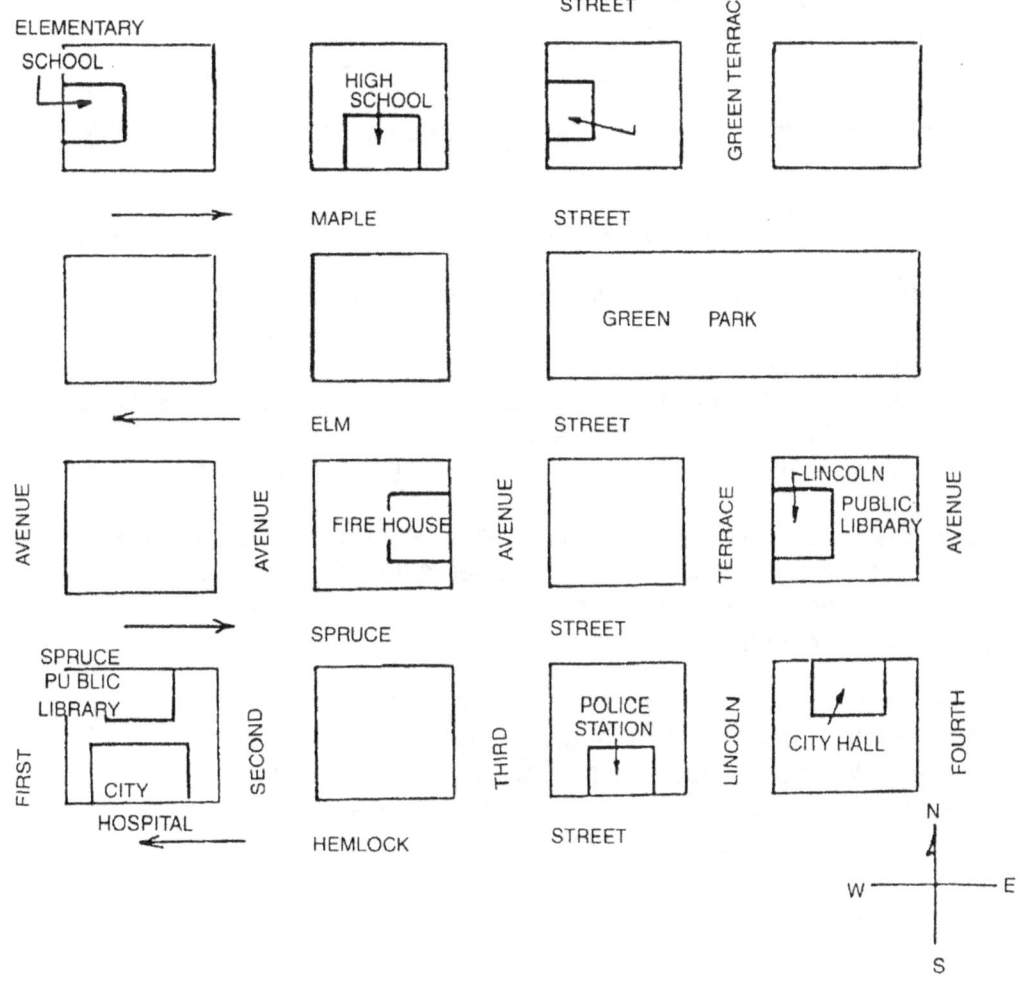

1. A woman whose handbag was stolen from her in Green Park asks a firefighter at the firehouse where to go to report the crime.
   The firefighter should tell the woman to go to the

   A. police station on Spruce Street
   B. police station on Hemlock Street
   C. city hall on Spruce Street
   D. city hall on Hemlock Street

2. A disabled senior citizen who lives on Green Terrace telephones the firehouse to ask which library is closest to her home.
   The firefighter should tell the senior citizen it is the

   A. Spruce Public Library on Lincoln Terrace
   B. Lincoln Public Library on Spruce Street
   C. Spruce Public Library on Spruce Street
   D. Lincoln Public Library on Lincoln Terrace

3. A woman calls the firehouse to ask for the exact location of City Hall.
   She should be told that it is on

   A. Hemlock Street, between Lincoln Terrace and Fourth Avenue
   B. Spruce Street, between Lincoln Terrace and Fourth Avenue
   C. Lincoln Terrace, between Spruce Street and Elm Street
   D. Green Terrace, between Maple Street and Pine Street

4. A delivery truck driver is having trouble finding the high school to make a delivery. The driver parks the truck across from the firehouse on Third Avenue facing north and goes into the firehouse to ask directions.
   In giving directions, the firefighter should tell the driver to go _____ to the school.

   A. north on Third Avenue to Pine Street and then make a right
   B. south on Third Avenue, make a left on Hemlock Street, and then make a right on Second Avenue
   C. north on Third Avenue, turn left on Elm Street, make a right on Second Avenue and go to Maple Street, then make another right
   D. north on Third Avenue to Maple Street, and then make a left

5. A man comes to the firehouse accompanied by his son and daughter. He wants to register his son in the high school and his daughter in the elementary school. He asks a firefighter which school is closest for him to walk to from the firehouse.
   The firefighter should tell the man that the

   A. high school is closer than the elementary school
   B. elementary school is closer than the high school
   C. elementary school and high school are the same distance away
   D. elementary school and high school are in opposite directions

Questions 6-8.

DIRECTIONS: Questions 6 through 8 are to be answered SOLELY on the basis of the following map and information. The flow of traffic is indicated by the arrows. If there is only one arrow shown, then traffic flows in the direction indicated by the arrow. If there are two arrows, then traffic flows in both directions. You must follow the flow of traffic

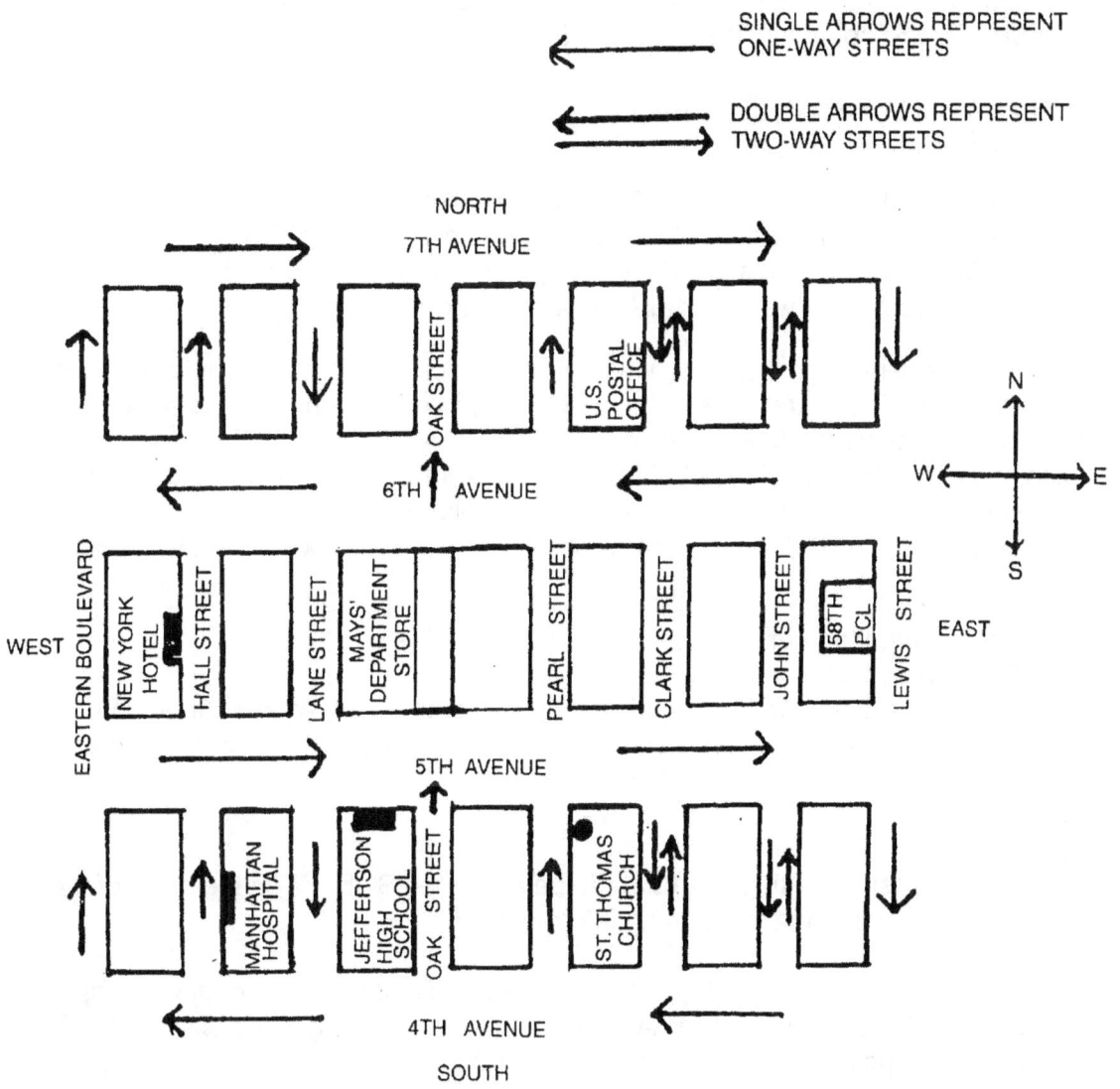

6. Traffic Enforcement Agent Fox was on foot patrol at John Street between 6th and 7th Avenues when a motorist driving southbound asked her for directions to the New York Hotel, which is located on Hall Street between 5th and 6th Avenues. Which one of the following is the SHORTEST route for Agent Fox to direct the motorist to take, making sure to obey all traffic regulations?
Travel _____ to the New York Hotel.

   A. north on John Street, then east on 7th Avenue, then north on Lewis Street, then west on 4th Avenue, then north on Eastern Boulevard, then east on 5th Avenue, then north on Hall Street
   B. south on John Street, then west on 6th Avenue, then south on Eastern Boulevard, then east on 5th Avenue, then north on Hall Street

6._____

C. south on John Street, then west on 6th Avenue, then south on Clark Street, then east on 4th Avenue, then north on Eastern Boulevard, then east on 5th Avenue, then north on Hall Street
D. south on John Street, then west on 4th Avenue, then north on Hall Street

7. Traffic Enforcement Agent Murphy is on motorized patrol on 7th Avenue between Oak Street and Pearl Street when Lt. Robertson radios him to go to Jefferson High School, located on 5th Avenue between Lane Street and Oak Street. Which one of the following is the SHORTEST route for Agent Murphy to take, making sure to obey all the traffic regulations?
Travel east on 7th Avenue, then south on _____, then east on 5th Avenue to Jefferson High School.

   A. Clark Street, then west on 4th Avenue, then north on Hall Street
   B. Pearl Street, then west on 4th Avenue, then north on Lane Street
   C. Lewis Street, then west on 6th Avenue, then south on Hall Street
   D. Lewis Street, then west on 4th Avenue, then north on Oak Street

8. Traffic Enforcement Agent Vasquez was on 4th Avenue and Eastern Boulevard when a motorist asked him for directions to the 58th Police Precinct, which is located on Lewis Street between 5th and 6th Avenues.
Which one of the following is the SHORTEST route for Agent Vasquez to direct the motorist to take, making sure to obey all traffic regulations.
Travel north on Eastern Boulevard, then east on _____ on Lewis Street to the 58th Police Precinct.

   A. 5th Avenue, then north
   B. 7th Avenue, then south
   C. 6th Avenue, then north on Pearl Street, then east on 7th Avenue, then south
   D. 5th Avenue, then north on Clark Street, then east on 6th Avenue, then south

Questions 9-13.

DIRECTIONS: Questions 9 through 13 are to be answered SOLELY on the basis of the following map and the following information.

Toll collectors answer motorists' questions concerning directions by reading a map of the metropolitan area. Although many alternate routes leading to destinations exist on the following map, you are to choose the MOST direct route of those given.

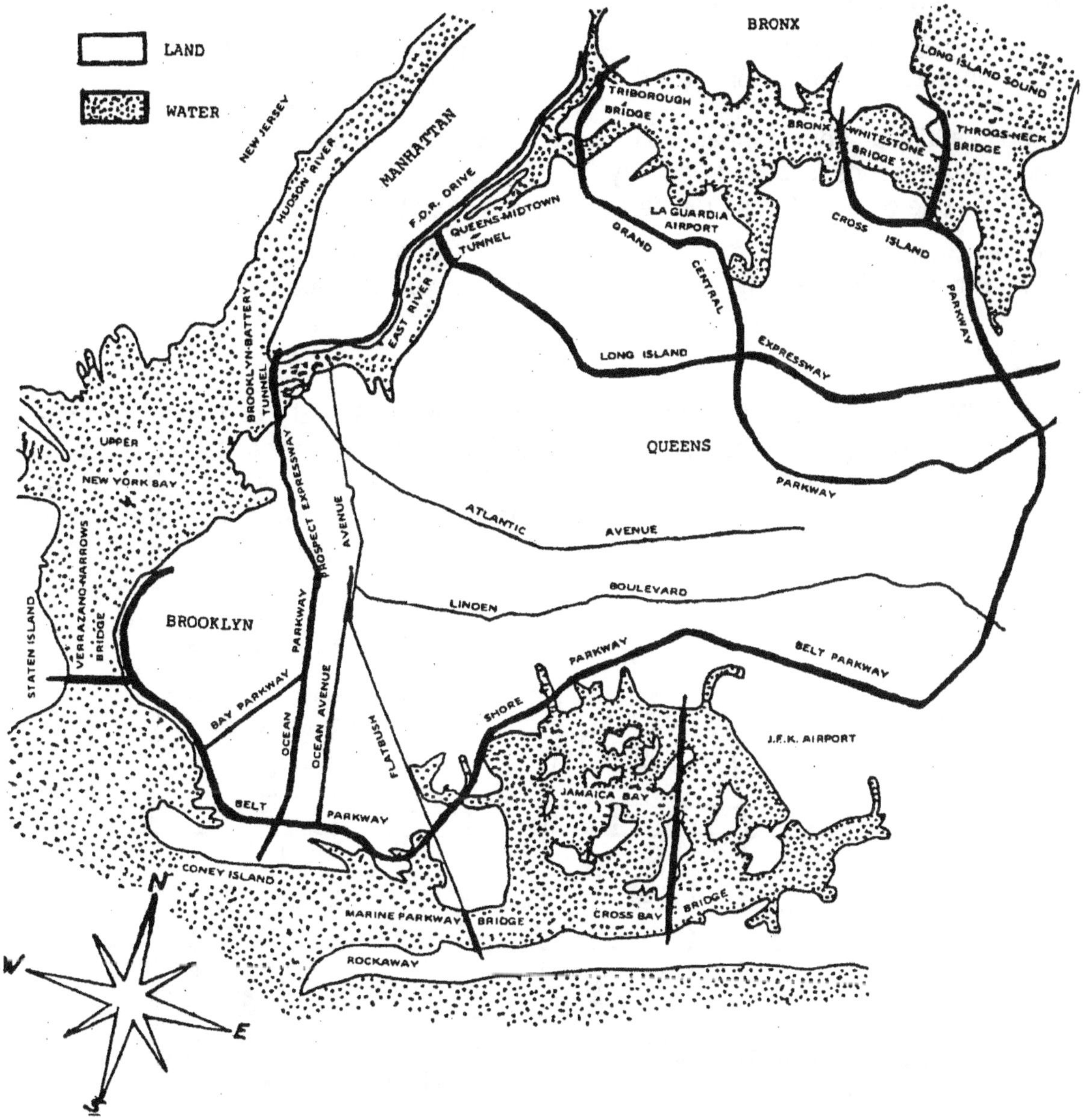

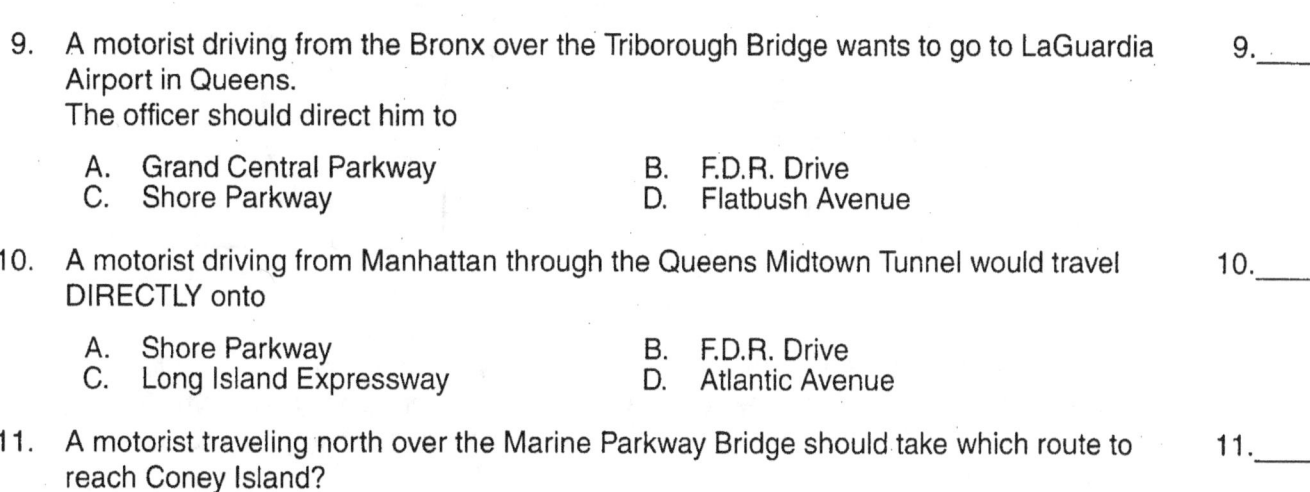

9. A motorist driving from the Bronx over the Triborough Bridge wants to go to LaGuardia Airport in Queens.
   The officer should direct him to

   A. Grand Central Parkway
   B. F.D.R. Drive
   C. Shore Parkway
   D. Flatbush Avenue

10. A motorist driving from Manhattan through the Queens Midtown Tunnel would travel DIRECTLY onto

    A. Shore Parkway
    B. F.D.R. Drive
    C. Long Island Expressway
    D. Atlantic Avenue

11. A motorist traveling north over the Marine Parkway Bridge should take which route to reach Coney Island?

    A. Shore Parkway East
    B. Belt Parkway West
    C. Linden Boulevard
    D. Ocean Parkway

12. Which facility does NOT connect the Bronx and Queens? 12.____

    A. Triborough Bridge
    B. Bronx-Whitestone Bridge
    C. Verrazano-Narrows Bridge
    D. Throgs-Neck Bridge

13. A motorist driving from Manhattan arrives at the toll booth of the Brooklyn-Battery Tunnel 13.____
    and asks directions to Ocean Parkway.
    To which one of the following routes should the motorist FIRST be directed?

    A. Atlantic Avenue
    B. Bay Parkway
    C. Prospect Expressway
    D. Ocean Avenue

Questions 14-16.

DIRECTIONS: Questions 14 through 16 are to be answered SOLELY on the basis of the following map. The flow of traffic is indicated by the arrows. If there is only one arrow shown, then traffic flows only in the direction indicated by the arrow. If there are two arrows, then traffic flows in both directions. You must follow the flow of traffic.

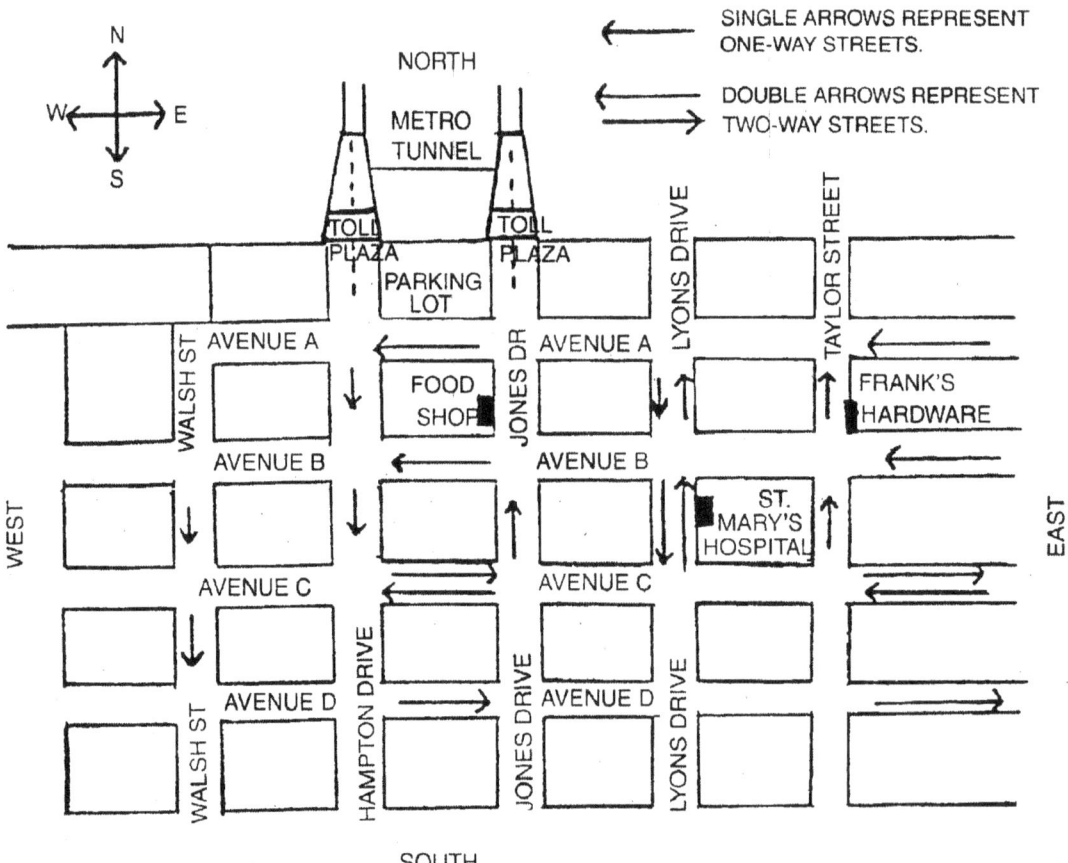

14. A motorist is exiting the Metro Tunnel and approaches the bridge and tunnel officer at the 14.____
    toll plaza. He asks the officer how to get to the food shop on Jones Drive. Which one of the following is the SHORTEST route for the motorist to take, making sure to obey all traffic regulations?
    Travel south on Hampton Drive, then left on _____ on Jones Drive to the food shop.

A. Avenue A, then right
B. Avenue B, then right
C. Avenue D, then left
D. Avenue C, then left

15. A motorist heading south pulls up to a toll booth at the exit of the Metro Tunnel and asks Bridge and Tunnel Officer Evans how to get to Frank's Hardware Store on Taylor Street. Which one of the following is the SHORTEST route for the motorist to take, making sure to obey all traffic regulations?
Travel south on Hampton Drive, then east on

    A. Avenue B to Taylor Street
    B. Avenue D, then north on Taylor Street to Avenue B
    C. Avenue C, then north on Taylor Street to Avenue B
    D. Avenue C, then north on Lyons Drive, then east on Avenue B to Taylor Street

16. A motorist is exiting the Metro Tunnel and approaches the toll plaza. She asks Bridge and Tunnel Officer Owens for directions to St. Mary's Hospital. Which one of the following is the SHORTEST route for the motorist to take, making sure to obey all traffic regulations?
Travel south on Hampton Drive, then _____ on Lyons Drive to St. Mary's Hospital.

    A. left on Avenue D, then left
    B. right on Avenue A, then left on Walsh Street, then left on Avenue D, then left
    C. left on Avenue C, then left
    D. left on Avenue B, then right

Questions 17-18.

DIRECTIONS: Questions 17 and 18 are to be answered SOLELY on the basis of the map which appears on the following page. The flow of traffic is indicated by the arrows. If there is only one arrow shown, then traffic flows only in the direction indicated by the arrow. If there are two arrows shown, then traffic flows in both directions. You must follow the flow of traffic.

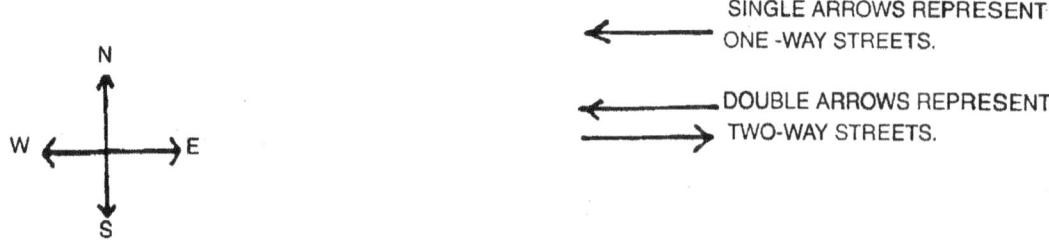

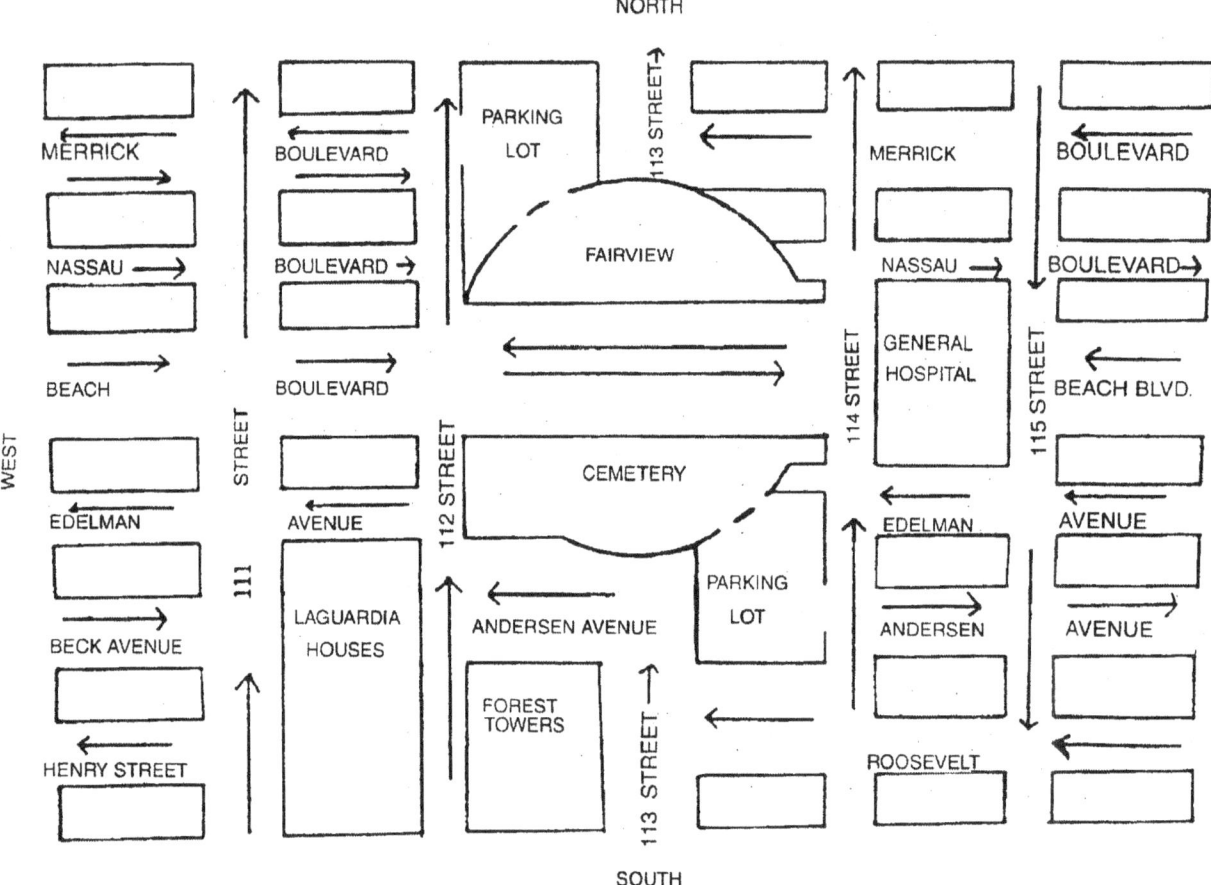

17. Police Officers Glenn and Albertson are on 111th Street at Henry Street when they are dispatched to a past robbery at Beach Boulevard and 115th Street.
Which one of the following is the SHORTEST route for the officers to follow in their patrol car, making sure to obey all traffic regulations?
Travel north on 111th Street, then east on _____ south on 115th Street.

    A. Edelman Avenue, then north on 112th Street, then east on Beach Boulevard, then north on 114th Street, then east on Nassau Boulevard, then one block
    B. Beach Boulevard, then north on 114th Street, then east on Nassau Boulevard, then one block
    C. Merrick Boulevard, then two blocks
    D. Nassau Boulevard, then south on 112th Street, then east on Beach Boulevard, then north on 114th Street, then east on Nassau Boulevard, then one block

17. ____

9 (#1)

18. Later in their tour, Officers Glenn and Albertson are driving on 114th Street. If they make a left turn to enter the parking lot at Andersen Avenue, and then make a u-turn, in what direction would they now be headed?

    A. North   B. South   C. East   D. West

18._____

Questions 19-20.

DIRECTIONS: Questions 19 and 20 are to be answered SOLELY on the basis of the following map. The flow of traffic is indicated by the arrows. If there is only one arrow shown, then traffic flows only in the direction indicated by the arrow. If there are two arrows shown, then traffic flows in both directions. You must follow the flow of traffic.

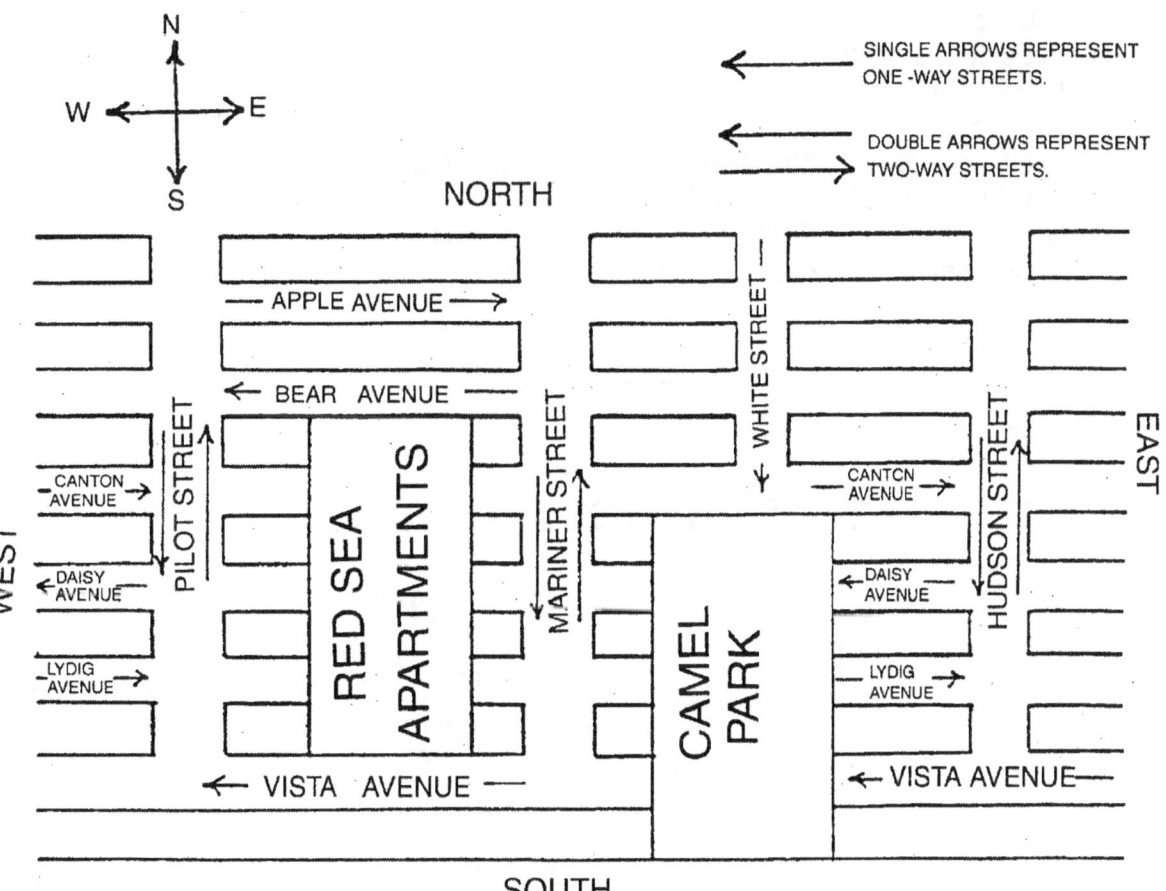

19. You are located at Apple Avenue and White Street. You receive a call to respond to the corner of Lydig Avenue and Pilot Street.
Which one of the following is the MOST direct route for you to take in your patrol car, making sure to obey all traffic regulations?
Travel _____ on Pilot Street.

  A. two blocks south on White Street, then one block east on Canton Avenue, then one block north on Hudson Street, then three blocks west on Bear Avenue, then three blocks south

  B. one block south on White Street, then two blocks west on Bear Avenue, then three blocks south

19._____

C. two blocks west on Apple Avenue, then four blocks south
D. two blocks south on White Street, then one block west on Canton Avenue, then three blocks south on Mariner Street, then one block west on Vista Avenue, then one block north

20. You are located at Canton Avenue and Pilot Street. You receive a call of a crime in progress at the intersection of Canton Avenue and Hudson Street.
Which one of the following is the MOST direct route for you to take in your patrol car, making sure to obey all traffic regulations?
Travel

   A. two blocks north on Pilot Street, then two blocks east on Apple Avenue, then one block south on White Street, then one block east on Bear Avenue, then one block south on Hudson Street
   B. three blocks south on Pilot Street, then travel one block east on Vista Avenue, then travel three blocks north on Mariner Street, then travel two blocks east on Canton Avenue
   C. one block north on Pilot Street, then travel three blocks east on Bear Avenue, then travel one block south on Hudson Street
   D. two blocks north on Pilot Street, then travel three blocks east on Apple Avenue, then travel two blocks south on Hudson Street

KEY (CORRECT ANSWERS)

1.	B	11.	B/D
2.	D	12.	C
3.	B	13.	C
4.	C	14.	D
5.	A	15.	C
6.	D	16.	C
7.	A	17.	B
8.	B	18.	C
9.	A	19.	B
10.	C	20.	D

READING COMPREHENSION
UNDERSTANDING AND INTERPRETING WRITTEN MATERIAL
EXAMINATION SECTION
TEST 1

DIRECTIONS: Each question or incomplete statement is followed by several suggested answers or completions. Select the one that BEST answers the question or completes the statement. *PRINT THE LETTER OF THE CORRECT ANSWER IN THE SPACE AT THE RIGHT.*

Questions 1-4.

DIRECTIONS: Questions 1 through 4 are to be answered SOLELY on the basis of the information given in the paragraph below.

Abandoned cars – with tires gone, chrome stripped away, and windows smashed – have become a common sight on the city's streets. In 2000, more than 72,000 were deposited at curbs by owners who never came back, an increase of 15,000 from the year before and more than 30 times the number abandoned a decade ago. In January 2001, the city Environmental Protection Administrator asked the State Legislature to pass a law requiring a buyer of a new automobile to deposit $100 and an owner of an automobile at the time the law takes effect to deposit $50 with the State Department of Motor Vehicles. In return, they would be given a certificate of deposit which would be passed on to each succeeding owner. The final owner would get the deposit money back if he could present proof that he has disposed of his car *in an environmentally acceptable manner.* The Legislature has given no indication that it plans to rush ahead on the matter.

1. The number of cars abandoned in the city streets in 1990 was MOST NEARLY

   A. 2,500   B. 12,000   C. 27,500   D. 57,000

2. The proposed law would require a person who owned a car bought before the law was passed to deposit

   A. $100 with the State Department of Motor Vehicles
   B. $50 with the Environmental Protection Administration
   C. $100 with the State Legislature
   D. $50 with the State Department of Motor Vehicles

3. The proposed law would require the State to return the deposit money ONLY when the

   A. original owner of the car shows proof that he sold it
   B. last owner of the car shows proof that he got rid of the car in a satisfactory way
   C. owner of a car shows proof that he has transferred the certificate of deposit to the next owner
   D. last owner of a car returns the certificate of deposit

4. The MAIN idea or theme of the above article is that

   A. a proposed new law would make it necessary for car owners in the State to pay additional taxes
   B. the State Legislature is against a proposed law to require deposits from automobile owners to prevent them from abandoning their cars
   C. the city is trying to find a solution for the increasing number of cars abandoned on its streets
   D. to pay for the removal of abandoned cars the city's Environmental Protection Administrator has asked the State to fine automobile owners who abandon their vehicles

Questions 5-7.

DIRECTIONS: Questions 5 through 7 are to be answered SOLELY on the basis of the information given in the paragraph below.

The regulations applying to parking meters provide that the driver is required to deposit the appropriate coin immediately upon parking and it is illegal for him to return at a later period to extend the parking time. If there is unused time on a parking meter, another car may be parked for a period not to exceed the unused time without the deposit of a coin. Operators of commercial vehicles are not required to deposit coins while loading or unloading expeditiously. By definition, a vehicle is considered parked even though there is a driver at the wheel and the meter must be used by the driver of such car.

5. According to the above paragraph, the regulations applying to parking meters do NOT

   A. allow the driver of a parked vehicle to stay in his car
   B. consider any loading or unloading of a vehicle as parking
   C. make any distinction between an unoccupied car and one with the driver at the wheel
   D. permit a driver who has parked a car at a meter with unused parking time to put a coin in the meter

6. According to the above paragraph, it is a violation of the parking meter regulations to

   A. load and unload slowly
   B. park commercial vehicles except for loading and unloading
   C. put a second coin in the meter in order to park longer
   D. use a parking space at any time without depositing a coin

7. The above paragraph CLEARLY indicates

   A. the number of minutes a vehicle may be parked
   B. the value of the coin that is to be put in the meter
   C. what is meant by a commercial vehicle
   D. when a car may be parked free

Questions 8-13.

DIRECTIONS: Questions 8 through 13 are to be answered on the basis of the information given in the paragraph below.

There are many types of reports. One of these is the field report, which requests information specified and grouped under columns or headings. A detailed, printed form is often used in submitting field reports. However, these printed, standardized forms provide a limited amount of space. The field man is required to make the decision as to how much of the information he has should go directly into the report and how much should be left for clarification if and when he is called in to explain a reported finding. In many instances, the addition of a short explanation of the finding might relieve the reader of the report of the necessity to seek an explanation. Therefore, the basic factual information asked for by the printed report form should often be clarified by some simple explanatory statement. If this is done, the reported finding becomes meaningful to the reader of the report who is far from the scene of the subject matter dealt with in the report. The significance of that which is reported finds its expression in the adoption of certain policies, improvements, or additions essential to furthering the effectiveness of the program.

8. According to the above paragraph, the field report asks for

   A. a detailed statement of the facts
   B. field information which comes under the heading of technical data
   C. replies to well-planned questions
   D. specific information in different columns

9. According to the above paragraph, the usual printed field report form

   A. does not have much room for writing
   B. is carefully laid out
   C. is necessary for the collection of facts
   D. usually has from three to four columns

10. According to the above paragraph, the man in the field MUST decide if

    A. a report is needed at all
    B. he should be called in to explain a reported finding
    C. he should put all the information he has into the report
    D. the reader of the report is justified in seeking an explanation

11. According to the above paragraph, the man in the field may be required to

    A. be acquainted with the person or persons who will read his report
    B. explain the information he reports
    C. give advice on specific problems
    D. keep records of the amount of work he completes

12. According to the above paragraph, the value of an explanatory statement added to the factual information reported in the printed forms is that it

    A. allows the person making the report to express himself briefly
    B. forces the person making the report to think logically
    C. helps the report reader understand the facts reported
    D. makes it possible to turn in the report later

13. According to the above paragraph, the importance of the information given by the field man in his report is shown by the

    A. adoption of policies and improvements
    B. effectiveness of the field staff
    C. fact that such a report is required
    D. necessary cost studies to back up the facts

13.___

Questions 14-15.

DIRECTIONS: Questions 14 and 15 are to be answered on the basis of the information contained in the following paragraph.

The driver of the collection crew shall at all times remain in or on a department vehicle in which there is revenue. In the event such driver must leave the vehicle, he shall designate one of the other members of the crew to remain in or on the vehicle. The member of the crew so designated by the driver shall remain in or on the vehicle until relieved by the driver or another member of the crew. The vehicle may be left unattended only when there is no revenue contained therein provided, however, that in that event the vehicle shall be locked. The loss of any vehicle or any of its contents, including revenue, resulting from any deviation from this rule, shall be the responsibility of the member or members of crew who shall be guilty of such deviation.

14. The vehicle of a collection crew may be left with no one in it only if

    A. it is locked
    B. there is a crew member nearby
    C. there is no money in it
    D. there is only one member in the crew

14.___

15. If money is stolen from an unattended vehicle of a collection crew, the employee held responsible is the

    A. driver
    B. one who left the vehicle unattended
    C. one who left the vehicle unlocked
    D. one who relieved the driver

15.___

Questions 16-18.

DIRECTIONS: Questions 16 through 18 are to be answered SOLELY on the basis of the information given in the paragraph below.

Safety belts provide protection for the passengers of a vehicle by preventing them from crashing around inside if the vehicle is involved in a collision. They operate on the principle similar to that used in the packaging of fragile items. You become a part of the vehicle package, and you are kept from being tossed about inside if the vehicle is suddenly decelerated. Many injury-causing collisions at low speeds, for example at city intersections, could have been injury-free if the occupants had fastened their safety belts. There is a double advantage to the driver in that it not only protects him from harm, but prevents him from being yanked away from the wheel, thereby permitting him to maintain control of the car.

5 (#1)

16. The principle on which seat belts work is that 16.____

   A. a car and its driver and passengers are fragile
   B. a person fastened to the car will not be thrown around when the car slows down suddenly
   C. the driver and passengers of a car that is suddenly decelerated will be thrown forward
   D. the driver and passengers of an automobile should be packaged the way fragile items are packaged

17. We can assume from the above passage that safety belts should be worn at all times because you can never tell when 17.____

   A. a car will be forced to turn off onto another road
   B. it will be necessary to shift into low gear to go up a hill
   C. you will have to speed up to pass another car
   D. a car may have to come to a sudden stop

18. Besides preventing injury, an ADDITIONAL benefit from the use of safety belts is that 18.____

   A. collisions are fewer
   B. damage to the car is kept down
   C. the car can be kept under control
   D. the number of accidents at city intersections is reduced

Questions 19-24.

DIRECTIONS: Questions 19 through 24 are to be answered on the basis of the following reading passage covering Procedures For Patrol.

PROCEDURES FOR PATROL

The primary function of all Parking Enforcement Agents assigned to patrol duty shall be to patrol assigned areas and issue summonses to violators of various sections of the City Traffic Regulations, which sections govern the parking or operation of vehicles. Parking Enforcement Agents occasionally may be called upon to distribute educational pamphlets and perform other work, at the discretion of the Bureau Chief.

Each Agent on patrol duty will be assigned a certain area (or areas) to be patrolled. These areas will be assigned during the daily roll call. Walking Cards will describe the street locations of the patrol and the manner in which the patrol is to be walked.

A Traffic Department vehicle will be provided for daily patrol assignments when necessary.

Each Agent shall accomplish an assigned field patrol in the following manner:

   a. Start each patrol at the location specified on the daily patrol sheet, and proceed as per walking instructions.
   b. Approach each metered space being utilized (each metered space in which a vehicle is parked). If the meter shows the expired flag, the member of the force shall prepare and affix a summons to the vehicle parked at meter.

c. Any vehicle in violation of any regulation governing the parking, standing, stopping, or movement of vehicles will be issued a summons.
d. No summons will be issued to a vehicle displaying an authorized vehicle identification plate of the Police Department unless the vehicle is parked in violation of the No Standing, No Stopping, Hydrant, Bus Stop, or Double Parking Regulations. Identification plates for Police Department automobiles are made of plastic and are of rectangular shape, 10 3/4" long, 3 3/4" high, black letters and numerals on a white background. The words *POLICE DEPT.* are printed on the face with the identification number. Identification plates for private automobiles are the same size and shape as those used on Police Department automobiles.

An Agent on patrol, when observing a person *feeding* a street meter (placing an additional coin in a meter so as to leave the vehicle parked for an additional period) shall prepare and affix a summons to the vehicle.

An Agent on patrol shall note on a computer card each missing or defective, out of order, or otherwise damaged meter.

19. Of the following, the work which the Parking Enforcement Agent performs MOST often is

   A. issuing summonses for parking violations
   B. distributing educational pamphlets
   C. assisting the Bureau Chief
   D. driving a city vehicle

20. The area to be covered by a Parking Enforcement Agent on patrol is

   A. determined by the Police Department
   B. regulated by the city Traffic Regulations
   C. marked off with red flags
   D. described on Walking Cards

21. A Parking Enforcement Agent reports a broken meter by

   A. issuing a summons
   B. making a mark on a computer card
   C. raising the flag on the broken meter
   D. attending a daily roll call

22. With respect to the use of an automobile for patrol duty,

   A. Parking Enforcement Agents must supply their own cars for patrol
   B. automobiles for patrol will be supplied by the Police Department
   C. Parking Enforcement Agents are permitted to park in a bus stop
   D. department vehicles will be provided when required for patrol

23. Parking Enforcement Agents sometimes issue summonses to drivers for *feeding* a street meter in violation of parking regulations.
    Which one of the following situations describes such a violation?
    A driver

   A. has moved from one metered space to another
   B. has parked next to a Police Department No Standing sign
   C. is parked by a meter which shows 30 minutes time still remaining
   D. has used a coin to reset the meter after his first time period expired

24. Vehicles displaying an authorized vehicle identification plate of the Police Department are allowed to park at expired meters.
Which one of the following statements describes the proper size of identification plates for private automobiles used for police work?
They

   A. are 10 3/4" long and 3 3/4" high
   B. have white letters and numerals on a black background
   C. are 3 3/4" long and 10 3/4" high
   D. have black letters and numerals on a white background

Questions 25-30.

DIRECTIONS: Questions 25 through 30 are to be answered on the basis of the following reading passage covering the Operation of Department Motor Vehicles.

OPERATION OF DEPARTMENT MOTOR VEHICLES

When operating a Traffic Department motor vehicle, a member of the force must show every courtesy to other drivers, obey all traffic signs and traffic regulations, obey all other lawful authority, and handle the vehicle in a manner which will foster safety practices in others and create a favorable impression of the Bureau, the Department, and the City. The operator and passengers MUST use the safety belts.

Driving Rules

   a. DO NOT operate a mechanically defective vehicle.
   DO NOT race engine on starting.
   DO NOT tamper with mechanical equipment.
   DO NOT run engine if there is an indication of low engine oil pressure, overheating, or no transmission oil.

   b. When parking on highway, all safety precautions must be observed.

   c. When parking in a garage or parking field, observe a maximum speed of 5 miles per hour. Place shift lever in park or neutral position, effectively apply hand brake, then shut off all ignition and light switches to prevent excess battery drain, and close all windows.

Reporting Defects

   a. Report all observed defects on Drivers' Vehicle Defect Card and on Monthly Vehicle Report Form 49 in sufficient detail so a mechanic can easily locate the source of trouble.
   b. Enter vehicle road service calls and actual time of occurrence on Monthly Vehicle Report.

Reporting Accidents

Promptly report all facts of each accident as follows: For serious accidents, including those involving personal injury, call your supervisor as soon as possible. Give all the appropriate information about the accident to your supervisor. Record vehicle registration information, including the name of the registered owner, the state, year, and serial number, and the classification marking on the license plates. Also record the operator's license number and other identifying information, and, if it applies, the injured person's age and sex. Give a full description of how the accident happened, and what happened following the accident, including the vehicles in collision, witnesses, police badge number, hospital, condition of road surface, time of day, weather conditions, location (near, far, center of intersection), and damage.

Repairs to Automobiles

When a Department motor vehicle requires repairs that cannot be made by the operator, or requires replacement of parts or accessories (including tires and tubes), or requires towing, the operator shall notify the District Commander.

When a Departmental motor vehicle is placed out of service for repairs, the Regional Commander shall assign another vehicle, if available.

Daily Operator's Report

The operator of a Department automobile shall keep a daily maintenance record of the vehicle, and note any unusual occurrences, on the Daily Operator's Report.

25. Parking Enforcement Agents who are assigned to operate Department motor vehicles on patrol are expected to

    A. disregard the posted speed limits to save time
    B. remove their seat belts on short trips
    C. show courtesy to other drivers on the road
    D. take the right of way at all intersections

26. The driver of a Department motor vehicle should

    A. leave the windows open when parking the vehicle in a garage
    B. drive the vehicle at approximately 10 miles per hour in a parking field
    C. be alert for indication of low engine oil pressure and overheated engine
    D. start a cold vehicle by racing the engine for 5 minutes

27. The reason that all defects on a Department vehicle that have been observed by its driver should be noted on a Monthly Vehicle Report Form 49 is:

    A. This action will foster better safety practices among other Agents
    B. The source of the defect may be located easily by a trained mechanic
    C. All the facts of an accident will be reported promptly
    D. The District Commander will not have to make road calls

28. If the driver of a Department vehicle is involved in an accident, an Accident Report should be made out. This Report should include a full description of how the accident happened.
    Which of the following statements would PROPERLY belong in an Accident Report?

    A. The accident occurred at the intersection of Broadway and 42nd Street.
    B. The operator of the Department motor vehicle replaced the windshield wiper.
    C. The vehicle was checked for gas and water before the patrol began.
    D. A bus passed two parked vehicles.

29. When a Department vehicle is disabled, whom should the operator notify? The

    A. Traffic Department garage
    B. Assistant Bureau Chief
    C. Police Department
    D. District Commander

30. The PROPER way for an operator of a Department vehicle to report unusual occurrences with respect to the operation of the vehicle is to

    A. follow the same procedures as for reporting a defect
    B. request the Regional Commander to assign another vehicle
    C. phone the Bureau Chief as soon as possible
    D. make a note of the circumstances on the Daily Operator's Report

KEY (CORRECT ANSWERS)

1.	A	16.	B
2.	D	17.	D
3.	B	18.	C
4.	C	19.	A
5.	C	20.	D
6.	C	21.	B
7.	D	22.	D
8.	D	23.	D
9.	A	24.	A
10.	C	25.	C
11.	B	26.	C
12.	C	27.	B
13.	A	28.	A
14.	C	29.	D
15.	B	30.	D

TEST 2

DIRECTIONS: Each question or incomplete statement is followed by several suggested answers or completions. Select the one that BEST answers the question or completes the statement. *PRINT THE LETTER OF THE CORRECT ANSWER IN THE SPACE AT THE RIGHT.*

Questions 1-4.

DIRECTIONS: Questions 1 through 4 are to be answered SOLELY on the basis of the information contained in the following passage.

Of those arrested in the city in 2003 for felonies or misdemeanors, only 32% were found guilty of any charge. Fifty-six percent of such arrestees were acquitted or had their cases dismissed. 11% failed to appear for trial, and 1% received other dispositions. Of those found guilty, only 7.4% received any sentences of over one year in jail. Only 50% of those found guilty were sentenced to any further time in jail. When considered with the low probability of arrests for most crimes, these figures make it clear that the crime control system in the city poses little threat to the average criminal. Delay compounds the problem. The average case took four appearances for disposition after arraignment. Twenty percent of all cases took eight or more appearances to reach a disposition. Forty-four percent of all cases took more than one year to disposition.

1. According to the above passage, crime statistics for 2003 indicate that

    A. there is a low probability of arrests for all crimes in the city
    B. the average criminal has much to fear from the law in the city
    C. over 10% of arrestees in the city charged with felonies or misdemeanors did not show up for trial
    D. criminals in the city are less likely to be caught than criminals in the rest of the country

2. The percentage of those arrested in 2003 who received sentences of over one year in jail amounted to MOST NEARLY

    A. .237   B. 2.4   C. 23.7   D. 24.0

3. According to the above passage, the percentage of arrestees in 2003 who were found guilty was

    A. 20% of those arrested for misdemeanors
    B. 11% of those arrested for felonies
    C. 50% of those sentenced to further time in jail
    D. 32% of those arrested for felonies or misdemeanors

4. According to the above paragraph, the number of appearances after arraignment and before disposition amounted to

    A. an average of four
    B. eight or more in 44% of the cases
    C. over four for cases which took more than a year
    D. between four and eight for most cases

Questions 5-6.

DIRECTIONS: Questions 5 and 6 are to be answered on the basis of the following paragraph.

A person who, with the intent to deprive or defraud another of the use and benefit of property or to appropriate the same to the use of the taker, or of any other person other than the true owner, wrongfully takes, obtains or withholds, by any means whatever, from the possession of the true owner or of any other person any money, personal property, thing in action, evidence of debt or contract, or article of value of any kind, steals such property and is guilty of larceny.

5. This definition from the Penal Law has NO application to the act of

   A. fraudulent conversion by a vendor of city sales tax money collected from purchasers
   B. refusing to give proper change after a purchaser has paid for an article in cash
   C. receiving property stolen from the rightful owner
   D. embezzling money from the rightful owner

6. According to the above paragraph, an auto mechanic who claimed to have a lien on an automobile for completed repairs and refused to surrender possession until the bill was paid

   A. *cannot* be charged with larceny because his repairs increased the value of the car
   B. *can* be charged with larceny because such actual possession can be construed to include intent to deprive the owner of use of the car
   C. *cannot* be charged with larceny because the withholding is temporary and such possession is not an evidence of debt
   D. *cannot* be charged with larceny because intent to defraud is lacking

Questions 7-12.

DIRECTIONS: Questions 7 through 12 are to be answered on the basis of the information given in the passage below. Assume that all questions refer to the same state described in the passage.

The courts and the police consider an *offense* as any conduct that is punishable by a fine or imprisonment. Such offenses include many kinds of acts—from behavior that is merely annoying, like throwing a noisy party that keeps everyone awake, all the way up to violent acts like murder. The law classifies offenses according to the penalties that are provided for them. In one state, minor offenses are called *violations*. A violation is punishable by a fine of not more than $250 or imprisonment of not more than 15 days, or both. The annoying behavior mentioned above is an example of a violation. More serious offenses are classified as *crimes*. Crimes are classified by the kind of penalty that is provided. A *misdemeanor* is a crime that is punishable by a fine of not more than $1,000 or by imprisonment of not more than 1 year, or both. Examples of misdemeanors include stealing something with a value of $100 or less, turning in a false alarm, or illegally possessing less than 1/8 of an ounce of a dangerous drug. A *felony* is a criminal offense punishable by imprisonment of more than 1 year. Murder is clearly a felony.

7. According to the above passage, any act that is punishable by imprisonment or by a fine is called a(n) 7.____

   A. offense B. violation C. crime D. felony

8. According to the above passage, which of the following is classified as a crime? 8.____

   A. Offense punishable by 15 days imprisonment
   B. Minor offense
   C. Violation
   D. Misdemeanor

9. According to the above passage, if a person guilty of burglary can receive a prison sentence of 7 years or more, burglary would be classified as a 9.____

   A. violation   B. misdemeanor
   C. felony   D. violent act

10. According to the above passage, two offenses that would BOTH be classified as misdemeanors are 10.____

    A. making unreasonable noise, and stealing a $90 bicycle
    B. stealing a $75 radio, and possessing 1/16 of an ounce of heroin
    C. holding up a bank, and possessing 1/4 of a pound of marijuana
    D. falsely reporting a fire, and illegally double-parking

11. The above passage says that offenses are classified according to the penalties provided for them. 11.____
    On the basis of clues in the passage, who probably decides what the maximum penalties should be for the different kinds of offenses?

    A. The State lawmakers   B. The City police
    C. The Mayor   D. Officials in Washington, D.C.

12. Of the following, which BEST describes the subject matter of the passage? 12.____

    A. How society deals with criminals
    B. How offenses are classified
    C. Three types of criminal behavior
    D. The police approach to offenders

Questions 13-20.

DIRECTIONS: Questions 13 through 20 are to be answered SOLELY on the basis of the following passage.

Auto theft is prevalent and costly. In 2005, 486,000 autos valued at over $500 million were stolen. About 28 percent of the inhabitants of Federal prisons are there as a result of conviction of interstate auto theft under the Dyer Act. In California alone, auto thefts cost the criminal justice system approximately $60 million yearly.

The great majority of auto theft is for temporary use rather than resale, as evidenced by the fact that 88 percent of autos stolen in 2005 were recovered. In Los Angeles, 64 percent of stolen autos that were recovered were found within two days, and about 80 percent within a week. Chicago reports that 71 percent of the recovered autos were found within four miles of the point of theft. The FBI estimates that 8 percent of stolen cars are taken for the purpose of stripping them for parts, 12 percent for resale, and 5 percent for use in another crime. Auto thefts are primarily juvenile acts. Although only 21 percent of all arrests for nontraffic offenses in 2005 were of individuals under 18 years of age, 63 percent of auto theft arrests were of persons under 18. Auto theft represents the start of many criminal careers; in an FBI sample of juvenile auto theft offenders, 41 percent had no prior arrest record.

13. In the above passage, the discussion of the reasons for auto theft does NOT include the percent of

   A. autos stolen by prior offenders
   B. recovered stolen autos found close to the point of theft
   C. stolen autos recovered within a week
   D. stolen autos which were recovered

14. Assuming the figures in the above passage remain constant, you may logically estimate the cost of auto thefts to the California criminal justice system over a five-year period beginning in 2005 to have been about _____ million.

   A. $200   B. $300   C. $440   D. $500

15. According to the above passage, the percent of stolen autos in Los Angeles which were not recovered within a week was _____ percent.

   A. 12   B. 20   C. 29   D. 36

16. According to the above passage, MOST auto thefts are committed by

   A. former inmates of Federal prisons   B. juveniles
   C. persons with a prior arrest record   D. residents of large cities

17. According to the above passage, MOST autos are stolen for

   A. resale   B. stripping of parts
   C. temporary use   D. use in another crime

18. According to the above passage, the percent of persons arrested for auto theft who were under 18

   A. equals nearly the same percent of stolen autos which were recovered
   B. equals nearly two-thirds of the total number of persons arrested for nontraffic offenses
   C. is the same as the percent of persons arrested for nontraffic offenses who were under 18
   D. is three times the percent of persons arrested for nontraffic offenses who were under 18

19. An APPROPRIATE title for the above passage is

   A. HOW CRIMINAL CAREERS BEGIN
   B. RECOVERY OF STOLEN CARS
   C. SOME STATISTICS ON AUTO THEFT
   D. THE COSTS OF AUTO THEFT

20. Based on the above passage, the number of cars taken for use in another crime in 2005 was

   A. 24,300   B. 38,880   C. 48,600   D. 58,320

Questions 21-22.

DIRECTIONS: Questions 21 and 22 are to be answered SOLELY on the basis of the following paragraph.

If the second or third felony is such that, upon a first conviction, the offender would be punishable by imprisonment for any term less than his natural life, then such person must be sentenced to imprisonment for an indeterminate term, the minimum of which shall be not less than one-half of the longest term prescribed upon a first conviction, and the maximum of which shall be not longer than twice such longest term, provided, however, that the minimum sentence imposed hereunder upon such second or third felony offender shall in no case be less than five years; except that where the maximum punishment for a second or third felony offender hereunder is five years or less, the minimum sentence must be not less than two years.

21. According to the above paragraph, a person who has a second felony conviction shall receive as a sentence for that second felony an indeterminate term

   A. not less than twice the minimum term prescribed upon a first conviction as a maximum
   B. not less than one-half the maximum term of his first conviction as a minimum
   C. not more than twice the minimum term prescribed upon a first conviction as a minimum
   D. with a maximum of not more than twice the longest term prescribed for a first conviction for this crime

22. According to the above paragraph, if the term for this crime for a first offender is up to three years, the possible indeterminate term for this crime as a second or third felony shall have a _____ of not _____ than _____ years.

   A. minimum; less; five
   B. maximum; more; five
   C. minimum; less; one and one-half
   D. maximum; less; six

23. A statute states: *A person who steals an article worth $1,000 or less where no aggravating circumstances accompany the act is guilty of petit larceny. If the article is worth more than $1,000, it may be grand larceny.*
   If all you know is that Edward Smith stole an article worth $1,000, it may reasonably be said that

   A. Smith is guilty of petit larceny
   B. Smith is guilty of grand larceny
   C. Smith is guilty of neither petit larceny nor grand larceny
   D. precisely what charge will be placed against Smith is uncertain

Questions 24-25.

DIRECTIONS: Questions 24 and 25 are to be answered on the basis of the following section of a law.

A person who, after having been three times convicted within this state of felonies or attempts to commit felonies, or under the law of any other state, government, or country, of crimes which if committed within this state would be felonious, commits a felony, other than murder, first or second degree, or treason, within this state, shall be sentenced upon conviction of such fourth, or subsequent, offense to imprisonment in a state prison for an indeterminate term the minimum of which shall be not less than the maximum term provided for first offenders for the crime for which the individual has been convicted, but, in any event, the minimum term upon conviction for a felony as the fourth or subsequent, offense shall be not less than fifteen years, and the maximum thereof shall be his natural life.

24. Under the terms of the above law, a person must receive the increased punishment therein provided if

   A. he is convicted of a felony and has been three times previously convicted of felonies
   B. he has been three times previously convicted of felonies, regardless of the nature of his present conviction
   C. his fourth conviction is for murder, first or second degree, or treason
   D. he has previously been convicted three times of murder, first or second degree, or treason

25. Under the terms of the above law, a person convicted of a felony for which the penalty is imprisonment for a term not to exceed ten years, and who has been three times previously convicted of felonies in this state, shall be sentenced to a term, the MINIMUM of which shall be

   A. 10 years
   B. 15 years
   C. indeterminate
   D. his natural life

KEY (CORRECT ANSWERS)

1.	C	11.	A
2.	B	12.	B
3.	D	13.	A
4.	A	14.	B
5.	C	15.	B
6.	D	16.	B
7.	A	17.	C
8.	D	18.	D
9.	C	19.	C
10.	B	20.	A

21. D
22. C
23. D
24. A
25. B

REPORT WRITING

EXAMINATION SECTION
TEST 1

DIRECTIONS: Each question or incomplete statement is followed by several suggested answers or completions. Select the one that BEST answers the question or completes the statement. *PRINT THE LETTER OF THE CORRECT ANSWER IN THE SPACE AT THE RIGHT.*

1. Police Officer Johnson responds to the scene of an assault and obtains the following information:
   Time of Occurrence: 8:30 P.M.
   Place of Occurrence: 120-18 119th Avenue, Apt. 2A
   Suspects: John Andrews, victim's ex-husband and unknown white male
   Victim: Susan Andrews
   Injury: Broken right arm
   Officer Johnson is preparing a complaint report on the incident.
   Which one of the following expresses the above information MOST clearly and accurately?

   A. Susan Andrews was assaulted at 120-18 119th Avenue, Apt. 2A. At 8:30 P.M., her ex-husband, John Andrews, and an unknown white male broke her arm.
   B. At 8:30 P.M., Susan Andrews was assaulted at 120-18 119th Avenue, Apt. 2A, by her ex-husband, John Andrews, and an unknown white male. Her right arm was broken.
   C. John Andrews, an unknown white male, and Susan Andrews' ex-husband, assaulted and broke her right arm at 8:30 P.M., at 120-18 119th Avenue, Apt. 2A.
   D. John Andrews, ex-husband of Susan Andrews, broke her right arm with an unknown white male at 120-18 119th Avenue, at 8:30 P.M. in Apt. 2A.

2. While on patrol, Officers Banks and Thompson see a man lying on the ground bleeding. Officer Banks records the following details about the incident:
   Time of Incident: 3:15 P.M.
   Place of Incident: Sidewalk in front of 517 Rock Avenue
   Incident: Tripped and fell
   Name of Injured: John Blake
   Injury: Head wound
   Action Taken: Transported to Merry Hospital
   Officer Banks is completing a report on the incident.
   Which one of the following expresses the above information MOST clearly and accurately?

   A. At 3:15 P.M., Mr. John Blake was transported to Merry Hospital. He tripped and fell, injuring his head on sidewalk in front of 517 Rock Avenue.
   B. Mr. John Blake tripped and fell on the sidewalk at 3:15 P.M. in front of 517 Rock Avenue. He was transported to Merry Hospital while he sustained a head wound.
   C. Mr. John Blake injured his head when he tripped and fell on the sidewalk in front of 517 Rock Avenue at 3:15 P.M. He was transported to Merry Hospital.
   D. A head was wounded on the sidewalk in front of 517 Rock Avenue at 3:15 P.M. Mr. John Blake tripped and fell and was transported to Merry Hospital.

3. When assigned to investigate a complaint, a police officer should
    I. Interview witnesses and obtain facts
    II. Conduct a thorough investigation of circumstances concerning the complaint
    III. Prepare a complaint report
    IV. Determine if the complaint report should be closed or referred for further investigation
    V. Enter complaint report on the Complaint Report Index and obtain a complaint report number at the station house

   While on patrol, Police Officer John is instructed by his supervisor to investigate a complaint by Mr. Stanley Burns, who was assaulted by his brother-in-law, Henry Traub. After interviewing Mr. Burns, Officer John learns that Mr. Traub has been living with Mr. Burns for the past two years. Officer John accompanies Mr. Burns to his apartment but Mr. Traub is not there. Officer John fills out the complaint report and takes the report back to the station house where it is entered on the Complaint Report Index and assigned a complaint report number. Officer John's actions were

   A. *improper,* primarily because he should have stayed at Mr. Burns' apartment and waited for Mr. Traub to return in order to arrest him
   B. *proper,* primarily because after obtaining all the facts, he took the report back to the station house and was assigned a complaint report number
   C. *improper,* primarily because he should have decided whether to close the report or refer it for further investigation
   D. *proper,* primarily because he was instructed by his supervisor to take the report from Mr. Burns even though it involved his brother-in-law

4. Police Officer Waters was the first person at the scene of a fire which may have been the result of arson. He obtained the following information:

   Place of Occurrence: 35 John Street, Apt. 27
   Time of Occurrence: 4:00 P.M.
   Witness: Daisy Logan
   Incident: Fire (possible arson)
   Suspect: Male, white, approximately 18 years old, wearing blue jeans and a plaid shirt, running away from the incident Officer Waters is completing a report on the incident.

   Which one of the following expresses the above information MOST clearly and accurately?

   A. At 4:00 P.M., Daisy Logan saw a white male, approximately 18 years old who was wearing blue jeans and a plaid shirt, running from the scene of a fire at 35 John Street, Apt. 27.
   B. Seeing a fire at 35 John Street, a white male approximately 18 years old, wearing blue jeans and a plaid shirt, was seen running from Apt. 27 at 4:00 P.M. reported Daisy Logan.
   C. Approximately 18 years old and wearing blue jeans and a plaid shirt, Daisy Logan saw a fire and a white male running from 35 John Street, Apt. 27 at 4:00 P.M.
   D. Running from 35 John Street, Apt. 27, the scene of the fire, reported Daisy Logan at 4:00 P.M., was a white male approximately 18 years old and wearing blue jeans and a plaid shirt.

5. Police Officer Sullivan obtained the following information at the scene of a two-car accident:

   Place of Occurrence: 2971 William Street
   Drivers and Vehicles Involved: Mrs. Wilson, driver of blue 2004 Toyota Camry; Mr. Bailey, driver of white 2001 Dodge
   Injuries Sustained: Mr. Bailey had a swollen right eye; Mrs. Wilson had a broken left hand

   Which one of the following expresses the above information MOST clearly and accurately?

   A. Mr. Bailey, owner of a white 2001 Dodge, at 2971 William Street, had a swollen right eye. Mrs. Wilson, with a broken left hand, is the owner of the blue 2004 Toyota Camry. They were in a car accident.
   B. Mrs. Wilson got a broken left hand and Mr. Bailey a swollen right eye at 2971 William Street. The vehicles involved in the car accident were a 2001 Dodge, white, owned by Mr. Bailey, and Mrs. Wilson's blue 2004 Toyota Camry.
   C. Mrs. Wilson, the driver of the blue 2004 Toyota Camry, and Mr. Bailey, the driver of the white 2001 Dodge, were involved in a car accident at 2971 William Street. Mr. Bailey sustained a swollen right eye, and Mrs. Wilson broke her left hand.
   D. Mr. Bailey sustained a swollen right eye and Mrs. Wilson broke her left hand in a car accident at 2971 William Street. They owned a 2001 white Dodge and a 2004 blue Toyota Camry.

6. Officer Johnson has issued a summons to a driver and has obtained the following information:

   Place of Occurrence: Corner of Foster Road and Woodrow Avenue
   Time of Occurrence: 7:10 P.M.
   Driver: William Grant
   Offense: Driving through a red light
   Age of Driver: 42
   Address of Driver: 23 Richmond Avenue

   Officer Johnson is making an entry in his Memo Book regarding the incident.
   Which one of the following expresses the above information MOST clearly and accurately?

   A. William Grant, lives at 23 Richmond Avenue at 7:10 P.M., went through a red light. He was issued a summons at the corner of Foster Road and Woodrow Avenue. The driver is 42 years old.
   B. William Grant, age 42, who lives at 23 Richmond Avenue, was issued a summons for going through a red light at 7:10 P.M. at the corner of Foster Road and Woodrow Avenue.
   C. William Grant, age 42, was issued a summons on the corner of Foster Road and Woodrow Avenue for going through a red light. He lives at 23 Richmond Avenue at 7:10 P.M.
   D. A 42-year-old man who lives at 23 Richmond Avenue was issued a summons at 7:10 P.M. William Grant went through a red light at the corner of Foster Road and Woodrow Avenue.

7. Police Officer Frome has completed investigating a report of a stolen auto and obtained the following information:

   Date of Occurrence: October 26, 2004
   Place of Occurrence: 51st Street and 8th Avenue
   Time of Occurrence: 3:30 P.M.
   Crime: Auto theft
   Suspect: Michael Wadsworth
   Action Taken: Suspect arrested

   Which one of the following expresses the above information MOST clearly and accurately?

   A. Arrested on October 26, 2004 was a stolen auto at 51st Street and 8th Avenue at 3:30 P.M. driven by Michael Wadsworth.
   B. For driving a stolen auto at 3:30 P.M., Michael Wadsworth was arrested at 51st Street and 8th Avenue on October 26, 2004.
   C. On October 26, 2004 at 3:30 P.M., Michael Wadsworth was arrested at 51st Street and 8th Avenue for driving a stolen auto.
   D. Michael Wadsworth was arrested on October 26, 2004 at 3:30 P.M. for driving at 51st Street and 8th Avenue. The auto was stolen.

8. Police Officer Wright has finished investigating a report of Grand Larceny and has obtained the following information:

   Time of Occurrence: Between 1:00 P.M. and 2:00 P.M.
   Place of Occurrence: In front of victim's home, 85 Montgomery Avenue
   Victim: Mr. Williams, owner of the vehicle
   Crime: Automobile broken into
   Property Taken: Stereo valued at $1,200

   Officer Wright is preparing a report on the incident. Which one of the following expresses the above information MOST clearly and accurately?

   A. While parked in front of his home Mr. Williams states that between 1:00 P.M. and 2:00 P.M. an unknown person broke into his vehicle. Mr. Williams, who lives at 85 Montgomery Avenue, lost his $1,200 stereo.
   B. Mr. Williams, who lives at 85 Montgomery Avenue, states that between 1:00 P.M. and 2:00 P.M. his vehicle was parked in front of his home when an unknown person broke into his car and took his stereo worth $1,200.
   C. Mr. Williams was parked in front of 85 Montgomery Avenue, which is his home, when it was robbed of a $1,200 stereo. When he came out, he observed between 1:00 P.M. and 2:00 P.M. that his car had been broken into by an unknown person.
   D. Mr. Williams states between 1:00 P.M. and 2:00 P.M. that an unknown person broke into his car in front of his home. Mr. Williams further states that he was robbed of a $1,200 stereo at 85 Montgomery Avenue.

9. Police Officer Fontaine obtained the following details relating to a suspicious package:

   Place of Occurrence: Case Bank, 2 Wall Street
   Time of Occurrence: 10:30 A.M.
   Date of Occurrence: October 10, 2004
   Complaint: Suspicious package in doorway
   Found By: Emergency Service Unit

   Officer Fontaine is preparing a report for department records.
   Which one of the following expresses the above information MOST clearly and accurately?

   A. At 10:30 A.M., the Emergency Service Unit reported they found a package on October 10, 2004 which appeared suspicious. This occurred in a doorway at 2 Wall Street, Case Bank.
   B. A package which appeared suspicious was in the doorway of Case Bank. The Emergency Service Unit reported this at 2 Wall Street at 10:30 A.M. on October 10, 2004 when found.
   C. On October 10, 2004 at 10:30 A.M., a suspicious package was found by the Emergency Service Unit in the doorway of Case Bank at 2 Wall Street.
   D. The Emergency Service Unit found a package at the Case Bank. It appeared suspicious at 10:30 A.M. in the doorway of 2 Wall Street on October 10, 2004.

10. Police Officer Reardon receives the following information regarding a case of child abuse:

    Victim: Joseph Mays
    Victim's Age: 10 years old
    Victim's Address: Resides with his family at 42 Columbia Street, Apt. 1B
    Complainant: Victim's uncle, Kevin Mays
    Suspects: Victim's parents

    Police Officer Reardon is preparing a report to send to the Department of Social Services.
    Which one of the following expresses the above information MOST clearly and accurately?

    A. Kevin Mays reported a case of child abuse to his ten-year-old nephew, Joseph Mays, by his parents. He resides with his family at 42 Columbia Street, Apt. 1B.
    B. Kevin Mays reported that his ten-year-old nephew, Joseph Mays, has been abused by the child's parents. Joseph Mays resides with his family at 42 Columbia Street, Apt. 1B.
    C. Joseph Mays has been abused by his parents. Kevin Mays reported that his nephew resides with his family at 42 Columbia Street, Apt. 1B. He is ten years old.
    D. Kevin Mays reported that his nephew is ten years old. Joseph Mays has been abused by his parents. He resides with his family at 42 Columbia Street, Apt. 1B.

11. While on patrol, Police Officer Hawkins was approached by Harry Roland, a store owner, who found a leather bag valued at $200.00 outside his store. Officer Hawkins took the property into custody and removed the following items:

2 Solex watches, each valued at	$500.00
4 14-kt. gold necklaces, each valued at	$315.00
Cash	$519.00
1 diamond ring, valued at	$400.00

Officer Hawkins is preparing a report on the found property.
Which one of the following is the TOTAL value of the property and cash found?

   A. $1,734   B. $3,171   C. $3,179   D. $3,379

12. While on patrol, Police Officer Blake observes a man running from a burning abandoned building. Officer Blake radios the following information:

Place of Occurrence:	310 Hall Avenue
Time of Occurrence:	8:30 P.M.
Type of Building:	Abandoned
Suspect:	Male, white, about 35 years old
Crime:	Arson

Officer Blake is completing a report on the incident.
Which one of the following expresses the above information MOST clearly and accurately?

   A. An abandoned building located at 310 Hall Avenue was on fire at 8:30 P.M. A white male, approximately 35 years old, was observed fleeing the scene.
   B. A white male, approximately 35 years old, at 8:30 P.M. was observed fleeing 310 Hall Avenue. The fire was set at an abandoned building.
   C. An abandoned building was set on fire. A white male, approximately 35 years old, was observed fleeing the scene at 8:30 P.M. at 310 Hall Avenue.
   D. Observed fleeing a building at 8:30 P.M. was a white male, approximately 35 years old. An abandoned building, located at 310 Hall Avenue, was set on fire.

13. Police Officer Winters responds to a call regarding a report of a missing person. The following information was obtained by the Officer:

Time of Occurrence:	3:30 P.M.
Place of Occurrence:	Harrison Park
Reported By:	Louise Dee - daughter
Description of Missing Person:	Sharon Dee, 70 years old, 5'5", brown eyes, black hair - mother

Officer Winters is completing a report on the incident. Which one of the following expresses the above information MOST clearly and accurately?

   A. Mrs. Sharon Dee, reported missing by her daughter, Louise, was seen in Harrison Park. The last time she saw her was at 3:30 P.M. She is 70 years old with black hair, brown eyes, and 5'5".
   B. Louise Dee reported that her mother, Sharon Dee, is missing. Sharon Dee is 70 years old, has black hair, brown eyes, and is 5'5". She was last seen at 3:30 P.M. in Harrison Park.
   C. Louise Dee reported Sharon, her 70-year-old mother at 3:30 P.M., to be missing after being seen last at Harrison Park. Described as being 5'5", she has black hair and brown eyes.

D. At 3:30 P.M. Louise Dee's mother was last seen by her daughter in Harrison Park. She has black hair and brown eyes. Louise reported Sharon is 5'5" and 70 years old.

14. While on patrol, Police Officers Mertz and Gallo receive a call from the dispatcher regarding a crime in progress.
    When the Officers arrive, they obtain the following information:
    Time of Occurrence: 2:00 P.M.
    Place of Occurrence: In front of 2124 Bristol Avenue
    Crime: Purse snatch
    Victim: Maria Nieves
    Suspect: Carlos Ortiz
    Witness: Jose Perez, who apprehended the subject
    The Officers are completing a report on the incident.
    Which one of the following expresses the above information MOST clearly and accurately?

    A. At 2:00 P.M., Jose Perez witnessed Maria Nieves. Her purse was snatched. The suspect, Carlos Ortiz, was apprehended in front of 2124 Bristol Avenue.
    B. In front of 2124 Bristol Avenue, Carlos Ortiz snatched the purse belonging to Maria Nieves. Carlos Ortiz was apprehended by a witness to the crime after Jose Perez saw the purse snatch at 2:00 P.M.
    C. At 2:00 P.M., Carlos Ortiz snatched a purse from Maria Nieves in front of 2124 Bristol Avenue. Carlos Ortiz was apprehended by Jose Perez, a witness to the crime.
    D. At 2:00 P.M., Carlos Ortiz was seen snatching the purse of Maria Nieves as seen and apprehended by Jose Perez in front of 2124 Bristol Avenue.

15. Police Officers Willis and James respond to a crime in progress and obtain the following information:
    Time of Occurrence: 8:30 A.M.
    Place of Occurrence: Corner of Hopkin Avenue and Amboy Place
    Crime: Chain snatch
    Victim: Mrs. Paula Evans
    Witness: Mr. Robert Peters
    Suspect: White male
    Officers Willis and James are completing a report on the incident.
    Which one of the following expresses the above information MOST clearly and accurately?

    A. Mrs. Paula Evans was standing on the corner of Hopkin Avenue and Amboy Place at 8:30 A.M. when a white male snatched her chain. Mr. Robert Peters witnessed the crime.
    B. At 8:30 A.M., Mr, Robert Peters witnessed Mrs. Paula Evans and a white male standing on the corner of Hopkin Avenue and Amboy Place. Her chain was snatched.
    C. At 8:30 A.M., a white male was standing on the corner of Hopkin Avenue and Amboy Place. Mrs. Paula Evans' chain was snatched, and Mr. Robert Peters witnessed the crime.

D. At 8:30 A.M., Mr. Robert Peters reported he witnessed a white male snatching Mrs. Paula Evans' chain while standing on the corner of Hopkin Avenue and Amboy Place.

16. Police Officers Cleveland and Logan responded to an assault that had recently occurred. The following information was obtained at the scene:

Place of Occurrence: Broadway and Roosevelt Avenue
Time of Occurrence: 1:00 A.M.
Crime: Attempted robbery, assault
Victim: Chuck Brown, suffered a broken tooth
Suspect: Lewis Brown, victim's brother

Officer Logan is completing a report on the incident.
Which one of the following expresses the above information MOST clearly and accurately?

   A. Lewis Brown assaulted his brother Chuck on the corner of Broadway and Roosevelt Avenue. Chuck Brown reported his broken tooth during the attempted robbery at 1:00 A.M.
   B. Chuck Brown had his tooth broken when he was assaulted at 1:00 A.M. on the corner of Broadway and Roosevelt Avenue by his brother, Lewis Brown, while Lewis was attempting to rob him.
   C. An attempt at 1:00 A.M. to rob Chuck Brown turned into an assault at the corner of Broadway and Roosevelt Avenue when his brother Lewis broke his tooth.
   D. At 1:00 A.M., Chuck Brown reported that he was assaulted during his brother's attempt to rob him. Lewis Brown broke his tooth. The incident occurred on the corner of Broadway and Roosevelt Avenue.

17. Police Officer Mannix has just completed an investigation regarding a hit-and-run accident which resulted in a pedestrian being injured. Officer Mannix has obtained the following information:

Make and Model of Car: Pontiac, Trans Am
Year and Color of Car: 2006, white
Driver of Car: Male, black
Place of Occurrence: Corner of E. 15th Street and 8th Avenue
Time of Occurrence: 1:00 P.M.

Officer Mannix is completing a report on the accident.
Which one of the following expresses the above information MOST clearly and accurately?

   A. At 1:00 P.M., at the corner of E. 15th Street and 8th Avenue, a black male driving a white 2006 Pontiac Trans Am was observed leaving the scene of an accident after injuring a pedestrian with the vehicle.
   B. On the corner of E. 15th Street and 8th Avenue, a white Pontiac, driven by a black male, a 2006 Trans Am injured a pedestrian and left the scene of the accident at 1:00 P.M.
   C. A black male driving a white 2006 Pontiac Trans Am injured a pedestrian and left with the car while driving on the corner of E. 15th Street and 8th Avenue at 1:00 P.M.
   D. At the corner of E. 15th Street and 8th Avenue, a pedestrian was injured by a black male. He fled in his white 2006 Pontiac Trans Am at 1:00 P.M.

18. The following details were obtained by Police Officer Dwight at the scene of a family dispute:

Place of Occurrence: 77 Baruch Drive
Victim: Andrea Valdez, wife of Walker
Violator: Edward Walker
Witness: George Valdez, victim's brother
Crime: Violation of Order of Protection
Action Taken: Violator arrested

Police Officer Dwight is preparing a report on the incident.
Which one of the following expresses the above information MOST clearly and accurately?

A. George Valdez saw Edward Walker violate his sister's Order of Protection at 77 Baruch Drive. Andrea Valdez's husband was arrested for this violation.
B. Andrea Valdez's Order of Protection was violated at 77 Baruch Drive. George Valdez saw his brother-in-law violate his sister's Order. Edward Walker was arrested.
C. Edward Walker was arrested for violating an Order of Protection held by his wife, Andrea Valdez. Andrea's brother, George Valdez, witnessed the violation at 77 Baruch Drive.
D. An arrest was made at 77 Baruch Drive when an Order of Protection held by Andrea Valdez was violated by her husband. George Valdez, her brother, witnessed Edward Walker.

19. The following details were obtained by Police Officer Jackson at the scene of a robbery:

Place of Occurrence: Chambers Street, northbound A platform
Victim: Mr. John Wells
Suspect: Joseph Miller
Crime: Robbery, armed with knife, wallet taken
Action Taken: Suspect arrested

Officer Jackson is completing a report on the incident.
Which one of the following expresses the above information MOST clearly and accurately?

A. At Chambers Street northbound A platform, Joseph Miller used a knife to remove the wallet of John Wells while waiting for the train. Police arrested him.
B. Mr. John Wells, while waiting for the northbound A train at Chambers Street, had his wallet forcibly removed at knifepoint by Joseph Miller. Joseph Miller was later arrested.
C. Joseph Miller was arrested for robbery. At Chambers Street, John Wells stated that his wallet was taken. The incident occurred at knifepoint while waiting on a northbound A platform.
D. At the northbound Chambers Street platform, John Wells was waiting for the A train. Joseph Miller produced a knife and removed his wallet. He was arrested.

20. Police Officer Bellows responds to a report of drugs being sold in the lobby of an apartment building. He obtains the following information at the scene:
    Time of Occurrence: 11:30 P.M.
    Place of Occurrence: 1010 Bath Avenue
    Witnesses: Mary Markham, John Silver
    Suspect: Harry Stoner
    Crime: Drug sales
    Action Taken: Suspect was gone when police arrived
    Officer Bellows is completing a report of the incident. Which one of the following expresses the above information MOST clearly and accurately?

    A. Mary Markham and John Silver witnessed drugs being sold and the suspect flee at 1010 Bath Avenue. Harry Stoner was conducting his business at 11:30 P.M. before police arrival in the lobby.
    B. In the lobby, Mary Markham reported at 11:30 P.M. she saw Harry Stoner, along with John Silver, selling drugs. He ran from the lobby at 1010 Bath Avenue before police arrived.
    C. John Silver and Mary Markham reported that they observed Harry Stoner selling drugs in the lobby of 1010 Bath Avenue at 11:30 P.M. The witnesses stated that Stoner fled before police arrived.
    D. Before police arrived, witnesses stated that Harry Stoner was selling drugs. At 1010 Bath Avenue, in the lobby, John Silver and Mary Markham said they observed his actions at 11:30 P.M.

21. While on patrol, Police Officer Fox receives a call to respond to a robbery. Upon arriving at the scene, he obtains the following information:
    Time of Occurrence: 6:00 P.M.
    Place of Occurrence: Sal's Liquor Store at 30 Fordham Road
    Victim: Sal Jones
    Suspect: White male wearing a beige parka
    Description of Crime: Victim was robbed in his store at gunpoint
    Officer Fox is completing a report on the incident. Which one of the following expresses the above information MOST clearly and accurately?

    A. I was informed at 6:00 P.M. by Sal Jones that an unidentified white male robbed him at gunpoint at 30 Fordham Road while wearing a beige parka at Sal's Liquor Store.
    B. At 6:00 P.M., Sal Jones was robbed at gunpoint in his store. An unidentified white male wearing a beige parka came into Sal's Liquor Store at 30 Fordham Road, he told me.
    C. I was informed at 6:00 P.M. while wearing a beige parka an unidentified white male robbed Sal Jones at gunpoint at Sal's Liquor Store at 30 Fordham Road.
    D. Sal Jones informed me that at 6:00 P.M. he was robbed at gunpoint in his store, Sal's Liquor Store, located at 30 Fordham Road, by an unidentified white male wearing a beige parka.

22. The following details were obtained by Police Officer Connors at the scene of a bank robbery:

Time of Occurrence: 10:21 A.M.
Place of Occurrence: Westbury Savings and Loan
Crime: Bank Robbery
Suspect: Male, dressed in black, wearing a black woolen face mask
Witness: Mary Henderson of 217 Westbury Ave.
Amount Stolen: $6141 U.S. currency

Officer Connors is completing a report on the incident. Which one of the following expresses the above information MOST clearly and accurately?

- A. At 10:21 A.M., the Westbury Savings and Loan was witnessed being robbed by Mary Henderson of 217 Westbury Avenue. The suspect fled dressed in black with a black woolen face mask. He left the bank with $6141 in U.S. currency.
- B. Dressed in black wearing a black woolen face mask, Mary Henderson of 217 Westbury Avenue saw a suspect flee with $6141 in U.S. currency after robbing the Westbury Savings and Loan. The robber was seen at 10:21 A.M.
- C. At 10:21 A.M., Mary Henderson of 217 Westbury Avenue, witness to the robbery of the Westbury Savings and Loan, reports that a male, dressed in black, wearing a black face mask, did rob said bank and fled with $6141 in U.S. currency.
- D. Mary Henderson, of 217 Westbury Avenue, witnessed the robbery of the Westbury Savings and Loan at 10:21 A.M. The suspect, a male, was dressed in black and was wearing a black woolen face mask. He fled with $6141 in U.S. currency.

23. At the scene of a dispute, Police Officer Johnson made an arrest after obtaining the following information:

Place of Occurrence: 940 Baxter Avenue
Time of Occurrence: 3:40 P.M.
Victim: John Mitchell
Suspect: Robert Holden, arrested at scene
Crime: Menacing
Weapon: Knife
Time of Arrest: 4:00 P.M.

Officer Johnson is completing a report of the incident.
Which one of the following expresses the above information
MOST clearly and accurately?

- A. John Mitchell was menaced by a knife at 940 Baxter Avenue. Robert Holden, owner of the weapon, was arrested at 4:00 P.M., twenty minutes later, at the scene.
- B. John Mitchell reports at 3:40 P.M. he was menaced at 940 Baxter Avenue by Robert Holden. He threatened him with his knife and was arrested at 4:00 P.M. at the scene.
- C. John Mitchell stated that at 3:40 P.M. at 940 Baxter Avenue he was menaced by Robert Holden, who was carrying a knife. Mr. Holden was arrested at the scene at 4:00 P.M.
- D. With a knife, Robert Holden menaced John Mitchell at 3:40 P.M. The knife belonged to him, and he was arrested at the scene of 940 Baxter Avenue at 4:00 P.M.

24. Officer Nieves obtained the following information after he was called to the scene of a large gathering:

Time of Occurrence: 2:45 A.M.
Place of Occurrence: Mulberry Park
Complaint: Loud music
Complainant: Mrs. Simpkins, 42 Mulberry Street, Apt. 25
Action Taken: Police officer dispersed the crowd

Officer Nieves is completing a report on the incident. Which one of the following expresses the above information MOST clearly and accurately?

- A. Mrs. Simpkins, who lives at 42 Mulberry Street, Apt. 25, called the police to make a complaint. A large crowd of people were playing loud music in Mulberry Park at 2:45 A.M. Officer Nieves responded and dispersed the crowd.
- B. Officer Nieves responded to Mulberry Park because Mrs. Simpkins, the complainant, lives at 42 Mulberry Street, Apt. 25. Due to a large crowd of people who were playing loud music at 2:45 A.M., he immediately dispersed the crowd.
- C. Due to a large crowd of people who were playing loud music in Mulberry Park at 2:45 A.M., Officer Nieves responded and dispersed the crowd. Mrs. Simpkins called the police and complained. She lives at 42 Mulberry Street, Apt. 25.
- D. Responding to a complaint by Mrs. Simpkins, who resides at 42 Mulberry Street, Apt. 25, Officer Nieves dispersed a large crowd in Mulberry Park. They were playing loud music. It was 2:45 A.M.

25. While patroling the subway, Police Officer Clark responds to the scene of a past robbery where he obtains the following information:

Place of Occurrence: Northbound E train
Time of Occurrence: 6:30 P.M.
Victim: Robert Brey
Crime: Wallet and jewelry taken
Suspects: 2 male whites armed with knives

Officer Clark is completing a report on the incident.
Which one of the following expresses the above information MOST clearly and accurately?

- A. At 6:30 P.M., Robert Brey reported he was robbed of his wallet and jewelry. On the northbound E train, two white males approached Mr. Brey. They threatened him before taking his property with knives.
- B. While riding the E train northbound, two white men approached Robert Brey at 6:30 P.M. They threatened him with knives and took his wallet and jewelry.
- C. Robert Brey was riding the E train at 6:30 P.M. when he was threatened by two whites. The men took his wallet and jewelry as he was traveling northbound.
- D. Robert Brey reports at 6:30 P.M. he lost his wallet to two white men as well as his jewelry. They were carrying knives and threatened him aboard the northbound E train.

13 (#1)

KEY (CORRECT ANSWERS)

1. B
2. C
3. C
4. A
5. C

6. B
7. C
8. B
9. C
10. B

11. D
12. A
13. B
14. C
15. A

16. B
17. A
18. C
19. B
20. C

21. D
22. D
23. C
24. A
25. B

TEST 2

DIRECTIONS: Each question or incomplete statement is followed by several suggested answers or completions. Select the one that BEST answers the question or completes the statement. *PRINT THE LETTER OF THE CORRECT ANSWER IN THE SPACE AT THE RIGHT.*

1. Police Officer Johnson has just finished investigating a report of a burglary and has obtained the following information:

    Place of Occurrence: Victim's residence
    Time of Occurrence: Between 8:13 P.M. and 4:15 A.M.
    Victim: Paul Mason of 1264 Twentieth Street, Apt. 3D
    Crime: Burglary
    Damage: Filed front door lock

    Officer Johnson is preparing a report of the incident. Which one of the following expresses the above information MOST clearly and accurately?

    A. Paul Mason's residence was burglarized at 1264 Twentieth Street, Apt. 3D, between 8:13 P.M. and 4:15 A.M. by filing the front door lock.
    B. Paul Mason was burglarized by filing the front door lock and he lives at 1264 Twentieth Street, Apt. 3D, between 8:13 P.M. and 4:15 A.M.
    C. Between 8:13 P.M. and 4:15 A.M., the residence of Paul Mason, located at 1264 Twentieth Street, Apt. 3D, was burglarized after the front door lock was filed.
    D. Between 8:13 P.M. and 4:15 A.M., at 1264 Twentieth Street, Apt. 3D, after the front door lock was filed, the residence of Paul Mason was burglarized.

    1.____

2. Police Officer Lowell has just finished investigating a burglary and has received the following information:

    Place of Occurrence: 117-12 Sutphin Boulevard
    Time of Occurrence: Between 9:00 A.M. and 5:00 P.M.
    Victim: Mandee Cotton
    Suspects: Unknown

    Officer Lowell is completing a report on this incident.
    Which one of the following expresses the above information MOST clearly and accurately?

    A. Mandee Cotton reported that her home was burglarized between 9:00 A.M. and 5:00 P.M. Ms. Cotton resides at 117-12 Sutphin Boulevard. Suspects are unknown.
    B. A burglary was committed at 117-12 Sutphin Boulevard reported Mandee Cotton between 9:00 A.M. and 5:00 P.M. Ms. Cotton said unknown suspects burglarized her home.
    C. Unknown suspects burglarized a home at 117-12 Sutphin Boulevard between 9:00 A.M. and 5:00 P.M. Mandee Cotton, homeowner, reported.
    D. Between the hours of 9:00 A.M. and 5:00 P.M., it was reported that 117-12 Sutphin Boulevard was burglarized. Mandee Cotton reported that unknown suspects are responsible.

    2.____

3. Police Officer Dale has just finished investigating a report of attempted theft and has obtained the following information:

   Place of Occurrence: In front of 103 W. 105th Street
   Time of Occurrence: 11:30 A.M.
   Victim: Mary Davis
   Crime: Attempted theft
   Suspect: Male, black, scar on right side of face
   Action Taken: Drove victim around area to locate suspect

   Officer Dale is preparing a report on the incident. Which one of the following expresses the above information MOST clearly and accurately?

   3._____

   A. Mary Davis was standing in front of 103 W. 105th Street when Officer Dale arrived after an attempt to steal her pocketbook failed at 11:30 A.M. Officer Dale canvassed the area looking for a black male with a scar on the right side of his face with Ms. Davis in the patrol car.
   B. Mary Davis stated that, at 11:30 A.M., she was standing in front of 103 W. 105th Street when a black male with a scar on the right side of his face attempted to steal her pocketbook. Officer Dale canvassed the area with Ms. Davis in the patrol car.
   C. Officer Dale canvassed the area by putting Mary Davis in a patrol car looking for a black male with a scar on the right side of his face. At 11:30 A.M. in front of 103 W. 105th Street, she said he attempted to steal her pocketbook.
   D. At 11:30 A.M., in front of 103 W. 105th Street, Officer Dale canvassed the area with Mary Davis in a patrol car who said that a black male with a scar on the right side of his face attempted to steal her pocketbook.

4. While on patrol, Police Officer Santoro received a call to respond to the scene of a shooting. The following details were obtained at the scene:

   Time of Occurrence: 4:00 A.M.
   Place of Occurrence: 232 Senator Street
   Victim: Mike Nisman
   Suspect: Howard Conran
   Crime: Shooting
   Witness: Sheila Norris

   Officer Santoro is completing a report on the incident.
   Which one of the following expresses the above information MOST clearly and accurately?

   4._____

   A. Sheila Norris stated at 4:00 A.M. she witnessed a shooting of her neighbor in front of her building. Howard Conran shot Mike Nisman and ran from 232 Senator Street.
   B. Mike Nisman was the victim of a shooting incident seen by his neighbor. At 4:00 A.M., Sheila Norris saw Howard Conran shoot him and run in front of their building. Norris and Nisman reside at 232 Senator Street.
   C. Sheila Norris states that at 4:00 A.M. she witnessed Howard Conran shoot Mike Nisman, her neighbor, in front of their building at 232 Senator Street. She further states she saw the suspect running from the scene.
   D. Mike Nisman was shot by Howard Conran at 4:00 A.M. His neighbor, Sheila Norris, witnessed him run from the scene in front of their building at 232 Senator Street.

5. Police Officer Taylor responds to the scene of a serious traffic accident in which a car struck a telephone pole, and obtains the following information:
   Place of Occurrence: Intersection of Rock Street and Amboy Place
   Time of Occurrence: 3:27 A.M.
   Name of Injured: Carlos Black
   Driver of Car: Carlos Black
   Action Taken: Injured taken to Beth-El Hospital
   Officer Taylor is preparing a report on the accident. Which one of the following expresses the above information MOST clearly and accurately?

   A. At approximately 3:27 A.M., Carlos Black drove his car into a telephone pole located at the intersection of Rock Street and Amboy Place. Mr. Black, who was the only person injured, was taken to Beth-El Hospital.
   B. Carlos Black, injured at the intersection of Rock Street and Amboy Place, hit a telephone pole. He was taken to Beth-El Hospital after the car accident which occurred at 3:27 A.M.
   C. At the intersection of Rock Street and Amboy Place, Carlos Black injured himself and was taken to Beth-El Hospital. His car hit a telephone pole at 3:27 A.M.
   D. At the intersection of Rock Street and Amboy Place at 3:27 A.M., Carlos Black was taken to Beth-El Hospital after injuring himself by driving into a telephone pole.

6. While on patrol in the Jefferson Housing Projects, Police Officer Johnson responds to the scene of a Grand Larceny.
   The following information was obtained by Officer Johnson:
   Time of Occurrence: 6:00 P.M.
   Place of Occurrence: Rear of Building 12A
   Victim: Maria Lopez
   Crime: Purse snatched
   Suspect: Unknown
   Officer Johnson is preparing a report on the incident.
   Which one of the following expresses the above information MOST clearly and accurately?

   A. At the rear of Building 12A, at 6:00 P.M., by an unknown suspect, Maria Lopez reported her purse snatched in the Jefferson Housing Projects.
   B. Maria Lopez reported that at 6:00 P.M. her purse was snatched by an unknown suspect at the rear of Building 12A in the Jefferson Housing Projects.
   C. At the rear of Building 12A, Maria Lopez reported at 6:00 P.M. that her purse had been snatched by an unknown suspect in the Jefferson Housing Projects.
   D. In the Jefferson Housing Projects, Maria Lopez reported at the rear of Building 12A that her purse had been snatched by an unknown suspect at 6:00 P.M.

7. Criminal Possession of Stolen Property 2nd Degree occurs when a person knowingly possesses stolen property with intent to benefit himself or a person other than the owner, or to prevent its recovery by the owner, and when the
    I. value of the property exceeds two hundred fifty dollars; or
    II. property consists of a credit card; or
    III. person is a pawnbroker or is in the business of buying, selling, or otherwise dealing in property; or
    IV. property consists of one or more firearms, rifles, or shotguns.

    Which one of the following is the BEST example of Criminal Possession of Stolen Property in the Second Degree?

    A. Mary knowingly buys a stolen camera valued at $225 for her mother's birthday.
    B. John finds a wallet containing $100 and various credit cards. John keeps the money and turns the credit cards in at his local precinct.
    C. Mr. Varrone, a pawnbroker, refuses to buy Mr. Cutter's stolen VCR valued at $230.
    D. Mr. Aquista, the owner of a toy store, knowingly buys a crate of stolen water pistols valued at $260.

8. Police Officer Dale has just finished investigating a report of menacing and obtained the following information:

    Time of Occurrence: 10:30 P.M.
    Place of Occurrence: (Hallway) 77 Hill Street
    Victim: Grace Jackson
    Suspect: Susan, white female, 30 years of age
    Crime: Menacing with a knife

    Officer Dale is preparing a report on the incident.
    Which one of the following expresses the above information MOST clearly and accurately?

    A. At 10:30 P.M., Grace Jackson was stopped in the hallway of 77 Hill Street by a 30-year-old white female known to Grace as Susan. Susan put a knife to Grace's throat and demanded that Grace stay out of the building or Susan would hurt her.
    B. Grace Jackson was stopped in the hallway at knifepoint and threatened to stay away from the building located at 77 Hill Street. The female who is 30 years of age known as Susan by Jackson stopped her at 10:30 P.M.
    C. At 10:30 P.M. in the hallway of 77 Hill Street, Grace Jackson reported a white female 30 years of age put a knife to her throat. She knew her as Susan and demanded she stay away from the building or she would get hurt.
    D. A white female 30 years of age known to Grace Jackson as Susan stopped her in the hallway of 77 Hill Street. She put a knife to her throat and at 10:30 P.M. demanded she stay away from the building or she would get hurt.

9. Police Officer Bennett responds to the scene of a car accident and obtains the following information from the witness:

    Time of Occurrence: 3:00 A.M.
    Victim: Joe Morris, removed to Methodist Hospital
    Crime: Struck pedestrian and left the scene of accident
    Description of Auto: Blue 2008 Pontiac, license plate BOT-3745

    Officer Bennett is preparing an accident report. Which one of the following expresses the above information MOST clearly and accurately?

A. Joe Morris, a pedestrian, was hit at 3:00 A.M. and removed to Methodist Hospital. Also a blue Pontiac, 2008 model left the scene, license plate BOT-3745.
B. A pedestrian was taken to Methodist Hospital after being struck at 3:00 A.M. A blue automobile was seen leaving the scene with license plate BOT-3745. Joe Morris was knocked down by a 2008 Pontiac.
C. At 3:00 A.M., Joe Morris, a pedestrian, was struck by a blue 2008 Pontiac. The automobile, license plate BOT-3745, left the scene. Mr. Morris was taken to Methodist Hospital.
D. Joe Morris, a pedestrian at 3:00 A.M. was struck by a Pontiac. A 2008 model, license plate BOT-3745, blue in color, left the scene and the victim was taken to Methodist Hospital.

10. At 11:30 A.M., Police Officers Newman and Johnson receive a radio call to respond to a reported robbery. The Officers obtained the following information:

Time of Occurrence: 11:20 A.M.
Place of Occurrence: Twenty-four hour newsstand at 2024 86th Street
Victim: Sam Norris, owner
Amount Stolen: $450.00
Suspects: Two male whites

Officer Newman is completing a complaint report on the incident.
Which one of the following expresses the above information MOST clearly and accurately?

A. At 11:20 A.M., it was reported by the newsstand owner that two male whites robbed $450.00 from Sam Norris. The Twenty-four hour newsstand is located at 2024 86th Street.
B. At 11:20 A.M., Sam Norris, the newsstand owner, reported that the Twenty-four hour newsstand located at 2024 86th Street was robbed by two male whites who took $450.00.
C. Sam Norris, the owner of the Twenty-four hour newsstand located at 2024 86th Street, reported that at 11:20 A.M. two white males robbed his newsstand of $450.00.
D. Sam Norris reported at 11:20 A.M. that $450.00 had been taken from the owner of the Twenty-four hour newsstand located at 2024 86th Street by two male whites.

11. While on patrol, Police Officers Carter and Popps receive a call to respond to an assault in progress. Upon arrival, they receive the following information:

Place of Occurrence: 27 Park Avenue
Victim: John Dee
Suspect: Michael Jones
Crime: Stabbing during a fight
Action Taken: Suspect arrested

The Officers are completing a report on the incident.
Which one of the following expresses the above information MOST clearly and accurately?

A. In front of 27 Park Avenue, Michael Jones was arrested for stabbing John Dee during a fight.
B. Michael Jones was arrested for stabbing John Dee during a fight in front of 27 Park Avenue.

C. During a fight, Michael Jones was arrested for stabbing John Dee in front of 27 Park Avenue.
D. John Dee was stabbed by Michael Jones, who was arrested for fighting in front of 27 Park Avenue.

12. Police Officer Gattuso responded to a report of a robbery and obtained the following information regarding the incident:

    Place of Occurrence: Princess Grocery, 6 Button Place
    Time of Occurrence: 6:00 P.M.
    Crime: Robbery of $200
    Victim: Sara Davidson, owner of Princess Grocery
    Description of Suspect: White, female, red hair, blue jeans, and white T-shirt
    Weapon: Knife

    Officer Gattuso is preparing a report on the incident.
    Which one of the following expresses the above information MOST clearly and accurately?

    A. Sara Davidson reported at 6:00 P.M. her store Princess Grocery was robbed at knifepoint at 6 Button Place. A white woman with red hair took $200 from her wearing blue jeans and a white T-shirt.
    B. At 6:00 P.M., a red-haired woman took $200 from 6 Button Place at Princess Grocery owned by Sara Davidson, who was robbed by the white woman. She was wearing blue jeans and a white T-shirt and used a knife.
    C. In a robbery that occurred at knifepoint, a red-haired white woman robbed the owner of Princess Grocery. Sara Davidson, the owner of the 6 Button Place store which was robbed of $200, said she was wearing blue jeans and a white T-shirt at 6:00 P.M.
    D. At 6:00 P.M., Sara Davidson, owner of Princess Grocery, located at 6 Button Place, was robbed of $200 at knifepoint. The suspect is a white female with red hair wearing blue jeans and a white T-shirt.

13. Police Officer Martinez responds to a report of an assault and obtains the following information regarding the incident :

    Place of Occurrence: Corner of Frank and Lincoln Avenues
    Time of Occurrence: 9:40 A.M.
    Crime: Assault
    Victim: Mr. John Adams of 31 20th Street
    Suspect: Male, white, 5'11", 170 lbs., dressed in gray
    Injury: Victim suffered a split lip
    Action Taken: Victim transported to St. Mary's Hospital

    Officer Martinez is completing a report on the incident. Which one of the following expresses the above information MOST clearly and accurately?

    A. At 9:40 A.M., John Adams was assaulted on the corner of Frank and Lincoln Avenues by a white male, 5'11", 170 lbs., dressed in gray, suffering a split lip. Mr. Adams lives at 31 20th Street and was transported to St. Mary's Hospital.
    B. At 9:40 A.M., John Adams was assaulted on the corner of Frank and Lincoln Avenues by a white male, 5'11", 170 lbs., dressed in gray, and lives at 31 20th Street. Mr. Adams suffered a split lip and was transported to St. Mary's Hospital.

C. John Adams, who lives at 31 20th Street, was assaulted at 9:40 A.M. on the corner of Frank and Lincoln Avenues by a white male, 5'11", 170 lbs., dressed in gray. Mr. Adams suffered a split lip and was transported to St. Mary's Hospital.
D. Living at 31 20th Street, Mr. Adams suffered a split lip and was transported to St. Mary's Hospital. At 9:40 A.M., Mr. Adams was assaulted by a white male, 5'11", 170 lbs., dressed in gray.

14. The following information was obtained by Police Officer Adams at the scene of an auto accident:

Date of Occurrence:	August 7, 2004
Place of Occurrence:	541 W. Broadway
Time of Occurrence:	12:45 P.M.
Drivers:	Mrs. Liz Smith and Mr. John Sharp
Action Taken:	Summons served to Mrs. Liz Smith

Officer Adams is completing a report on the accident. Which one of the following expresses the above information MOST clearly and accurately?

A. At 541 W. Broadway, Mr. John Sharp and Mrs. Liz Smith had an auto accident at 12:45 P.M. Mrs. Smith received a summons on August 7, 2004.
B. Mrs. Liz Smith received a summons at 12:45 P.M. on August 7, 2004 for an auto accident with Mr. John Sharp at 541 W. Broadway.
C. Mr. John Sharp and Mrs. Liz Smith were in an auto accident. At 541 W. Broadway on August 7, 2004 at 12:45 P.M., Mrs. Smith received a summons.
D. On August 7, 2004 at 12:45 P.M. at 541 W. Broadway, Mrs. Liz Smith and Mr. John Sharp were involved in an auto accident. Mrs. Smith received a summons.

15. Police Officer Gold and his partner were directed by the radio dispatcher to investigate a report of a past burglary. They obtained the following information at the scene:

Date of Occurrence:	April 2, 2004
Time of Occurrence:	Between 7:30 A.M. and 6:15 P.M.
Place of Occurrence:	124 Haring Street, residence of victim
Victim:	Mr. Gerald Palmer
Suspect:	Unknown
Crime:	Burglary
Items Stolen:	Assorted jewelry, $150 cash, TV, VCR

Officer Gold must complete a report on the incident. Which one of the following expresses the above information MOST clearly and accurately?

A. Mr. Gerald Palmer stated that on April 2, 2004, between 7:30 A.M. and 6:15 P.M., while he was at work, someone broke into his house at 124 Haring Street and removed assorted jewelry, a VCR, $150 cash, and a TV.
B. Mr. Gerald Palmer stated while he was at work that somebody broke into his house on April 2, 2004 and between 7:30 A.M. and 6:15 P.M. took his VCR, TV, assorted jewelry, and $150 cash. His address is 124 Haring Street.
C. Between 7:30 A.M. and 6:15 P.M. on April 2, 2004, Mr. Gerald Palmer reported an unknown person at 124 Haring Street took his TV, VCR, $150 cash, and assorted jewelry from his house. Mr. Palmer said he was at work at the time.
D. An unknown person broke into the house at 124 Haring Street and stole a TV, VCR, assorted jewelry, and $150 cash from Mr. Gerald Palmer. The suspect broke in on April 2, 2004 while he was at work, reported Mr. Palmer between 7:30 A.M. and 6:15 P.M.

16. While on patrol, Police Officers Morris and Devine receive a call to respond to a reported burglary. The following information relating to the crime was obtained by the Officers:

Time of Occurrence: 2:00 A.M.
Place of Occurrence: 2100 First Avenue
Witness: David Santiago
Victim: John Rivera
Suspect: Joe Ryan
Crime: Burglary, DVD player stolen

The Officers are completing a report on the incident.
Which one of the following expresses the above information MOST clearly and accurately?

- A. David Santiago, the witness reported at 2:00 A.M. he saw Joe Ryan leave 2100 First Avenue, home of John Rivera, with a DVD player.
- B. At 2:00 A.M. David Santiago reported that he had seen Joe Ryan go into 2100 First Avenue and steal a DVD player. John Rivera lives at 2100 First Avenue.
- C. David Santiago stated that Joe Ryan burglarized John Rivera's house at 2100 First Avenue. He saw Joe Ryan leaving his house at 2:00 A.M. with a DVD player.
- D. David Santiago reported that at 2:00 A.M. he saw Joe Ryan leave John Rivera's house, located at 2100 First Avenue, with Mr. Rivera's DVD player.

16.____

17. When a police officer responds to an incident involving the victim of an animal bite, the officer should do the following in the order given:
    I. Determine the owner of the animal
    II. Obtain a description of the animal and attempt to locate it for an examination if the owner is unknown
    III. If the animal is located and the owner is unknown, comply with the Care and Disposition of Animal procedure
    IV. Prepare a Department of Health Form 480BAA and deliver it to the Desk Officer with a written report
    V. Notify the Department of Health by telephone if the person has been bitten by an animal other than a dog or cat.

Police Officer Rosario responds to 1225 South Boulevard where someone has been bitten by a dog. He is met by John Miller who informs Officer Rosario that he was bitten by a large German Shepard. Mr. Miller also states that he believes the dog belongs to someone in the neighborhood but does not know who owns it. Officer Rosario searches the area for the dog but is unable to find it.
What should Officer Rosario do NEXT?

- A. Locate the owner of the animal.
- B. Notify the Department of Health by telephone.
- C. Prepare a Department of Health Form 480BAA.
- D. Comply with the Care and Disposition of Animal procedure.

17.____

18. The following details were obtained by Police Officer Howard at the scene of a hit-and-run accident:

    Place of Occurrence: Intersection of Brown Street and Front Street
    Time of Occurrence: 11:15 A.M.
    Victim: John Lawrence
    Vehicle: Red Chevrolet, license plate 727PQA
    Crime: Leaving the scene of an accident

    Officer Howard is completing a report on the incident. Which one of the following expresses the above information MOST clearly and accurately?

    A. A red Chevrolet, license plate 727PQA, hit John Lawrence. It left the scene of the accident at 11:15 A.M. at the intersection of Brown and Front Streets.
    B. At 11:15 A.M., John Lawrence was walking at the intersection of Brown Street and Front Street when he was struck by a red Chevrolet, license plate 727PQA, which left the scene.
    C. It was reported at 11:15 A.M. that John Lawrence was struck at the intersection of Brown Street and Front Street. The red Chevrolet, license plate 727PQA, left the scene.
    D. At the intersection of Brown Street and Front Street, John Lawrence was the victim of a car at 11:15 A.M. which struck him and left the scene. It was a red Chevrolet, license plate 727PQA.

18.____

19. Police Officer Donnelly has transported an elderly male to Mt. Hope Hospital after finding him lying on the street. At the hospital, Nurse Baker provided Officer Donnelly with the following information:

    Name: Robert Jones
    Address: 1485 E. 97th St.
    Date of Birth: May 13, 1935
    Age: 73 years old
    Type of Ailment: Heart condition

    Officer Donnelly is completing an Aided Report.
    Which one of the following expresses the above information MOST clearly and accurately?

    A. Mr. Robert Jones, who is 73 years old, born on May 13, 1935, collapsed on the street. Mr. Jones, who resides at 1485 E. 97th Street, suffers from a heart condition.
    B. Mr. Robert Jones had a heart condition and collapsed today on the street, and resides at 1485 E. 97th Street. He was 73 years old and born on May 13, 1935.
    C. Mr. Robert Jones, who resides at 1485 E. 97th Street, was born on May 13, 1935, and is 73 years old, was found lying on the street from a heart condition.
    D. Mr. Robert Jones, born on May 13, 1935, suffers from a heart condition at age 73 and was found lying on the street residing at 1485 E. 97th Street.

19.____

20. Police officers on patrol are often called to a scene where a response from the Fire Department might be necessary.
    In which one of the following situations would a request to the Fire Department to respond be MOST critical?

20.____

10 (#2)

- A. A film crew has started a small fire in order to shoot a scene on an October evening.
- B. Two manhole covers blow off on a September afternoon.
- C. Homeless persons are gathered around a trash can fire on a February morning.
- D. A fire hydrant has been opened by people in the neighborhood on a July afternoon.

21. Police Officer Johnson arrives at the National Savings Bank five minutes after it has been robbed at gunpoint.
    The following are details provided by eyewitnesses: <u>Suspect</u>
    Sex: Male
    Ethnicity: White
    Height: 5'10" to 6'2"
    Weight: 180 lbs. to 190 lbs.
    Hair Color: Blonde
    Clothing: Black jacket, blue dungarees
    Weapon: .45 caliber revolver
    Officer Johnson is completing a report on the incident.
    Which one of the following expresses the above information MOST clearly and accurately?
    A white male

    - A. weighing 180-190 lbs. robbed the National Savings Bank. He was white with a black jacket with blonde hair, is 5'10" to 6'2", and blue dungarees. The robber was armed with a .45 caliber revolver.
    - B. weighing around 180 or 190 lbs. was wearing a black jacket and blue dungarees. He had blonde hair and had a .45 caliber revolver, and was 5'10" to 6'2". He robbed the National Savings Bank.
    - C. who was 5'10" to 6'2" and was weighing 180 to 190 lbs., and has blonde hair and wearing blue dungarees and a black jacket with a revolver, robbed the National Savings Bank.
    - D. armed with a .45 caliber revolver robbed the National Savings Bank. The robber was described as being between 180-190 lbs., 5'10" to 6'2", with blonde hair. He was wearing a black jacket and blue dungarees.

21.____

22. While on patrol, Police Officer Rogers is approached by Terry Conyers, a young woman whose pocketbook has been stolen. Ms. Conyers tells Officer Rogers that the following items were in her pocketbook at the time it was taken:
    4 Traveler's checks, each valued at $20.00
    3 Traveler's checks, each valued at $25.00
    Cash of $212.00
    1 wedding band valued at $450.00
    Officer Rogers is preparing a Complaint Report on the robbery.
    Which one of the following is the TOTAL value of the property and cash taken from Ms. Conyers?

    A. $707   B. $807   C. $817   D. $837

22.____

23. While on patrol, Police Officer Scott is dispatched to respond to a reported burglary. Two burglars entered the home of Mr. and Mrs. Walker and stole the following items:
    3 watches valued at $65.00 each
    1 amplifier valued at $340.00
    1 television set valued at $420.00
    Officer Scott is preparing a Complaint Report on the burglary.
    Which one of the following is the TOTAL value of the property stolen?

    A. $707	B. $825	C. $920	D. $955

24. While on patrol, Police Officer Smith is dispatched to investigate a grand larceny. Deborah Paisley, a businesswoman, reports that her 2000 Porsche was broken into. The following items were taken:
    1 car stereo system valued at $2,950.00
    1 car phone valued at $1,060.00
    Ms. Paisley's attache case valued at $200.00 was also taken from the car in the incident. The attache case contained two new solid gold pens valued at $970.00 each. Officer Smith is completing a Complaint Report.
    Which one of the following is the TOTAL dollar value of the property stolen from Ms. Paisley's car?

    A. $5,180	B. $5,980	C. $6,040	D. $6,150

25. Police Officer Grundig is writing a Complaint Report regarding a burglary and assault case. Officer Grundig has obtained the following facts:
    Place of Occurrence: 2244 Clark Street
    Victim: Mrs. Willis
    Suspect: Mr. Willis, victim's ex-husband
    Complaint: Unlawful entry; head injury inflicted with a bat
    Officer Grundig is completing a report on the incident. Which one of the following expresses the above information MOST clearly and accurately?

    A. He had no permission or authority to do so and it caused her head injuries, when Mr. Willis entered his ex-wife's premises. Mrs. Willis lives at 2244 Clark Street. He hit her with a bat.
    B. Mr. Willis entered 2244 Clark Street, the premises of his ex-wife. He hit her with a bat, without permission and authority to do so. It caused Mrs. Willis to have head injuries.
    C. After Mr. Willis hit his ex-wife, Mrs. Willis, at 2244 Clark Street, the bat caused her to have head injuries. He had no permission nor authority do so so.
    D. Mr. Willis entered his ex-wife's premises at 2244 Clark Street without her permission or authority. He then struck Mrs. Willis with a bat, causing injuries to her head.

KEY (CORRECT ANSWERS)

1. C
2. A
3. B
4. C
5. A

6. B
7. D
8. A
9. C
10. C

11. B
12. D
13. C
14. D
15. A

16. D
17. C
18. B
19. A
20. B

21. D
22. C
23. D
24. D
25. D

PREPARING WRITTEN MATERIAL
EXAMINATION SECTION
TEST 1

DIRECTIONS: The sentences numbered 1 to 10 deal with some phase of police activity. They may be classified most appropriately under one of the following four categories:
A. *Faulty* because of incorrect grammar
B. *Faulty* because of incorrect punctuation
C. *Faulty* because of incorrect use of a word
D. *Correct*

Examine each sentence carefully. Then, in the correspondingly numbered space on the right, print the capital letter preceding the option which is the best of the four suggested above.

(All incorrect sentences contain only one type of error. Consider a sentence correct if it contains none of the types of errors mentioned, even though there may be other correct ways of expressing the same thought.)

1. The Department Medal of Honor is awarded to a member of the Police Force who distinguishes himself inconspicuously in the line of police duty by the performance of an act of gallantry. 1.____

2. Members of the Detective Division are charged with: the prevention of crime, the detection and arrest of criminals, and the recovery of lost or stolen property. 2.____

3. Detectives are selected from the uniformed patrol forces after they have indicated by conduct, aptitude, and performance that they are qualified for the more intricate duties of a detective. 3.____

4. The patrolman, pursuing his assailant, exchanged shots with the gunman and immortally wounded him as he fled into a nearby building. 4.____

5. The members of the Traffic Division has to enforce the Vehicle and Traffic Law, the Traffic Regulations, and ordinances relating to vehicular and pedestrian traffic. 5.____

6. After firing a shot at the gunman, the crowd dispersed from the patrolman's line of fire. 6.____

7. The efficiency of the Missing Persons Bureau is maintained with a maximum of public personnel due to the specialized training given to its members. 7.____

8. Records of persons arrested for violations of Vehicle and Traffic Regulations are transmitted upon request to precincts, courts, and other authorized agencies. 8.____

9. The arresting officer done all he could to subdue the perpetrator without physically injuring him. 9._____

10. The Deputy Commissioner is authorized to exercise all of the powers and duties of the Police Commissioner in the latter's absence. 10._____

KEY (CORRECT ANSWERS)

1.	C	6.	A
2.	B	7.	C
3.	D	8.	D
4.	C	9.	A
5.	A	10.	D

TEST 2

DIRECTIONS: Questions 1 through 4 consist of sentences concerning criminal law. Some of the sentences contain errors in English grammar or usage, punctuation, spelling, or capitalization. (A sentence does not contain an error simply because it could be written in a different manner.

Choose answer
- A. if the sentence contains an error in English grammar or usage
- B. if the sentence contains an error in punctuation
- C. if the sentence contains an error in spelling or capitalization
- D. if the sentence does not contain any errors

1. The severity of the sentence prescribed by contemporary statutes—including both the former and the revised New York Penal Laws—do not depend on what crime was intended by the offender.

2. It is generally recognized that two defects in the early law of *attempt* played a part in the birth of *burglary*: (1) immunity from prosecution for conduct short of the last act before completion of the crime, and (2) the relatively minor penalty imposed for an attempt (its being a common law misdemeanor) vis-à-a the completed offense.

3. The first sentence of the statute is applicable to employees who enter their place of employment, invited guests, and all other persons who have an express or implied license or privilege to enter the premises.

4. Contemporary criminal codes in the United States generally divide burglary into various degrees, differentiating the categories according to place, time, and other attendent circumstances.

1.____
2.____
3.____
4.____

KEY (CORRECT ANSWERS)

1. A
2. D
3. D
4. C

TEST 3

DIRECTIONS: For each of the sentences numbered 1 through 10, select from the options given below the MOST applicable choice, and print the letter of the correct answer in the space at the right.

    A. The sentence is correct.
    B. The sentence contains a spelling error only
    C. The sentence contains an English grammar error only
    D. The sentence contains *both* a spelling error and an English grammar error

1. Every person in the group is going to do his share.   1._____
2. The man who we selected is new to Duke University.   2._____
3. She is the older of the four secretaries on the two staffs that are to be combined.   3._____
4. The decision has to be made between him and I.   4._____
5. One of the volunteers are too young for this complecated task, don't you think?   5._____
6. I think your idea is splindid and it will improve this report considerably.   6._____
7. Do you think this is an exagerated account of the behavior you and me observed this morning?   7._____
8. Our supervisor has a clear idea of excelence.   8._____
9. How many occurences were verified by the observers?   9._____
10. We must complete the typing of the draft of the questionaire by noon tomorrow.   10._____

KEY (CORRECT ANSWERS)

1. A   6. B
2. C   7. D
3. C   8. B
4. C   9. B
5. D   10. B

TEST 4

DIRECTIONS: Questions 1 through 3 are based on the following paragraph, which consists of three numbered sentences.

Edit each sentence to insure clarity of meaning and correctness of grammar without substantially changing the meaning of the sentence.

Examine each sentence and then select the option which changes the sentence to express BEST the thought of the sentence.

(1) Unquestionably, a knowledge of business and finance is a good advantage to audit committee members but not essential to all members. (2) Other factors also carry weight; for example, at least one member must have the ability to preside over meetings and to discuss things along constructive lines. (3) In the same way, such factors as the amount of time a member can be able to devote to duties or his rating on the score of motivation, inquisitiveness, persistence, and disposition towards critical analysis are important.

1. In the first sentence, the word
   A. "good" should be changed to "distinct"
   B. "good" should be omitted
   C. "and" should be changed to "or"
   D. "are" should be inserted between the words "but" and "not"

2. In the second sentence, the
   A. word "factors" should be changed to "things"
   B. words "preside over" should be changed to "lead at"
   C. phrase "discuss things" should be changed to "direct the "discussion"
   D. word "constructive" should be changed to "noteworthy"

3. In the third sentence, the
   A. word "amount" should be changed to "period"
   B. words "amount of" should be changed to "length of"
   C. word "can" should be changed to "will"
   D. word "same" should be changed to "similar

KEY (CORRECT ANSWERS)

1. A
2. C
3. C

TEST 5

DIRECTIONS: Each question or incomplete statement is followed by several suggested answers or completions. Select the one that BEST answers the question or completes the statement. *PRINT THE LETTER OF THE CORRECT ANSWER IN THE SPACE AT THE RIGHT.*

1. Of the following, the MOST acceptable close of a business letter would usually be:
    A. Cordially yours,
    B. Respectfully Yours,
    C. Sincerely Yours,
    D. Yours very truly,

2. When writing official correspondence to members of the armed forces, their titles should be used
    A. both on the envelope and in the inside address
    B. in the inside address, but not on the envelope
    C. neither on the envelope nor in the inside address
    D. on the envelope but not in the inside address

3. Which one of the following is the LEAST important advantage of putting the subject of a letter in the heading to the right of the address? It
    A. makes filing of the copy easier
    B. makes more space available in the body of the letter
    C. simplifies distribution of letters
    D. simplifies determination of the subject of the letter

4. Generally, when writing a letter, the use of precise words and concise sentences is
    A. *good*, because less time will be required to write the letter
    B. *bad*, because it is most likely that the reader will think the letter is unimportant and will not respond favorably
    C. *good*, because it is likely that your desired meaning will be conveyed to the reader
    D. *bad*, because your letter will be too brief to provide adequate information

5. Of the following, it is MOST appropriate to use a form letter when it is necessary to answer many
    A. requests or inquiries from a single individual
    B. follow-up letters from individuals requesting additional information
    C. requests or inquiries about a single subject
    D. complaints from individuals that they have been unable to obtain various types of information

KEY (CORRECT ANSWERS)

1. D
2. A
3. B
4. C
5. C

TEST 6

DIRECTIONS: Each question or incomplete statement is followed by several suggested answers or completions. Select the one that BEST answers the question or completes the statement. *PRINT THE LETTER OF THE CORRECT ANSWER IN THE SPACE AT THE RIGHT.*

1. The one of the following sentences which is LEAST acceptable from the viewpoint of correct usage is:
   A. The police thought the fugitive to be him.
   B. The criminals set a trap for whoever would fall into it.
   C. It is ten years ago since the fugitive fled from the city.
   D. The lecturer argued that criminals are usually cowards.
   E. The police removed four bucketfuls of earth from the scene of the crime.

   1.____

2. The one of the following sentences which is LEAST acceptable from the viewpoint of correct usage is:
   A. The patrolman scrutinized the report with great care.
   B. Approaching the victim of the assault, two bruises were noticed by the patrolman.
   C. As soon as I had broken down the door, I stepped into the room.
   D. I observed the accused loitering near the building, which was closed at the time.
   E. The storekeeper complained that his neighbor was guilty of violating a local ordinance.

   2.____

3. The one of the following sentences which is LEAST acceptable from the viewpoint of correct usage is:
   A. I realized immediately that he intended to assault the woman, so I disarmed him.
   B. It was apparent that Mr. Smith's explanation contained many inconsistencies.
   C. Despite the slippery condition of the street, he managed to stop the vehicle before injuring the child.
   D. Not a single one of them wish, despite the damage to property, to make a formal complaint.
   E. The body was found lying on the floor.

   3.____

KEY (CORRECT ANSWERS)

1. C
2. B
3. D

PREPARING WRITTEN MATERIAL

PARAGRAPH REARRANGEMENT
COMMENTARY

The sentences that follow are in scrambled order. You are to rearrange them in proper order and indicate the letter choice containing the correct answer at the space at the right.

Each group of sentences in this section is actually a paragraph presented in scrambled order. Each sentence in the group has a place in that paragraph; no sentence is to be left out. You are to read each group of sentences and decide upon the best order in which to put the sentences so as to form a well-organized paragraph.

The questions in this section measure the ability to solve a problem when all the facts relevant to its solution are not given.

More specifically, certain positions of responsibility and authority require the employee to discover connection between events sometimes, apparently, unrelated. In order to do this, the employee will find it necessary to correctly infer that unspecified events have probably occurred or are likely to occur. This ability becomes especially important when action must be taken on incomplete information.

Accordingly, these questions require competitors to choose among several suggested alternatives, each of which presents a different sequential arrangement of the events. Competitors must choose the MOST logical of the suggested sequences.

In order to do so, they may be required to draw on general knowledge to infer missing concepts or events that are essential to sequencing the given events. Competitors should be careful to infer only what is essential to the sequence. The plausibility of the wrong alternatives will always require the inclusion of unlikely events or of additional chains of events which are NOT essential to sequencing the given events.

It's very important to remember that you are looking for the best of the four possible choices, and that the best choice of all may not even be one of the answers you're given to choose from.

There is no one right way to solve these problems. Many people have found it helpful to first write out the order of the sentences, as they would have arranged them, on their scrap paper before looking at the possible answers. If their optimum answer is there, this can save them some time. If it isn't, this method can still give insight into solving the problem. Others find it most helpful to just go through each of the possible choices, contrasting each as they go along. You should use whatever method feels comfortable and works for you.

While most of these types of questions are not that difficult, we've added a higher percentage of the difficult type, just to give you more practice. Usually there are only one or two questions on this section that contain such subtle distinctions that you're unable to answer confidently. And you then may find yourself stuck deciding between two possible choices, neither of which you're sure about.

EXAMINATION SECTION
TEST 1

DIRECTIONS: Each question consists of several sentences which can be arranged in a logical sequence. For each question, select the choice which places the numbered sentences in the MOST logical sequence. *PRINT THE LETTER OF THE CORRECT ANSWER IN THE SPACE AT THE RIGHT.*

1. I. A body was found in the woods.
    II. A man proclaimed innocence.
    III. The owner of a gun was located.
    IV. A gun was traced.
    V. The owner of a gun was questioned.
    The CORRECT answer is:
    A. IV, III, V, II, I
    B. II, I, IV, III, V
    C. I, IV, III, V, II
    D. I, III, V, II, IV
    E. I, II, IV, III, V

    1.____

2. I. A man is in a hunting accident.
    II. A man fell down a flight of steps.
    III. A man lost his vision in one eye.
    IV. A man broke his leg.
    V. A man had to walk with a cane.
    The CORRECT answer is:
    A. II, IV, V, I, III
    B. IV, V, I, III, II
    C. III, I, IV, V, II
    D. I, III, V, II, IV
    E. I, III, II, IV, V

    2.____

3. I. A man is offered a new job.
    II. A woman is offered a new job.
    III. A man works as a waiter.
    IV. A woman works as a waitress.
    V. A woman gives notice.
    The CORRECT answer is:
    A. IV, II, V, III, I
    B. IV, II, V, I, III
    C. II, IV, V, III, I
    D. III, I, IV, II, V
    E. IV, III, II, V, I

    3.____

4. I. A train let the station late.
    II. A man was late for work.
    III. A man lost his job.
    IV. Many people complained because the train was late.
    V. There was a traffic jam.
    The CORRECT answer is:
    A. V, II, I, IV, III
    B. V, I, IV, II, III
    C. V, I, II, IV, III
    D. I, V, IV, II, III
    E. II, I, IV, V, III

    4.____

5.
   I. The burden of proof as to each issue is determined before trial and remains upon the same party throughout the trial.
   II. The jury is at liberty to believe one witness' testimony as against a number of contradictory witnesses.
   III. In a civil case, the party bearing the burden of proof is required to prove his contention by a fair preponderance of the evidence.
   IV. However, it must be noted that a fair preponderance of evidence does not necessarily mean a greater number of witnesses.
   V. The burden of proof is the burden which rests upon one of the parties to an action to persuade the trier of the facts, generally the jury, that a proposition he asserts is true.
   VI. If the evidence is equally balanced, or if it leaves the jury in such doubt as to be unable to decide the controversy either way, judgment must be given against the party upon whom the burden of proof rests.
   The CORRECT answer is:
   A. III, II, V, IV, I, VI   B. I, II, VI, V, III, IV   C. III, IV, V, I, II, VI
   D. V, I, III, VI, IV, II   E. I, V, III, VI, IV, II

6.
   I. If a parent is without assets and is unemployed, he cannot be convicted of the crime of non-support of a child.
   II. The term *sufficient ability* has been held to mean sufficient financial ability.
   III. It does not matter if his unemployment is by choice or unavoidable circumstances.
   IV. If he fails to take any steps at all, he may be liable to prosecution for endangering the welfare of a child.
   V. Under the penal law, a parent is responsible for the support of his minor child only if the parent is of *sufficient ability*.
   VI. An indigent parent may meet his obligation by borrowing money or by seeking aid under the provisions of the Social Welfare Law.
   The CORRECT answer is:
   A. VI, I, V, III, II, IV   B. I, III, V, II, IV, VI   C. V, II, I, III, VI, IV
   D. I, VI, IV, V, II, III   E. II, V, I, III, VI, IV

7.
   I. Consider, for example, the case of a rabble rouser who urges a group of twenty people to go out and break the windows of a nearby factory.
   II. Therefore, the law fills the indicated gap with the crime of *inciting to riot*.
   III. A person is considered guilty of inciting to riot when he urges ten or more persons to engage in tumultuous and violent conduct of a kind likely to create public alarm.
   IV. However, if he has not obtained the cooperation of at least four people, he cannot be charged with unlawful assembly.
   V. The charge of inciting to riot was added to the law to cover types of conduct which cannot be classified as either the crime of *riot* or the crime of *unlawful assembly*.
   VI. If he acquires the acquiescence of at least four of them, he is guilty of unlawful assembly even if the project does not materialize.
   The CORRECT answer is:
   A. III, V, I, VI, IV, II   B. V, I, IV, VI, II, III   C. III, IV, I, V, II, VI
   D. V, I, IV, VI, III, II   E. V, III, I, VI, IV, II

8. I. If, however, the rebuttal evidence presents an issue of credibility, it is for the jury to determine whether the presumption has, in fact, been destroyed.
    II. Once sufficient evidence to the contrary is introduced, the presumption disappears from the trial.
    III. The effect of a presumption is to place the burden upon the adversary to come forward with evidence to rebut the presumption.
    IV. When a presumption is overcome and ceases to exist in the case, the fact or facts which gave rise to the presumption still remain.
    V. Whether a presumption has been overcome is ordinarily a question for the court.
    VI. Such information may furnish a basis for a logical inference.
    The CORRECT answer is:
    A. IV, VI, II, V, I, III   B. III, II, V, I, IV, VI   C. V, III, VI, IV, II, I
    D. V, IV, I, II, VI, III   E. II, III, V, I, IV, VI

    8.____

9. I. An executive may answer a letter by writing his reply on the face of the letter itself instead of having a return letter typed.
    II. This procedure is efficient because it saves the executive's time, the typist's time, and saves office file space.
    III. Copying machines are used in small offices as well as large offices to save time and money in making brief replies to business letters.
    IV. A copy is made on a copying machine to go into the company files, while the original is mailed back to the sender.
    The CORRECT answer is:
    A. I, II, IV, III   B. I, IV, II, III   C. III, I, IV, II   D. III, IV, II, I

    9.____

10. I. Most organizations favor one of the types but always include the others to a lesser degree.
    II. However, we can detect a definite trend toward greater use of symbolic control.
    III. We suggest that our local police agencies are today primarily utilizing material control.
    IV. Control can be classified into three types: physical, material, and symbolic.
    The CORRECT answer is:
    A. IV, II, III, I   B. II, I, IV, III   C. III, IV, II, I   D. IV, I, III, II

    10.____

11. I. Project residents had first claim to this use, followed by surrounding neighborhood children.
    II. By contrast, recreation space within the project's interior was found to be used more often by both groups.
    III. Studies of the use of project grounds in many cities showed grounds left open for public use were neglected and unused, both by residents and by members of the surrounding community.
    IV. Project residents had clearly laid claim to the play spaces, setting up and enforcing unwritten rules for use.
    V. Each group, by experience, found their activities easily disrupted by other groups, and their claim to the use of space for recreation difficult to enforce.

    11.____

The CORRECT answer is:
A. IV, V, I, II, III
B. V, II, IV, III, I
C. I, IV, III, II, V
D. III, V, II, IV, I

12. I. They do not consider the problems correctable within the existing subsidy formula and social policy of accepting all eligible applicants regardless of social behavior.
   II. A recent survey, however, indicated that tenants believe these problems correctable by local housing authorities and management within the existing financial formula.
   III. Many of the problems and complaints concerning public housing management and design have created resentment between the tenant and the landlord.
   IV. This same survey indicated that administrators and managers do not agree with the tenants.
   The CORRECT answer is:
   A. II, I, III, IV   B. I, III, IV, II   C. III, II, IV, I   D. IV, II, I, III

13. I. In single-family residences, there is usually enough distance between tenants to prevent occupants from annoying one another.
   II. For example, a certain small percentage of tenant families has one or more members addicted to alcohol.
   III. While managers believe in the right of individuals to live as they choose, the manager becomes concerned when the pattern of living jeopardizes others' rights.
   IV. Still others turn night into day, staging lusty entertainments which carry on into the hours when most tenants are trying to sleep.
   V. In apartment buildings, however, tenants live so closely together that any misbehavior can result in unpleasant living conditions.
   VI. Other families engage in violent argument.
   The CORRECT answer is:
   A. III, II, V, IV, VI, I
   B. I, V, II, VI, IV, III
   C. II, V, IV, I, III, VI
   D. IV, II, V, VI, III, I

14. I. Congress made the commitment explicit in the Housing Act of 194, establishing as a national goal the realization of a *decent home and suitable environment for every American family*.
   II. The result has been that the goal of decent home and suitable environment is still as far distant as ever for the disadvantaged urban family.
   III. In spite of this action by Congress, federal housing programs have continued to be fragmented and grossly underfunded.
   IV. The passage of the National Housing Act signaled a few federal commitment to provide housing for the nation's citizens.
   The CORRECT answer is:
   A. I, IV, III, II   B. IV, I, III, II   C. IV, I, II, III   D. II, IV, I, III

15.
I. The greater expense does not necessarily involve *exploitation*, but it is often perceived as exploitative and unfair by those who are aware of the price differences involved, but unaware of operating costs.
II. Ghetto residents believe they are *exploited* by local merchants, and evidence substantiates some of these beliefs.
III. However, stores in low-income areas were more likely to be small independents, which could not achieve the economies available to supermarket chains and were, therefore, more likely to charge higher prices, and the customers were more likely to buy smaller-sized packages which are more expensive per unit of measure.
IV. A study conducted in one city showed that distinctly higher prices were charged for goods sold in ghetto stores in other areas.

The CORRECT answer is:
A. IV, II, I, III   B. IV, I, III, II   C. II, IV, III, I   D. II, III, IV, I

15.____

KEY (CORRECT ANSWERS)

1.	C	6.	C	11.	D
2.	E	7.	A	12.	C
3.	B	8.	B	13.	B
4.	B	9.	C	14.	B
5.	D	10.	D	15.	C

CAMPUS SECURITY

COMMENTARY

This section describes the structure of the campus security office and appraises its function through an examination of its legal apparatus and by the relationships it has maintained with other components of institutional life.

The findings are based upon research in the legal status of the security office and the authority of the security officer; questions as to the structure, the functioning, and the relationships of the security office; and the assessment of the campus security function and its ability to be supportive to students.

In particular, this summary takes cognizance of the inconsequential role heretofore delegated to the security officer and the significant part he may yet play as the threat to the security of the campus accelerates.

1. The history of the campus security office reflects a variety of service tasks distributed among several functionaries which ultimately came to be housed together. From the early fire-watching days to traffic control and student disorder, it has been a body generally utilized "for" but rarely considered "of" the university. Campus security officers and their predecessors have been long cast in roles of menial activities with minimal responsibilities. Never having attained recognition and legitimacy as a part of the total university community, they continue to exercise an uncertain authority amidst a questioning constituency.

2. The uncertainty that has always surrounded the role of the campus security officer is best evidenced in the limitations placed upon his authority. Until recent years few of the state legislatures bestowed direct arrest authority upon a campus security officer. The authority was obtained derivatively as a result of deputization by the local municipal police department or by the sheriff. Although many state legislatures now permit the governing bodies of higher education, such as the boards of regents, to designate campus security officers with peace officers' authority, deputization continues.

3. This situation exists inasmuch as the authority obtained through the governing bodies is usually of a narrow range and it has not yet had the benefit of adequate court testing and judicial approval. Some few states permit private colleges to obtain similar appointments, generally through application to the governor, but the rule among private colleges has been to rely on deputization for their campus security authority.

4. Among the states requiring mandatory training for entering police officers, several do not yet consider a campus security officer subject to the standards imposed upon peace officers. Moreover, the federal government specifically excludes many campus security officers from the benefits of available training scholarships. Virtually no organized, state-wide specialized training programs for campus security officers are either required under the law or are afforded under state auspices.

5. The law is well established in regard the right of institutions of higher educations to control traffic and parking within their own disciplinary machinery. The courts have upheld the colleges' imposition of reasonable penalties for such violations and have provided the civil court system as an appeal tribunal.

6. Adequate legal precedent exists upon which a campus security officer may enter a residence hall in search of contraband without benefit of a search warrant. The

case law condoning such entry is predicated upon several theories. The major legal premise is that the institution must be afforded the flexibility of access to all buildings in order to properly govern itself. The student is also considered only a temporary occupant of the premises and by his enrollment "waives" certain rights. The privilege of entry is available to administrators and may be delegated to law enforcement officers in the pursuit of a reasonable investigation. The erosion of the "in loco parentis" doctrine and recent judicial pronouncements suggest that the privilege of entry without a warrant may not be arbitrarily invoked.

7. The formalized role of the campus security office in major stress situations such as organized or spontaneous campus disorder is to provide intelligence upon which administrators may make decisions, to serve as liaison with outside police agencies, and to gather evidence for later use against students violating the law. Although the press of events may force campus security officers into confrontation situations, the plans for responding to campus disorders do not generally contemplate such a role. The campus security office's early involvement is aimed primarily at delay so that student personnel officers and the executive officer may have the opportunity to use whatever personal, persuasive influence they can marshal. In the event the institutional executive determines that outside force is necessary, the campus security serves as a communications liaison to interpret the tactical decisions demanded by the outside police agencies in terms of the goals aspired to by the executive.

8. While the complexities of a campus-wide disorder may impose limitations upon the involvement of the security officer, his ability to respond to the normal, foreseeable, routine, enforcement contingencies also remains open to question. The profile of the campus security function discloses many characteristics that suggest only a minimal ability to satisfy ordinary campus needs.

9. Particularly among small institutions and especially private colleges, the training is limited, the equipment is meager, and the advantages over the local police nonexistent. The security force generally lacks specialists within the department, has a minimum of sophisticated equipment, and what little intelligence is available is obtained from outside police sources. Students and female officers are scarcely used and only in short demand.

10. All components of the university recognize that the campus security force most effectively performs the tasks requiring the least specialty training. Building and ground patrol, parking, and traffic control are at the top rank, in that order, while the duties involving criminal investigation and student disorders are the areas least effectively performed.

11. It is apparent to security officers that the presence of larger student bodies, more vehicles on campus, more buildings to patrol, a rise in the individual crime rate, and the potential for disorder arising from student demonstrations call for an increased professional staff.

12. Administrative changes are sought by security officers with almost 60.0 percent favoring a centralized, state-wide coordinating body and almost 70.0 percent requesting a chain of command which would lead directly to the president. None of the other respondent groups (faculty, students, administrators) evinces strong support for these propositions.

13. There is no consensus among the campus groups as to the personnel changes which would most improve performance. The security officers and the administrators ranked salary increase as the top priority personnel change, whereas the students and the faculty selected specialized training in human behavior as their first

choice. Inasmuch as the campus security office services a select clientele in a unique setting, the projected changes need not be weighed against the prototype sought for the law enforcement officer employed to exercise order among the general population.

14. The campus security office has virtually no involvement in policy-making beyond traffic regulations and has little contact in a formal setting with students and faculty. A good working relationship seems to exist with the office of student affairs and other administrators as well as with the outside police agencies.

15. The strong support indicated by all four groups (campus security, faculty, students, and administrators) for the proposition that too few channels of communication exist between the campus security office and the students is evidenced by the lack of security officer participation in student educational programs, by the failure of the campus security office to meet regularly with student committees, and by the security office's absence in the process of establishing student codes of conduct and student discipline procedures. Students involved in off-campus arrests cannot look for security office assistance except to a small extent at schools in the under-10,000 population brackets.

16. Although administrative support for the campus security office as a policy-making body is absent, there is evidence showing regular committee meetings with the office of student affairs and other administration groups. A continuing exchange of information exists with the office of student affairs concerning problem students, and a concurring belief is held by all four groups that the administrators and the office of student affairs would support the action of the campus security office in a disorder situation.

17. The working relationship with administrators also extends to outside police agencies. The local police are available for many manpower and investigative services, and, in some instances, campus violations of the municipal and state law may be handled by security officers within the framework of the school's discipline structure rather than requiring students to face criminal prosecution. Despite the amicable ties between the campus security force and the local police, the security officer joined with the other three groups in unequivocally asserting that the over-reaction by outside police agencies was the occurrence most likely to change an orderly student demonstration into a campus disorder.

18. The aspirations of the campus security officer to contribute to the educational goals of the institution and to participate in its traditional customs finds little of a responsive chord among other components on campus. Although 40.0 percent of the security officers considered the aiding of students in the educational process as an appropriate goal, only 18.0 percent of the students and 6.0 percent of the faculty voiced agreement. The campus security officer viewed himself as the interpreter of the function of police agencies in our society, but the concept had only scattered support with the students and the faculty.

19. There was mixed sentiment toward the campus security officer's enforcement role. Some of the characteristics deemed the antithesis of higher education tradition were attributed to him. For instance, all of the groups identified him with an authoritarian enforcement approach. In addition, 50.0 percent of the student were critical of his use of informers and about 25.0 percent of all groups suggested that uniforms be replaced with civilian-like attire. Despite the 70.0 percent of the security officers seeking increased authority, there was a reluctance to increase campus security authority or to allow participation in student discipline policy-making. The suggestion that the campus security office is a policing agency and as such is

unacceptable to the academic community averaged but a 30.0 percent acceptance among all four groups. While the campus security office was not totally repudiated because of its law enforcement posture, nonetheless it has not been afforded peer status by the other components of the campus society.

20. The anticipation that a supportive relationship can be maintained with students while performing enforcement duties is an unfulfilled expectation. This was apparent to all four groups in their over-70.0 percent recognition that duties such as searching residence halls for contraband are inimical to maintaining a compatible association, and, as well, in their almost 50.0 percent recognition of the stress created in using necessary force against student disorders. Duties involving building and grounds patrol, traffic control, and criminal investigation are performed in less strained settings, permitting a more harmonious relationship.

21. The image of the campus security officer that is transmitted to the student represents order and authority. The uniform, the weapons, and the equipment are synonymous with discipline and control. From the student point of view, the product is not conducive to a mutuality of interest. The absence of joint educational programs and regularly scheduled committee meetings also negates the development of any meaningful interchange. The failure of campus security to offer assistance to students in need of aid as a result of an off-campus arrest may further estrange the two groups. The differential in educational background and age also widens the chasm.

22. Students do not go so far as to state that the campus security officer is too low in the status hierarchy to maintain their respect but they strongly favor supervisory controls such as student ombudsmen and a joint faculty-student committee to review the performance of the campus security officer.

23. The campus security officer as presently constituted is not trained to provide supportive services for students, is not given a status role by the administration which would engender a high regard, and does not participate in policy making or become involved in aspects of the educational process.

24. Little recognition is attainable to the security officer other than that arising from his enforcement activities. There are few if any common grounds existing between him and the student from which a symbiotic relationship may develop.

25. In some few critical areas, the results reflected similar percentage support among the four groups. However, the internal consistency check to determine agreement among the four groups within each institution showed that in only 2 of the 16 selected items were there affirmative responses suggesting consistent agreement within each of the schools. The item of greatest support had 82 of the 89 schools with all four groups agreeing to the truism that the campus security goal is to provide protection for property and person.

Fifty schools had all components in agreement that the overreaction by outside police agencies may change orderly demonstrations into a campus disorder. The other items showed considerably lower internal consistency scores. The diversity of attitude among the component groups that comprise the educational institutions of higher learning and the lack of unanimity within each institution suggest a searching reexamination of the campus security model.

www.ingramcontent.com/pod-product-compliance
Lightning Source LLC
Chambersburg PA
CBHW082044300426
44117CB00015B/2605